UNIVERSITY BUDGETING FOR CRITICAL MASS AND COMPETITION

by
L.R. Jones
III

PRAEGER

PRAEGER SPECIAL STUDIES • PRAEGER SCIENTIFIC

New York • Philadelphia • Eastbourne, UK
Toronto • Hong Kong • Tokyo • Sydney

Library of Congress Cataloging in Publication Data

Jones, L.R.
  University budgeting for critical mass and
competition.

  Bibliography: p.
  Includes index.
  1. Public universities and colleges — United States —
Finance. 2. Higher education and state — United States.
3. State aid to higher education — United States.
4. Budgets — United States — States. I. Title.
LB2328.6.J66 1985   378′.02   84-26416
ISBN 0-03-062776-1 (alk. paper)

Published in 1985 by Praeger Publishers
CBS Educational and Professional Publishing, a Division of CBS Inc.
521 Fifth Avenue, New York, NY 10175 USA

Printed in the United States of America on acid-free paper

INTERNATIONAL OFFICES

Orders from outside the United States should be sent to the appropriate address listed below. Orders from areas not listed below should be placed through CBS International Publishing, 383 Madison Ave., New York, NY 10175 USA

Australia, New Zealand
Holt Saunders, Pty, Ltd., 9 Waltham St., Artarmon, N.S.W. 2064, Sydney, Australia

Canada
Holt, Rinehart & Winston of Canada, 55 Horner Ave., Toronto, Ontario, Canada M8Z 4X6

Europe, the Middle East, & Africa
Holt Saunders, Ltd., 1 St. Anne's Road, Eastbourne, East Sussex, England BN21 3UN

Japan
Holt Saunders, Ltd., Ichibancho Central Building, 22-1 Ichibancho, 3rd Floor, Chiyodaku, Tokyo, Japan

Hong Kong, Southeast Asia
Holt Saunders Asia, Ltd., 10 Fl, Intercontinental Plaza, 94 Granville Road, Tsim Sha Tsui East, Kowloon, Hong Kong

Manuscript submissions should be sent to the Editorial Director, Praeger Publishers, 521 Fifth Avenue, New York, NY 10175 USA

Preface

Research on the critical mass portion of this book began when I was a budget and planning analyst in the chancellor's office at the University of California, Berkeley, in the mid-1970s. A number of individuals aided and influenced my research, including Lyman Glenny, who helped arrange a Sproul Fellowship to support my dissertation, Martin Trow, Guy Benveniste, Earl Cheit, Robert Biller, Todd La Porte, Fred Balderston, West Churchman, Frank Bowen, Allan Sindler, Loris Davanzo, Sidney Suslow, Gerry Sasek, David Hopkins, George Weathersby, Clark Kerr, and Aaron Wildavsky. In particular, I am grateful to Errol Mauchlan for employing me in the Berkeley budget office while I was a graduate student and for patiently explaining the advantages of a critical mass approach to resource planning and decision making at the University of California. To the best of my knowledge, the concept of applying critical mass to academic budgeting in universities originated in academic planning at Berkeley in the mid-1960s. Key participants were Raymond Bressler, Jr., Errol Mauchlan, and the late Sidney Suslow.

The second half of the book, which focuses on state government budgeting and regulation of higher education, is the product of a dozen years of field research, work experience, reading, participant observation, and discussion. I am especially appreciative of the insights and help provided by close friends Fred Thompson and William Zumeta, who contributed to Chapter Six. In addition, I would like to thank Al Loeb, who helped teach me to prepare, scrutinize, and control higher education budgets as a budget and policy analyst in the California State Department of Finance, and also Alan Post, John Vasconcellos, William Pickens, and Dan Cothran. Arthur Marmaduke provided financial support from the California Student Aid Commission to this research in its infancy. Robert Cope, Richard Hill, Bryan Downes, and Charles Levine also contributed ideas to this work. Joann Brady, Lorrie McCoy, Linda Lynch, Bobbie Squires, Mary Williams, and Dan Wood are thanked for their assistance in manuscript preparation.

This book is dedicated to G. P. J. for her love,
support, and painstaking efforts to improve my writing
and thinking.

L. R. Jones
University of Oregon

Contents

LIST OF TABLES AND FIGURES

One
Management of Universities under Resource Uncertainty

Many universities and state governments presently find themselves in the throes of managing under conditions of financial restraint. As a result of demographic trends that have reduced the size of the traditional college-age cohort of young people seeking advanced education, the impact of inflation on budgets, and reductions in federal and state financial support, public universities are learning to cope with resource scarcity. Likewise, state governments continue to struggle in allocating scarce resources in a way that preserves quality and integrity in the provision of public services.

This book presents alternative and competing views on budgeting for public universities under conditions of financial resource scarcity and uncertainty. The first perspective is that of university management. Part I of the book describes and evaluates a critical mass strategy for university academic budgeting, resource planning, and management. Part II provides an analysis of state government budgetary and program policy for universities.

The purpose of this book is not to reconcile alternative and competing views on the appropriate methods for resource allocation in postsecondary education. Rather, the attempt is to improve our understanding of university and state government budgetary objectives and strategies and the manner in which each may be interpreted to serve the public interest.

COMPETITION OVER BUDGETARY CONTROL
AND PROGRAM AUTHORITY

The essence of the countervailing prescriptive arguments presented here is that to remain vital in a period of
resource restraint, universities should attempt to negotiate
budgets and allocate financial resources internally using
critical mass program and resource criteria somewhat, but
not entirely, independent of student demand. On the other
hand, in order to achieve state objectives of financial control, state governments should attempt to negotiate and
allocate higher-education budgets and supporting academic
program plans on a student-unit subsidy basis.

The strategic financial and program objectives of
universities and state government, while united in attempting to serve the public interest, are viewed as competing
along the dimensions of control and authority. This conflict is most poignant in the financial resource negotiation
and decision process, that is, in budgeting. Universities
would prefer to manage themselves and spend public money
as freely as possible from state government financial control
and regulatory policy constraints. Universities also prefer
incremental or growing budgetary appropriations over decremental budgets.

On the other hand, for a variety of reasons related
to financial and program accountability and the need to
enforce norms of cost-effectiveness across government, state
officials generally prefer to have greater, rather than less,
control over university budgetary and program priorities.
They also perceive it necessary to cut university budget
appropriations to help balance state budgets strained by
recession-produced reductions in state revenues in nominal/
constant dollars, enrollment drops or shifts, inflation, and
increased expenditure demand from other state government
service areas. University budget reductions may also be
made by state officials out of a concern for equity in resource allocation where other service programs supported
by state government have to be cut as well.

Although some of the budgetary pressure on public
universities that characterized the late 1970s and early
1980s has been alleviated as a result of national economic
recovery in the mid-1980s, budgetary constraints in many
universities continue due to enrollment decline or stability
and redistribution as student instructional preferences
have shifted. State government budgetary stress and en-

rollment changes, coupled with the downward trend in federal financial assistance and research sponsorship for universities, which became more acute in the early 1980s, continue to threaten the financial condition of universities in the near future. Under such conditions, the competition in postsecondary education over budgetary control and program policy authority is likely to remain and, perhaps, to increase in intensity.

An attempt to reconcile competing views of how university funding and program priorities should be established and whether budgetary and regulatory leverage should be exerted by state government to control academic program distribution, content, and university management practices would be to misrepresent the way in which the world appears to operate. Universities and state government officials compete and often disagree strongly over budgetary and program policy. Much of this competition appears inevitable and even necessary to achieve budgetary equilibrium in state expenditure policy and to meet public service demand across a broad range of service areas. However, the view rendered here is that reforms should be made in both university and state government budgetary planning, negotiation, and decision-making practices. The changes suggested here are intended to clarify our understanding of how the public may be better served in post-secondary education through a reduction in conflict over centralization of control, but not through lessened competition for scarce resources.

FINANCIAL RESTRAINT IN UNIVERSITIES

Conditions of financial restraint present problems related to both internal institutional management and external affairs. On the one hand, universities face the task of developing internal resource planning and budgeting systems that produce the programmatic information necessary to enable definition of institutional priorities to guide budget allocation and program reduction decision making. Resource planning systems are expected to enable participation of academic units and the faculty as a whole in developing program review criteria, retrenchment, and reallocation priorities. The budget and planning process is also expected to provide the information system and data base to permit comprehensive and equitable institutional program evaluation.

To survive retrenchment in a manner that maintains their vitality, higher education institutions also now find it necessary to develop more explicit and successful operational marketing strategies to deal with the student constituencies, governments, private and nonprofit organizations that provide their lifeblood of financial resources. Improved external marketing entails more than improved public relations and advertising. In fact, such efforts are likely to be productive only where institutions invest in market research to determine the nature of consumer demand and the degree of political and constituent support for the services they produce. Assessment of market competition, of the degree of consumer segmentation, of differential demand and support patterns, and of demand price elasticity across income and age groups in response to changes in tuition and fee levels entails a considerable investment in market analysis.

Further, public higher education institutions find it necessary to develop methods to improve internal marketing of their budgets to state governments to prevent withdrawal of financial support based upon strict student enrollment budget formulas. In this regard institutions need to present cogent and persuasive arguments that in addition to student enrollment demand, program quality, and breadth criteria ought to be heeded by state legislators and executives as they prepare to wield the budget axe.

To university managers, the challenge to develop academic budgeting and planning processes and long-range plans that articulate program reallocation, financial and marketing strategies to increase the probability of maintaining institutional quality and program breadth is formidable. The purpose of Part I of this book is in part to describe and analyze a resource management process that performs the functions of academic budgeting and program resource planning, internal program review, and program priority setting. This system is intended to integrate with the development and execution of external financial and marketing strategies to meet the demands of an era of restraint.

The critical mass approach to academic resource budgeting and planning is both a resource management process and an academic program information system. It enables institutions to define the criteria for program review and priority setting and to develop performance-oriented measures that translate into data for budgetary decision making.

Through the definition of institutional mission, critical mass program size, and core resources necessary to support critical mass programs, institutions become better able to compare academic unit performance in instruction and research. Additionally, the definition of critical mass program size and core resources permits public universities and colleges to defend themselves better and to negotiate more effectively against attacks on programs and financial resources by state government executive and legislative officials, budgeteers, and program review staff.

The critical mass approach to resource planning and decision making supplies the rationale and the programmatic and budgetary information necessary to argue effectively against state government attempts to reduce financial support due to declining student enrollment. Further, where student enrollment is steady or increasing, the critical mass approach enables proactive and systematic budgeting and planning for growth and internal redistribution of financial resources so that universities can meet the challenges posed by changes in student composition, educational preferences, instructional and research technology, and other factors related to the production and marketing of university services.

The use of what may be termed rational systems management in universities is discussed in Chapter Two as a means of placing in perspective the critical mass resource decision model presented and evaluated in Chapter Three. The issues addressed initially are whether the development of systems for use on the academic side of university management is necessary or appropriate and if so, under what conditions such systems would appear advantageous or disadvantageous in terms of both internal management and state government relations. Chapter Four constitutes a description and analysis of how public universities recognize and attempt to manage financial stress. It indicates in part how universities might adapt to resource scarcity and environmental change.

STATE GOVERNMENT BUDGETARY AND PROGRAM POLICY CONTROL

State government officials possess a number of instruments of policy to influence and control the behavior of universities. These instruments include budgetary policy determined largely by governors, by executive finance and

budget officials, particularly where item-veto authority
exists, by legislative budget and policy committees, and
by legislative analytical-support officials. Through the
establishment of administrative rules, executive-branch
program review and evaluation, the passage of legislation
and legislative oversight, state governments influence future budgetary policy and the manner in which institutional
programs are undertaken and provided. State educational
coordinating commissions attempt to regulate the provision
of institutional services by universities, both at individual
institutions and within multicampus state systems through
budgetary and program review and degree program approval. Often these agencies also attempt to regulate competition for students through direct regulation of supply
and market entry.

Officials in the executive and legislative branches
of state government sometimes become involved in issues of
university management and academic program authority in
the context of budget negotiation, in review of university
program expansion proposals, in analysis of capital project
planning, and under special circumstances where the public becomes aroused over university activities. Under the
worst of circumstances from the view of university faculty
and administrators, state officials may attempt to influence
or control academic instructional and research program content. State judicial decisions and opinions exert an increasingly important influence over university policy and
management practices. Other examples of state government
influence over university structure, behavior, and performance may be identified.

The second portion of this book provides perspectives on state government budgetary and regulatory control.
Several themes are developed. The first is that the state
may use a number of strategic approaches to influence university instructional practices, specifically with regard to
stimulating or retarding instructional innovation and adaptation to student preferences. The enrollment market strategy discussed in Chapter Five would reduce the scope of
centralized state program and policy controls but would improve capacities for influencing institutional responsiveness
through refined fiscal control. This use of fiscal control
in the form of per-unit subsidies rather than program review and regulatory controls may be argued to serve the
interests of state government and, in the long run, universities as well. Advantages to universities from such a system might include improved clarity in state policy and bud-

getary incentives regarding university behavior and performance, on the one hand, and greater institutional authority and autonomy in program and service delivery decision making on the other.

Chapter Six argues that budgetary controls are often incorrectly applied by state government budgeteers because they misunderstand the objectives of control. The theory of budgetary control presented in this chapter indicates under what conditions various ex ante and ex post budgetary controls may be applied to achieve state objectives and where controls seem to be a waste of time and effort for central budget staffs and universities. The economic rationale for experimentation with per-unit subsidies in state budgeting follows, presented in the context of a budgetary control theory.

The issue of regulatory control exerted by state government, higher education boards, and commissions over interinstitutional competition in new educational service markets is explored in Chapter Seven. Employing an industrial organization approach, a theme is developed that while there may be some valid arguments for direct regulation of market entry and instructional program development under conditions of rapid enrollment growth, there is no advantage to regulation to prevent interinstitutional competition in periods of stable, shifting, or declining enrollment.

Chapter Eight summarizes the reforms in university and state government budgetary and program control methods appropriate for postsecondary management under conditions of resource scarcity and environmental uncertainty.

The purpose of this book is to improve our understanding of budgeting and control of the academic side of university activity. To gain perspective on how responsibility for resource planning, budgeting, and control developed in universities, the following section presents a brief historical overview of how the academic management function in universities evolved.

INSTITUTIONAL ORIGINS AND
DEVELOPMENT OF GOVERNANCE

The origins of institutions for advanced learning appear to lie in the academies of ancient Greece. The Sophists taught oratory, grammar, logic, and philosophy

in schools as early as the fifth century B.C.[1] Pythagoreans researched and taught mathematics, astronomy, and
metaphysics in formal schools. The theories of Empedocles,
Anaxagoras, and Democritus anticipated the development of
atomic theory.[2] The philosophers Protagoras of Abdera,
Gorgias of Leontenium, and Hippias of Elis all contributed
to the tradition of formalized transmission of knowledge,
which was inherited by the Academy of Plato and the
Lyceum of Aristotle. Plato's Academy served as a model
of what has been termed the Oxford approach to institutional organization and communication of advanced knowledge, dedicated to teaching the humanities. The schools
of the Sophists and Pythagoreans emphasized the teaching
of applied theory, ideas which could be used directly to
enhance practical "success in life" for their students, an
approach which led to development of the tradition of professional schools. The origins of university academic organization per se, thus, are found in the design of curricula in the Greek schools and academies.

The origins of academic management as a function
may be viewed generally to rest in the development of
mechanisms for governance of colleges and universities at
the end of the Middle Ages in Europe. The universities of
Bologna, Salerno, Salamanca, Paris, Oxford, and Cambridge
utilized different modes of governance and management. At
the University of Bologna, student-faculty guilds planned
curricula, instruction, and research. Kerr describes the
emergence of administrations:

> The original medieval universities had at
> the start nothing that could be identified
> as a separate administration, but one quick-
> ly developed. The guild of masters of stu-
> dents selected a rector; and later there
> were deans of the faculties. At Oxford and
> Cambridge, there came to be the masters
> of the colleges.[3]

In England, creation of the University Grants Committee stimulated the growth of an administrative structure
of vice-chancellors at Oxford and Cambridge that dealt with
planning and administration of the entire university. The
University of Paris was governed and managed by faculty
peers.[4] Hofstadter and Metzger trace the origins of the
lay governing board model, which has prevailed in the

United States, from seventeenth-century Holland.5   With
respect to lay boards, however, the distinction between
governance and management must be made.   Most lay
boards have not engaged in institutional management in
public institutions of higher education beyond setting policy priorities.   Exception to this notion can be found in
some contemporary community college lay boards that exert
significant impact on institutional academic management.
However, our focus is on universities rather than all of
higher education.

The academic specialization that developed in European universities in the seventeenth, eighteenth, and nineteenth centuries reveals the degree to which institutions
sought to satisfy particular curricular objectives in addition to simply reflecting the character of the societies
within which they evolved.   The University of Bologna became a center for study of the law; the University of
Salerno provided specialized instruction in medicine.   Establishment of the University of Berlin in 1809 is regarded
as a significant event in the specialized development of
the modern university.   At Berlin, departments consisting
of faculty teaching in specific subject areas were organized.
Separate graduate-level instruction and university research
institutes were created.   Academic management prescribed
the general nature and organization of instruction and research activity.   Disciplinary planning and management
were performed at the departmental level.

In the United States, the colonial and revolutionary
period witnessed establishment of colleges and universities
based on the Oxford model.   The history of institutional
governance and management during this period is the history of the development of individual institutions.6   Thomas
Jefferson adopted the elective system at the University of
Virginia and developed the campus library as a component
of the institution.   Academic management at Virginia, Harvard, Yale, Michigan, and Brown was accomplished by
faculty, influenced strongly in some cases by institutional
founders such as Thomas Jefferson.   It was not until after
the Civil War that U.S. institutions began to adopt the
organizationally sophisticated Berlin model of university
instruction and research within departments, schools, and
colleges.   Johns Hopkins University, established in 1876,
was the first U.S. university to be organized in this manner, emphasizing graduate instruction and research.   Harvard, Michigan, Columbia, the University of California,

and numerous other public and private institutions soon
followed this approach in the latter quarter of the nineteenth century.[7] Veysey notes some of the important influences on how the U.S. university developed after the
Civil War:

> Since its leaders lacked the "feel" of what
> the public might be willing to accept, new
> ideas from Europe could penetrate with
> fewer impedances. Indeed, it was the
> luxury of widespread public indifference
> which permitted such a variety of abstract
> conceptions of the university to blossom
> immediately after 1865. In this fluid time,
> before the pressure of numbers had irrevo-
> cably descended, entire universities might
> even be founded or reorganized in the
> names of such particular conceptions. Presi-
> dents and professors could engage in de-
> bate among themselves over the guiding aim
> of the university with the feeling that their
> words really mattered. It could be hoped
> that deeply held convictions would realize
> themselves in institutional structures.[8]

The 20-year period prior to World War I has been
characterized as the first "golden age" of U.S. academe.
However, higher education in the United States suffered
after the Civil War until the 1890s. It is only in positive
retrospect that this period is viewed as one of development.
Institutional faculty and administrators were not confident
that Americans valued higher education during this period.
In the quarter century after the Civil War, despite a nearly 25 percent growth in the nation's population, enrollments in higher education grew less than 5 percent. Americans were not yet imbued with the spirit of higher education. As Veysey points out, "In 1885 less than a quarter
of all American congressmen were college graduates, as
compared with 38% ten years earlier."[9] It was the emergence of U.S. business and industry, along with enactment
of the Morrill Land Grant Act of 1862, that created an at-
mosphere in which Americans began to seek higher education as a means of social and economic mobility. Indus-
trialization and the national decision to increase agricul-
turally related research and instruction had a direct impact

on academic management, asserting a demand for professional education in addition to the humanities and the physical and nascent social sciences taught at that time in U.S. universities. The Morrill Act was written specifically to elicit the development of "agriculture and mechanical" instruction. By and large, however, until the 1890s universities pursued their development without much general public interest or support.

THE ROLE OF THE EXECUTIVE

Governance and management of higher education institutions at the turn of the century and for the several decades following was carried out most directly by strong institutional presidents and chancellors such as Gilman at Johns Hopkins, Eliot at Harvard, Hutchins at Chicago, and Wheeler at the University of California. If it is accepted that the initial phase of academic planning and management consists of institutional goal setting, then a first step in the historical development of the university academic management process was the expression and examination of values as a precursor to specification of institutional goals. The articulation of values by presidents of major U.S. universities at the turn of the century was crucial to the development of institutions. Whether the president was Upton Sinclair's "universal father" or the "initiator" of James Morrill, he stimulated an interest in public values among politicians, faculty, and the general public. This expression of values influenced the development of the academic character of universities.[10] Conflict between populist and academic views of the university that arose in this period were manifested in the approaches to institutional development preferred by presidents and their administrations versus those preferred by university faculty.

> Academic executives emerged with a battle-scarred sensitivity to the subject of public opinion. Knowing its power, fearing its force, these men could develop an almost obsequious habit of submissiveness to it. But, secondly, the very aloofness of many academic concerns from public sympathy tended also to attract men to the university who sought to separate themselves

from the other elements of the society. This
second kind of academic man, more often a
professor than a president, relished the
distinctiveness of the higher learning. He
wished to build the university in an almost
deliberately unpopular style. While naturally he hoped to win the loyalties of a
certain number of students, he assumed
that these students would have to meet the
standards he imposed, not that he should
have to go forward to bargain with them.
The academic life, for this kind of believer
in the university, must set its own terms.[11]

The means by which faculty sought to retain control of
their disciplines was to organize more carefully into "scientific schools" to prove that "science had its own, carefully
segregated, place within the institution and that no wholesale revision of curricula needed to be fueled from above."[12]

The more decentralized modern university that emerged
after World War I posed some challenging management problems: how could all this diverse activity be held together
to form an interdependent and cohesive set of relationships?
The establishment of research units in the new university
created an organizational entity that was difficult to incorporate into the formalized planning and management process
of universities. Holding together the rapidly expanding em-
pire of the emerging modern university became the responsibility of presidents and administrators. Responsibility for
academic management sifted into several categories. Presidents articulated broad values and set major policies and
academic program priorities, such as the emphasis on graduate instruction and research. Faculties, on the other hand,
divided into specialized working groups, developing their
curricular and disciplinary interests. Academic resource
management and the outlines of budgetary decision processes developed in this context.

Academic administration in the emerging university
developed under the president. Administrations were com-
prised of deans, support staff, and cadres of senior pro-
vessors in whom the president had trust. As Veysey notes,
"administration connoted a certain state of mind; it meant
these people in the university community who characteris-
tically thought in terms of institutional management or organizational planning."[13] One of the early practitioners

of institutional administration was Eliot at Harvard, who had a strong concern for budgets and public relations. Eliot's book University Administration was published in 1908, and a number of articles on academic and general institutional management were published soon thereafter. Typewriters, administrative forms to maintain records of teaching appointments, university catalogues and course announcements, annual reports, and numerous other accoutrements of administration became part of the presidents' aegis in large universities before World War I.

Competition between university administrators and academic units and faculty began to grow as a consequence of the conflict between presidents and faculty over the mission of the university. This competition and conflict was stimulated by the inquisitiveness of the administrator, propelled by the president, and by the administrator's sense of role.

> If the administrator had confined his purview to the financial and technical aspects of the university, conflict might not have appeared. But such restraint on his part would have been inconceivable, for few financial questions lacked some academic bearing as long as departments begged for money. The normal need of deciding matters of tenure and promotion would have caused emotions to rise, had there been no other form of executive interference, for when these practical questions presented themselves the dream of a "republic of letters" retreated most abjectly into the realm of theory. As it was, many academic executives claimed the abstract right to judge the performance of professors quite comprehensively. Bureaucratic administration was the structural device which made possible the new epoch of institutional empire-building without recourse to specific shared values. Thus, while unity of purpose disintegrated, a uniformity of standardized practices was coming into being.[14]

Different styles of academic management may be contrasted in U.S. universities after the First World War.

Academic resource planning and management was carried out either by small and informal groups composed of faculty and administrators or by the personal aristocracy of presidents and administrators working independently of the faculty. Competition for prestige among U.S. universities had a marked influence on the development of the academic management function. As universities were ranked according to the quality and breadth of their curricula, the quality of their graduate education, the strength of their faculty, their libraries, and so forth, institutional development could no longer proceed without the setting of priorities. Creation of professional academic societies and organizations (for example, the American Association of Land Grant Colleges and Universities in 1887) before and after World War I also exercised an influence on the emergence of the academic management function in universities. These factors caused a professionalization of academic management independent of faculty involvement.

The boom in student enrollments that began in the 1890s and resumed later in the 1920s exerted considerable pressure for institutions to plan and manage higher education institutions, which grew from approximately 30,000 in 1870 to 1.1 million by 1930 while institutions grew in number from 500 to 1,400.[15] This growth, coupled with adoption of the elective system, created a need for curriculum and student-flow planning. Planning of this nature pressed the level of administrative coordination far beyond Hutchins' view of the organization of a university as departments with interconnected heating systems. During this period, some institutional presidents were careful not to emphasize the bureaucratic nature of their institutions to the general public or to their faculties for fear of provoking reaction against activities that were absolutely necessary in their eyes. The centralization of academic management proceeded, protected by university presidents.

In the 1930s, U.S. higher education encountered a period of reduced growth related generally to the Great Depression. While the trend to mass education had begun in the 1920s, only well-to-do families could afford to send their children to universities in the 1930s. This period of slowed growth may be likened to that of the 1970s and 1980s in that it enabled institutions to evaluate themselves and their previous growth more carefully. This period was not, however, one of tranquil deliberation. Conflict between administrations and faculties over governance and management, greater clamor for student involvement, intense interest in foreign and domestic policy, and threats of reduced state spending, among other things, created pressures in universities that stimulated the maturation of procedures for administration control.

> Colleges and universities . . . were harassed from all sides—by state bureaucracies that imposed repressive controls, by demands for cutbacks in expenditures, by attacks on their nature and function from the radicals of the right and left, by student dissent and faculty distress, by scapegoat treatment from demagoguery on platform and in press. There is undoubtedly a resemblance between conditions producing the loss of priority status in the current situation and events in the thirties—but the virulence of criticism in the Depression far surpassed what is now encountered.[16]

POSTWAR DEVELOPMENTS

The influx of federal monies for research into universities during and after World War II may be regarded as one of the primary influences on the development of the contemporary university. Many federally financed projects required very specific academic and scientific control that operated outside the mainstream of management for the university campus or multicampus system of which they were a part. During the war, universities also provided coursework on federal contract, especially in engineering, science, management, and related defense training. Some of the curricula developed in this period were retained after the war ended.

Universities and colleges experienced continued enrollment loss until the late 1940s. Because institutional curricula had been changed in some cases to accommodate the military effort, many institutions consciously reviewed their programs during this period to determine the appropriate content of university curricula. Even greater emphasis on administrative management and control was to come soon thereafter with the boom in WW II veteran-student enrollments financed under the G.I. Bill. In accommodating enrollment growth, and as a result of increasing interaction with the federal and state governments, university administration became a major component of the university. Kerr characterizes this change as follows:

> By force of circumstance if not by choice, [administration becomes] a more prominent feature of the university. As the institution becomes larger, administration becomes ·more formalized and separated as a distinct function; as the institution becomes more complex, the role of administration becomes more central in integrating it; as it becomes more related to the once external world, the administration assumes the burden of these relationships.[17]

Resource planning and management as an explicit function emerged in universities only in the last 30 years. This is not to say that Eliot's administrative transformation of Harvard and Harper's efforts at Chicago did not involve management. However, the specialization of effort in academic management in universities is a relatively recent phenomenon.

During the 1950s and 1960s, university academic management coalesced further in response to student enrollment demand and increased federal contract and grant funding. Faculty in departments determined which courses would be taught and by whom, and which new areas of research should be explored. However, as Jencks and Riesman have noted, while the faculty retained formal power over the institutions through academic senates and departmental academic planning, the budgetary and personnel decision making shifted steadily to administrators representing presidents and lay boards of trustees.[18] At the same time, the complexities of decision in the modern university tended to push decision-making authority to presidents and their administrative staffs. The shift of authority to professional academic administrators may be compared to the managerial revolution in business and industry. What is distinctive organizationally about this shift in universities is that in many cases the top management that gained power tended to represent the middle management of the organization, that is, the faculty. Because most university presidents and high-level administrators began their careers as academics, they have tended to view institutions as assemblages of scholars and scientists. Loyalty to faculty at times had been observed to cause administrators to be captive to the "prejudices of their faculty."[19] This is not to imply that competition and conflict between academic administration and faculty was reduced. However, the role of the university president in mitigating and orchestrating relations between faculty and administrators may be viewed as a potential advantage for universities relative to other organizations due to the background and academic understanding possessed by many presidents. It may also be noted that while the ascendance of professional administrations in general has led to considerable resentment over usurpation of rights and responsibilities among faculty, it has also provided a useful insulation for the faculty to protect the productive core of the university organization. When there are system failures, it is convenient to blame incompetent administrators. When resources are not received or allocated as faculty would wish, it is the president and the administrators who bear the brunt of criticism. More on the changing administrative role of university presidents will be noted in Chapter Eight.

CONTEMPORARY ACADEMIC RESOURCE MANAGEMENT

In the last decade, increased requirements for planning and accountability in budgeting, academic and non-academic program review, personnel administration, student admissions procedures, and faculty workload have caused academic institutions to expand their management capacities. As Clark Kerr noted in his postscript to The Uses of the University in 1972, the change in public and political sympathy for academe has exerted considerable influence on university administrations. The "minor counter-revolt" of undergraduate students in 1963 became a major revolt against academic institutions as symbols of a corrupted society through the late 1960s and early 1970s. Public resentment over student unrest was manipulated by politicians while, at the same time, "the university was accelerating its racing car named Science, hardly noticing that the public was ready to reduce the supply of gas."[20]

During the late 1960s and early 1970s, many state government officials became critical of the universities for their tolerance of student activism, and also for their purported fiscal irresponsibility. Although it took a few years to translate such political and social value judgments into bureaucratic action, state-level officials have challenged the fiscal and management integrity of universities. Audit and program review findings have been utilized in budget negotiation to limit and reduce state appropriations to universities. In addition to their use in reducing budgets, audit and other studies have been employed to publicly discredit universities, imploring them to become more frugal, effective, and responsible. The actions of the public in voting for expenditure-reducing alterations of taxation policies have added to these pressures directly or indirectly, for example, Proposition 13 in California.

In eroding public confidence in universities, state executives have to some extent altered the sense of trust and esteem citizens have traditionally exhibited toward higher education institutions. This confidence and pride had been most evident in the period 1947 to 1955 and in the early and mid-1960s when enrollments and public expenditures for higher education grew rapidly. The tradition of tuition-free or low-tuition public higher education before 1970 was sincere testimony to the social commitment to higher education, especially given the regressivity of the income redistributional effect resulting from such policies. As political rhetoric weakened university support from its general constituency, criticism of management practices has reinforced adversaries and neutralized supporters of higher education in state legislatures. Coalitions of adversaries have been forged of fiscal conservatives wanting to reduce university budgets and populist liberals who sympathize with characterizations of universities as educationally elitist and unresponsive to student needs.[21] In short, the environment had become more threatening for universities. Reductions in federal government spending for research added to the financial threat for research-oriented universities.

External threat and the increasing complexity of academic disciplines created a need within universities to order information about academic organization for purposes of improving internal management and external relations. One of the ways in which complex organizations attempt to deal with threat and uncertainty is to engage in planning and management control. Under circumstances of reduced resources, priority setting becomes more necessary. The environmental context described above has caused many higher education institutions to devote more attention to the resource management function. Environmental threat poses significant challenges both to university organization and to strategic resource planning and management. The purpose of this book is to assist universities in responding to these challenges. Part of this effort is directed to indicate how state governments may achieve public educational objectives while reducing their control over university management decision making.

NOTES

1. C. Kerr, The Uses of the University (Cambridge, Mass.: Harvard University Press, 1961), 9.

2. J. Bentley, Philosophy: An Outline-History (Paterson, N.J.: Littlefield, Adams, 1964), 7.

3. Kerr, Uses of the University, 27.

4. Ibid., 28.

5. R. Hofstadter and W. Metzger, The Development of Academic Freedom in the United States (New York: Columbia University Press, 1955), 61, 71.

6. Kerr, Uses of the University, 28.

7. Ibid., 13.

8. L. Veysey, "Stability and Experiment in the American Undergraduate Curriculum," in Content and Context, ed. C. Kaysen, The Carnegie Commission on Higher Education (San Francisco: McGraw-Hill, 1973), 3.

9. L. Veysey, The Emergence of the American University (Chicago: The University of Chicago Press, 1965), 4.

10. U. Sinclair, The Goose-Step: A Study of American Education (Pasadena, Calif.: Upton Sinclair, 1923), 382-84; J. Morrill, The Ongoing State University (Minneapolis: University of Minnesota Press, 1960), 48.

11. Veysey, Emergence of the American University, 17.

12. Ibid., 49.

13. Ibid., 305; see also W. DeVane, Higher Education in Twentieth-Century America (Cambridge, Mass.: Harvard University Press, 1965), 14-33.

14. Veysey, Emergence of the American University, 309, 311.

15. D. Henry, Challenges Past, Challenges Present (San Francisco: Jossey-Bass, 1975), 5.

16. Ibid., 37.

17. Kerr, Uses of the University, 28.

18. C. Jencks and D. Riesman, The Academic Revolution (New York: Doubleday, 1968), 16–17.

19. Ibid., 27.

20. Kerr, Uses of the University, 134–35.

21. M. Trow, "The Public and Private Lives of Higher Education," Daedalus 104 (Winter 1975):125.

PART I
Critical Mass
Resource Management
in Universities

Under conditions of fiscal stress and restraint institutions propose resource allocation changes that are not strictly tied to institutional enrollment levels. These proposals often focus attention on the resource impact of internal shifts in student demand and the desirability of maintaining minimum, or "critical mass," levels of academic program breadth and quality. Part I addresses the academic budgeting and resource planning procedures needed to advance nonenrollment-driven resource maintenance and acquisition proposals in institutional and state-level budgets and strategic academic plans.

The purpose of the critical mass academic resource management system presented here is to facilitate analysis, priority setting, and negotiation of academic program alternatives. The critical mass approach establishes an institution-wide decision process and information system for setting priorities in academic program development through (a) analysis of existing breadth and depth of faculty expertise in instruction and research at the subdisciplinary level and (b) through identification of subdisciplinary areas in which academic units would like to provide instruction and research in the future. Critical mass denotes the level of course offerings and research which academic units could not reduce and still maintain programs that fulfill their own objectives, compatible with the overall mission of their institution. Critical mass program size and core resource requirements are established by academic unit faculty and then negotiated with institutional administrations and state government.

The critical mass resource planning and decision process is designed for application in medium- and large-sized universities in which formal, comprehensive, and integrated academic resource management systems do not operate presently. Its purpose is to improve institutional capacities for proactive academic program management under financial constraints. Further, implementation of the critical mass approach would assist the development of university marketing strategies and sharpen the market research attentiveness in institutions to changes in public educational preferences.

Two

Systems Management in Universities: Competing Paradigms of Adaptation and Control

An evolution in the modes of governance, resource planning, and management in higher education institutions has occurred historically as the range and depth of human knowledge has expanded. Universities and colleges have reflected increasing social complexity in their transformation into more complex organizations. An important element in this transformation has been the shift in management responsibility from faculty engaged in teaching and research to full-time academic administrators.

As higher education institutions have become more complex, both within themselves and in the nature of their relationships to the outside world, university administrators have established more complex procedures to plan and manage. In establishing these procedures, and sometimes as a result of pressure by external agencies, universities have created internal administrative systems to manage the admission, registration, and counting of students; the employment and maintenance of personnel records on faculty, administrative, and other staff; academic program development and review; evaluation of faculty and staff performance; utilization of physical space; budgeting, accounting, and payroll, and numerous other tasks.   In the language of organization theory, such instrumentation may be referred to as rationalized management systems (RMS).[1]

The use of RMS in complex organizations in the second half of the twentieth century evidences

1. a growing intellectual and organizational recognition of the importance of planning and policy coordination
2. the application of systems analysis to policy choice
3. the introduction of systems analysis and control theory in management practice
4. the attempt to rationalize budget control by the use of program-oriented budgeting processes.

The development of "systems thinking" as a means for solving problems has been described as a process of breaking problems into component parts, with each component analyzed and understood according to its particular characteristics.[2] The application of systems analysis to define and resolve problems in complex organizations also appears to have been influenced by concepts developed in the physical and biological sciences, for example, the subsystems of atomic theory, the systems of living organisms, and evolution.

Effective use of RMS appears, however, to be dependent upon the ability of systems to accurately capture the subtle characteristics of the organizations or functions intended to be better managed. Further, to quote Benveniste, "Rationalization exercises are only useful when the problem is formulated in such a way that there is sufficient information to yield a solution."[3] In many areas of public management, application of RMS appears to have been very useful. For example, in analyzing the manpower and supply resources necessary for reforestation, the United States Forest Service has used RMS to increase human and forest productivity.[4] The use of RMS in weapons development in the Department of Defense has sometimes been held as an example of successful systems and cost-benefit analysis application. In these examples it may be argued that the problem components and desired results could be measured quantitatively relatively easily. Thus, many note that a prime criterion for successful use of RMS is the ability to relate accurately the inputs and outputs of systems, and to relate them quantitatively.

The initial issue addressed in this chapter is the extent to which RMS are useful in universities and colleges to improve academic resource planning, budgeting resource management, decision making, and, ultimately, the quality of institutional performance. The most obvious problem in application of RMS to education lies in clear and unambiguous identification of results. Applying a production

function model to higher education institutions, the "inputs"
for a university can be quantitatively measured in terms
of numbers of students, amounts of dollars appropriated to
institutions (the price paid by the state for instruction in
an economic sense), per-student expenditures by governments and by students, faculty salaries, and other variables. The production functions of institutions, that is,
how institutions accomplish their tasks, can be measured
through the use of quantitative measures, or "proxies,"
such as student credit units, student and faculty full-time
equivalencies (FTEs), weekly faculty-student contact hours,
numbers of research publications, and other measures.

Leaving aside for a moment the major issues of the
accuracy and appropriateness of quantitative proxies as
measurements for teaching, learning, and the advancement
of knowledge, a major problem remains in the measurement
of output in higher education. Certainly, there are some
convenient quantitative output proxies used to measure university performance, for example, number of degrees
granted, student enrollment, and future earnings of students. In addition, there are means for quantitatively relating inputs to outputs, such as rate of return on dollar
investments by students to obtain degrees relative to additional future income gained by having a degree and being
better educated.[5]

Application of the economic theory of the firm in
production function modeling to higher education has been
examined by a number of researchers in the past decade
or so.[6] The model has been applied to predict the behavior of institutions with some success. Hypotheses such
as that higher education institution executives act as
"revenue maximizers" and that institutions do what the
financial systems pay them to do (response to financial
incentives) irrespective of conflicting administrative guidelines and political rhetoric have been examined.[7] Price,
demand and demand elasticity, employment demand, and
other factors have been analyzed relative to the costs of
education, numbers of degrees achieved, and other output
measures. However, this type of analysis has not overcome
entirely the problem of output measurement.

According to Hanushek and others, higher education
outputs may be divided into cognitive and noncognitive
categories.[8] Cognitive outputs are measurable through student achievement tests. The value added to a student's
breadth and depth of knowledge can be tested to some

extent by longitudinal analysis, for example, through comparison of test scores before and after university attendance. Noncognitive benefits, such as improved citizen-
ship, are not easily measured, although proxies such as
voting behavior are available for use in this regard.
Sophisticated quantitative analysis in this area consistent-
ly runs into the problem of simultaneous equation bias,
that is, that independent variables relate and overlap in
ways that cannot be controlled, partially because the
ranges of variables are very broad, and also because of
problems of sensitivity and inability to measure some variables with tight confidence in the results. In short, it
has been difficult to accurately relate input and output
variables in higher education in ways that unambiguously
guide academic resource planning and decision making at
the institutional or state level.

Benveniste has argued that the use of "rationalization exercises are valuable when . . . objectives can be
easily specified . . . [and when] we can measure important components of the inputs, process and output variables."[9] This does not appear to be the case for higher
education. However, even where this is not possible, there
may still be some value in the use of RMS:

> Rationalization exercises are important in
> the context of rising levels of external un-
> certainty if and when . . . they provide
> ways of thinking about decisions involving
> many variables as long as goals are agreed
> to, are clear and measurable, and as long
> as we know what it is we are doing . . .
> they provide mechanisms of articulation
> when the relations between components are
> well understood, and a willingness to co-
> operate emerges from this knowledge.[10]

The fact that successful relation of input and process variables to output variables in higher education has
not been accomplished has not prevented the use of RMS
and numerous quantitative proxies for resource planning
and decision making in higher education. There is, however, a growing body of literature in higher education
which protests this usage both in terms of its limited relevance and its inaccuracy in portraying the truly important
aspects of institutional educational activity.

Martin Trow has criticized the application of economics, budgeting and management control, and quantitative methods to higher education, decrying planners for believing that true outputs of higher education are measurable.[11] Conceding the use of quantitative proxies as necessary at systemwide, state, and federal levels to keep central systems analysts from sticking their noses too deeply into the "private lives" of institutions, he decries the leveling effect that RMS use tends to have on how government budgeteers, decision makers, and the general public regard higher education. He notes that the particular strength of higher education is its pluralism. In essence, he asks RMS zealots to remember what James March and Herbert Simon pointed out two decades ago, that organizations are not made up of offices, telephones, data systems, computer terminals, or even rules in the Weberian sense.[12] Rather, they are made up of people. Trow asks those who use RMS in resource management to remember that the full-time equivalent faculty (FTEF) and full-time equivalent students (FTES) they manipulate are real, live faculty and students, and that the keys to teaching and learning, to the extent that they are known, cannot be generalized beyond certain levels of abstraction. In assessing the relationship between institutional diversity and the leveling tendency of bureaucratic analysis of higher education resource use he observes,

> For one thing, the maintenance of high levels of diversity involves an equally higher measure of . . . "slack"--that is to say, resources which cannot be specifically allocated to or justified by current demand. Central authority, in part because it also centralizes responsibility in the service of narrow conceptions of efficiency, tends to trim programs to meet current rather than uncertain future needs.
> In addition, central authorities are governed by broad norms of equity which prescribe equal treatment for equivalent "units" under a single governing body. This is, in a sense, the same norm that says that to a parent all children are of equal worth and deserve equal treatment. But diversity rests very often on unequal

> treatment, on unequal support, on unequal
> forms of rules and unequal application of
> rules.   That is what diversity is about,
> and the serious application of norms of
> equitable treatment tends to have a marked
> leveling effect on component units and pro-
> grams, reducing at least some dimensions
> of their genuine diversity.   These norms of
> equity are especially strong when resources
> are constrained.   It is one thing to admin-
> ister inequalities when all budgets are ris-
> ing; it is quite a different and more diffi-
> cult matter when budgets are constant or
> falling.[13]

With regard to arguments that there is little evidence to suggest that higher education produces external
benefits for society, Trow provides a number of additional
arguments against the use of quantitative analysis.[14]   For
example, he argues that "a good deal of what has made
great universities really creative has been a function of
bad data collection.   Much of the best as well as the worst
in higher education has flourished in, indeed required, a
decent obscurity."[15]

This view may be understood to reflect the work of
Bennis, Likert, Argyris, and other human relations organizational theorists to the effect that creativity and change
in organizations are related to the ability to engage in
risk-taking behavior.[16]   Bennis has asserted that when
people are closely watched, when their performance is
closely monitored, their task accomplishment may increase.
However, motivation to think about how to improve job performance is diminished along with job satisfaction.   The
risks involved in attempting creative thinking and practice
may be too great and the obstacles to high performance too
formidable when production pressure or other types of
stress are heavy.   The extent of productivity loss will be
reflected in risk aversion and self-justifying behavior distributed differentially in organizations relative to the application of such stress.   In fact, this behavior may be
observed in higher education institutions operating under
severe financial restraint.

Among the diversity of institutions in our society,
universities have been traditionally regarded as places in
which experimentation was not only encouraged but stimu-

lated as a way of life. However, the bureaucratic application of rationalized management systems in higher education often appears overly control oriented, revealing anti-
intellectual tendencies in generalization about the behavior
of students, faculty, and higher education institutions.
There appears to be a bias held by certain elements of
government and society that faculty and students are provided too much freedom to decide how to teach, to learn,
and to organize their professional and personal lives in
universities. Some narrow-mindedness about higher education institutions is understandably strong among central
government decision makers and officials, who are unable
to comprehend higher education production activity and are
ideologically biased against the social objectives of higher
education as it is presently constituted. However, such
biases may be viewed as socially counterproductive where
they restrict creativity in the search for new knowledge and
better understanding of different approaches to social problem solving.[17]

Bias exercised by elected officials, government budgeteers, and administrators in considering the academic
resource proposals and policies of institutions can exert
profound influence on the manner in which higher education institutions obtain and manage financial and human
resources. Although the biases of government officials toward higher education have not been studied as thoroughly
as is needed, observers of state government higher education program and financial policy formation have noted
factors that may explain characteristics of the behavior of
government officials, that is, that their values, social
views, and political attitudes are to a considerable extent
a product of limited educational and professional experience.[18] Trow has noted that "the democratization of higher
education . . . has broken the near monopoly of the leading state universities on the higher education of state
legislators . . . and professionals in state government."[19]
He explains that fewer numbers of state-level budgeteers,
planners, and decision makers have graduated from the
"leading" universities, and as a result, many are "not
quite so respectful" of high-prestige public institutions in
their "claims to resources and autonomy."[20] He goes on to
speculate as follows:

> They went to institutions which got by on
> less (and often resented it), and which

also were accustomed to a good deal more
direct state intervention and control. As
these people come to positions of influence
and authority, they often do not see why
the leading research university might not
also profit from closer public scrutiny, and
perhaps also from a smaller differential
advantage in per capita support for staff
and students.

The character, quality and perspectives of these professional administrators,
growing in numbers and in influence over
the life of universities from their positions
in state departments and coordinating commissions, is of great importance. My im-
pression is that many are what might be
called "populist-technocrats." Their views
are markedly egalitarian, hostile to elite
values and institutions. They identify with
the interests of "the people" over and
against the universities, and tend to be
more sympathetic to the non-selective public institutions. They serve these values,
within political and organizational constraints, through the manipulation of the
new techniques of rationalized management,
with its steady focus on measurable outputs,
and thus on the "efficiency" and "productivity," of colleges and universities. Underlying this stance is a conception of higher
education as a machine for the production
of "socially desireable ends," which are
seen as short-term and broadly popular.
Thus their sophisticated techniques are in
the service of populist values.[21]

From a broader social perspective, it must be observed that in many state governments and among many
citizens there is great pride in universities and colleges.
However, there also is considerable skepticism about university efficiency and management capability. Further,
there is some jealousy and resentment of academic autonomy.
The environment of trust that permitted the establishment
and expansion of the higher education segment of the education industry has clearly been eroded in the past decade.

The influence of public opinion in reaction to perceived university political radicalism during the Vietnam War era and more recently with nuclear disarmament demonstrations, and the manipulation of the press by political actors in some instances, certainly has contributed to the loss in confidence in higher education institutions. However, some government and public displeasure with universities may result from the opinion that universities are not managed well, and this view may be correct in more instances than academics and friends of higher education would care to admit.

The tendency toward intervention by government officials in internal institutional management over the last decade is very evident. Reorganization of budgetary, financial, and accounting systems in many public university systems has occurred in response to pressure from the state governors and legislators. The development of management systems in universities is testimony to the desire on the part of state decision makers to find out more clearly how institutions spend state-appropriated funds. This curiosity is inevitable and is not limited to financial matters. Appropriations are spent within or in support of academic programs and, therefore, if state executives, legislators, and planners wish to judge present effectiveness in the use of financial resources and proposals for new program funding, they naturally feel they must know more about academic programs. Increasingly, this concern centers on relating financial inputs to production functions under norms of efficiency, rather than to educational outputs or outcomes.

One of the major effects of increasing state concern over higher education expenditure and efficiency over the last decade has been the mobilization of structures and processes on behalf of institutions to respond to the challenges and questions posed by central government. As education budget and planning staffs in state capitals have grown in size and skill and have become better able to examine institutional affairs, university systems have responded by strengthening their administrative capacities for response in defense of their missions, objectives, and programs. As the size and skills of central university budget and planning offices have grown, so has the flow of questions concerned with the internal behavior and activities of academic units increased. The result of this vastly expanded demand for information has been a corresponding growth in the externally related administrative workload of university academic administrators and academic unit chairpersons and faculty.

An effect perceived as even more important by some institutional faculty and administrators is that the funds consumed by this mobilization have reduced the monies available for teaching and research activities and for direct academic support. This fact has become painfully evident to many institutions during the budget squeeze experienced over the last five years. An important management issue has become, how can institutional decision makers respond to central planning and information pressures while not themselves becoming the very threat against which they are supposed to be insulating the academic segment of universities?

It may be argued that there are several essential differences in the administrative inquisitiveness of central government versus university decision makers and staff. These differences relate to motives, decision incentives, and knowledge about universities as complex organizations. Elected officials are motivated by the desire for reelection. They attempt to reward constituents and to influence agencies of government with this primary objective in mind. The budget, analytical, and other staffs that serve elected officials are used, among other things, to maximize the chances of remaining in office and to maintain the political power rewards of continued incumbency. Where the public perceive discretionary income to be falling and taxes to be too burdensome, and are also concerned with overregulation and the bureaucratization of government, popular support is provided for restraint of government spending.

Political demand for restraint, preferences for new government program and service priorities on the part of some elected officials, and revenue shortfalls resulting from weakness in the economy have created incentives for government analysts to search out ways to reduce higher education budget appropriations. These incentives have resulted in the exertion of considerable pressure to justify resources on the basis of promised increases in efficiency. The pressure for efficiency, in turn, stimulates the development of information and management systems intended to evaluate the extent to which efficiency norms are met, and to tie this achievement or lack thereof to marginal budgetary appropriation adjustments (increments or decrements).

Earlier in this chapter it was noted that the use of rational management systems and an exclusive interest in efficiency can confuse rather than clarify the manner in which resources inputs relate to production activities and outputs in higher education. Although institutional academic decision makers face incentives that should cause them to attempt to understand how and why academic units perform as they do ·given some sophistication of knowledge about the behavior of complex organizations), state-level decision makers and staff appear to be faced with few incentives to try to understand the subtle and significant characteristics and differences that exist within and between academic units, fields, and disciplines. In fact, pressure to reallocate and/or reduce budget appropriations in most instances appears to result in efforts to avoid complexity while pressing for efficiency as measured by simple quantitative performance indexes such as student enrollment per full-time faculty. This occurs in part because the job of the budget cutter is easier when the rules of the resource acquisition or reduction game are simple, where they can be set or changed unilaterally from the center, and where the budget rule changes are designed explicitly either to reduce resource inputs or to extract commitments for increases in production for the same amount of financial resource input.

From the view of institutional decision makers, the operational objectives in playing the budget efficiency-control game are to protect the existing resource base, to obtain additional resources or minimize reduction, to resist control over how existing and new resources are expended, to reduce pressure for more information from central government decision makers and staff, and to maintain the power and authority for the institution and its units to set their own objectives.

An obvious danger in collecting more information about academic performance is that public universities will not be able to prevent acquisition and utilization of poor-quality information by political adversaries and central government budget controllers to reduce budgets. This fear is based upon the presumption that central government decision makers will not know how to interpret much of the information provided and, further, that they face incentives to use it to recommend decisions based upon their own, rather than university, values and priorities. The issue of confidentiality of information in public organizations is complicated by legal and procedural questions, many of which are still being tested in courts of law. And, while it may be axiomatic to presume that if information exists in some finite and organized form in a public organization, staff in a competing central government organization can obtain the information they desire if they know what they want, it is another step to presume that this information will be used appropriately in resource decision making.

In the context of the model for resource planning and decision making presented in this book, the gains accruing from better knowledge about academic unit planning would not be outweighed by the negative effects on the instructional and research activities of the university that might result from too much data collection or misuse of critical information by central state university or decision makers. In fact, the approach described in Chapter Three is intended to reduce the overall amount of administrative data collected in universities through systematic identification and collection of only that information to be used in decision making—that is, if data initially assembled are found not to be useful, then their collection should be terminated—and through organization of academic resource planning, budgeting, and program review activities and information collection into one integrated system, rather than in separate systems as is the case at most higher education institutions.

The caveats expressed earlier in this chapter regarding the use of RMS may be understood to hold for the critical mass approach to academic resource planning and decision making presented in the next chapter. However, applying the criterion that RMS are likely to be useful only when the problems they are intended to resolve are formulated so that the information provided by the instruments enable a solution to be developed, the critical mass approach would appear to serve and protect higher education institutions from resource loss far better than most are presently protected. Further, the critical mass approach is intended to supply the information necessary to enable development of resource defense and acquisition strategies from within, based upon the principle of identification and exploitation of comparative advantage, instead of having program reduction priorities mandated externally by central government agencies.

The critical mass approach anticipates the incentives for misuse of information and strategic misrepresentation of data by state budget offices and other control agency staff. It takes the position that the best defense to protect the purposeful slack in a university's resource base is a good offense. Further, it assumes that the rationale for insulating universities against withdrawal of uncommitted or flexibly allocatable resources is that higher education institutions need to adapt continually to socio-economic, political, and cultural changes in their environments, as do most complex organizations, and that such adaptation requires some slack resources. In addition, the critical mass approach to resource planning and decision making assumes that some resources must be reallocated within universities to maintain their adaptability, particularly under conditions of financial restraint.

From one view, where an environment of trust exists in relationships between government resource allocators and program-providing agencies, there is little need for formal methods of evaluation and accountability, in part because the costs of operating such systems exceed their benefits. In other words, universities must be trusted to use their resources wisely. A competing view would argue that like any other public agency dependent on public funding, universities must be fully evaluatable and accountable for the financial resources they consume. As noted, there are a number of difficult problems inherent in attempting to evaluate institutions that have hundreds of missions and objectives. Virtually every academic unit has a different mission and attempts to satisfy a different academic, professional, and consumer constituency. Because of this, evaluation and accountability systems are far more likely to provide meaningful information to stimulate adaptation, and much more apt to be responsive to public preferences, if they are implemented from within than from without, and from the bottom up instead of from the top down.

None of the views regarding the rationale for systems development in universities provided above presumes that state decision makers and staff will face different incentives in budgeting than they encounter presently. Instead, the critical mass approach assumes that the purposefulness of protecting academic resources, and the freedom to determine academic program priorities, will be understood clearly only by higher education institutional managers and faculty. Indeed, this appears to be inevitable given that state-level decision makers operate at such a distance from the essential and highly pluralistic research and teaching activities of academic units. An appreciation of this distance can be understood by the fact that in many instances even faculty colleagues within the same academic unit do not understand very well how and why their fellow faculty are pursuing their work.

Academic departments typically operate as loosely aggregated groups of entrepreneurs united by common support services such as secretarial staff and office equipment and, most importantly, a core instructional curriculum. However, the instructional curriculum often indicates more cohesion and interrelatedness within academic units than exists, given the diverse professional backgrounds, research interests, methodological skills, and pedagogical philosophies of faculties. In addition, faculty typically differ to a great degree in attitudes toward academic management, governance, and academic politics. To assume that such complex organizations may be understood and then guided programmatically at great distance (for example, by state government officials or by systemwide administrators in multicampus universities) is both perplexing and wrong. Thus, one premise articulated here and in subsequent chapters is that in order to preserve academic self-guidance, better use of rational management systems must be undertaken by universities to stimulate allocation of resources to their best use and to avoid mismanagement by central government and multi-institutional university decision makers. While universities do not lend themselves easily to management because of their social, political, and cultural diversity and the multiplicity of the products and services they provide, better management of academic resources is a necessity. This is particularly the case given a social environment and economic condition where spending restraint is a highly marketable political commodity.

NOTES

1. G. Benveniste, Bureaucracy (Berkeley, Calif.: Glendessary Press, 1977), 5.
2. C. Churchman, The Systems Approach (New York: Dell, 1969).
3. Benveniste, Bureaucracy, 6.

4. H. Kaufman, The Forest Ranger: A Study in Administrative Behavior (Baltimore: Johns Hopkins University Press, 1967).

5. R. Eckaus, Estimating the Returns to Education: A Disaggregated Approach (New York: McGraw-Hill, 1973). Eckaus demonstrates that the highest rate of return in dollars on student investment in higher education in the past has been for achievers of bachelor's degrees, with negative returns for many types of graduate education.

6. E. Hanushek, "Regional Differences in the Structure of Earnings," Review of Economics and Statistics 5 (May 1973):204-13.

7. R. Radner and L. Miller, Supply and Demand in United States Higher Education (San Francisco: McGraw-Hill, 1975).

8. Hanushek, "Regional Differences."

9. Benveniste, Bureaucracy.

10. Ibid., 7.

11. See, for example, M. Trow, "Reflections on the Transition from Mass to Universal Higher Education," Daedalus 99 (Spring 1970):1-42; M. Trow, "The Public and Private Lives of Higher Education," Daedalus 104 (Winter 1975):113-27.

12. J. March and H. Simon, Organizations (New York: Wiley, 1958).

13. M. Trow, "The Implications of Low Growth Rates for Higher Education," Higher Education 5 (1976):377-96.

14. Trow, "Public and Private Lives." Trow notes as follows: "This is indeed the assumption underlying the work of economists on manpower planning and theories of human capital." See, for example, the essays in L. Solmon and P. Taubman, eds., Does College Matter: Some Evidence on the Impacts of Higher Education (New York: Academic Press, 1973). "Very little empirical evidence exists on external benefits. Economists who analyze public policy toward higher education have shown an increasing tendency to regard the absence of good, hard quantified data in this area as indirect evidence that no such benefits exist. This may be more a reflection of the deficiencies in the economists' education or the narrowness of their perspective: some things in this world cannot be quantified," 35-36.

15. Trow, "Public and Private Lives," 143.

16. W. Bennis, Changing Organizations (New York: McGraw-Hill, 1966).

17.   S. Lipset, <u>Political Man</u> (Cambridge, Mass.: Harvard University Press, 1960).

18.   Benveniste, <u>Bureaucracy</u>.

19.   Trow, "Public and Private Lives," 123.

20.   Ibid.

21.   Ibid.

Three

The Critical Mass Approach
to Academic Resource Planning
and Decision Making

The topic of academic budgeting and planning has probably never been so thoroughly discussed in the academic community as during the past five years, not even in the rapid-growth era of the 1960s. Accepting conditions of slow or no growth, resource reduction, and budgetary pressure from state governments, many colleges and universities have given greater attention to internal program review and resource reallocation over the past decade.[1] This chapter describes an approach to academic resource planning and decision making appropriate to the context of financial restraint faced by research-oriented colleges and universities in the 1980s.

For the purposes of this exploration, institutional academic resource planning can be defined as an interactive process in which institutional and academic unit program goals, and the financial means for achieving these goals, are negotiated among faculty, administrators, and other parties within and outside the university. Academic budgeting and planning entails deciding how finite resources will be allocated, setting the conditions under which instruction, research, and supporting services will be provided. Thus, academic budgeting and planning integrate budgetary planning, decision making, academic program review, and elements of academic administration.

The purposes of the critical mass resource allocation decision model presented in this chapter are to facilitate planning, negotiation, and budgeting of academic program alternatives under conditions of financial restraint and to

enable academic units and universities and colleges, especially public institutions, to justify resource acquisition,
retention, and allocation on a basis other than student
enrollments. Under the model, critical mass program size
and "core" resource requirements are negotiated between
academic units and institutional administrators similar to
the ways in which budgets and plans are now negotiated,
except that proposals are reviewed and resources are allocated on the basis of better-defined academic program and
disciplinary characteristics than are presently available in
most institutions. Resource negotiation is designed to operate within the context of a highly defined institutional
planning process. In addition, implementation of the model
at the institutional level enables the university or multiuniversity system to negotiate its budget with state officials based upon critical mass resource requirements. The
model provides both proactive and reactive strategies that
may be employed by institutions to fit the opportunities
and constraints presented by the nature of the funding
relationship between universities and state governments.
The critical mass approach to resource decision making is
intended to aid higher education institutions in adapting
to different economic conditions and to changes in government funding priorities.

GENESIS OF THE CRITICAL MASS APPROACH

The term critical mass is defined in physics generally as the mass of fissionable material required to produce a self-sustaining sequence of fission reactions in a
system, or the minimum mass of fissionable material that
will sustain a chain reaction. It is reputed that the term
critical mass was first used in physics by Lise Meitner
and Otto Frisch in 1939, explaining the nuclear chemistry
experiments of Hahn and Strassman conducted in Germany
in 1938.[2]
The concept of critical mass applied to academic
planning and program analysis is used to denote the size
and sufficiency of academic program- resources at several
different organizational levels. At academic unit, university, or multicampus levels, it defines the minimum necessary
program breadth and corresponding financial resources required to fulfill the educational mission and objectives of
the institution and of a larger university system where

applicable. The model assumes that consensus prevails on institutional mission and objectives for an individual university or among campuses within a multicampus university, and also that the university system is operating in conformance with state postsecondary education master plans where they exist. The critical mass concept is defined in a specific operational sense subsequently in this chapter.

The genesis of the critical mass concept applied to university resource planning lies in the early development of academic programs in major research-oriented universities and colleges in the nineteenth and early part of the twentieth centuries. The notion that a discipline ought to have certain curricula, taught by faculty with knowledge and research experience in particular subdisciplinary areas, was commonly held by the prominent faculty members around whom departments were formed in many universities.[3] This tradition had been inherited to a considerable extent from European universities, especially from the "German model" established at the University of Berlin in the early nineteenth century and implemented initially in the United States at Johns Hopkins and elsewhere.[4]

In the period from the mid-1950s to the late 1960s, when higher education enrollments were growing rapidly, it became evident to some institutional executives, budget staff, and faculty responsible for academic planning and resource allocation that use of quantitative proxies in program and budget proposals by academic units such as student-faculty ratios, numbers of courses taught, or the ratio of courses taught to faculty were not sufficient for instructional decision making. Similar observations were made about problems and apparent inconsistencies in budgeting diverse university research activities.[5] This was especially evident for decisions on allocation of faculty positions and academic support resources.

As proposals for development of new programs were advanced in the 1960s, attempts to plan and budget for new programs on the basis of student-faculty ratios demonstrated predictable inadequacy. Justifications for new programs and for growth of existing programs were based on generalized faculty and curricular needs, augmented by projected data on student demand and faculty workload. As program planning and budgeting methodology developed, a tendency in universities and colleges was to develop data on program costs which were often, due to their level of generalization, inadequate for academic program and sub-

program resource allocation, and to incorporate program
cost data into formulas, which came to be regarded at institutional and state government levels as proper tools for
resource allocation. Such academic program resource allocation approaches treated departments and disciplines with
unacceptable uniformity, as if one were shifting "the same
eggs between different boxes."[6] While acknowledging that,
in some limited cases, faculty and curricula could be
mobile between academic units, the critical mass approach
recognizes that budgeting and planning for academic units
requires actual information about faculty expertise and the
breadth, depth, and subdisciplinary organization of academic disciplines.

CRITICAL MASS OPERATIONAL DEFINITION

The approach to resource planning and allocation
presented here is a programmatically-based alternative to
existing academic budgeting and planning procedures used
typically in many medium- and large-sized research-oriented
universities. The central assumption upon which the model
rests is that academic resource allocation should be based
upon an exact understanding of existing instructional and
research program attributes and performance, rather than
methods that are limited in predictive accuracy and do not
provide a detailed understanding of academic program
depth and breadth. The critical mass approach is intended
to indicate differences in the organization of faculty, curricula, and research activity in different academic units
at single institutions and differences in organization of
the same or similar disciplines between institutions. The
critical mass approach assumes that curricula are designed
and provided by academic units in response to student demand, but that student demand is not, nor should it be,
the most important factor in determining the subdisciplinary
composition of academic unit instructional and research
programs. Rather, subdisciplinary curricular resource allocation should be based upon faculty judgment of how
their specific subdisciplines are changing, and also on
how their programs should be constituted to implement a
strategy of comparative advantage relative to the curricular
characteristics of programs offered by other academic units
in the same institution and at other academic institutions.

It is assumed here that in a single- or multicampus university, academic resource allocation should be based upon the following: institutional and systemwide program differentiation and delineation of functions between institutions; requirements that academic programs reflect distinct differences in institutional educational missions; the need to provide institutional and multicampus systemwide decision makers with a programmatic overview of institutional disciplinary strengths and weaknesses to guide complimentary program differentiation, development, or curtailment across an institution or a multicampus system; the necessity for accurate projection of resource requirements where there are increases or decreases in instructional demand; and the need to predict the effects on academic unit instructional demand that result from the addition or reduction of students in existing or new instructional programs (induced workload measures).

For purposes of definition, an academic unit is an administrative entity composed of faculty offering instruction in the titled subject matter of that unit. The term academic unit is used to describe departments, divisions, schools, colleges, institutes, centers, and other academic organizational forms extant in contemporary universities. Where it is important to distinguish between types of units, greater specificity is employed. Instructional program is used in this context to describe the major and degree programs offered by universities through their departments, schools, colleges, interdisciplinary, and independent graduate programs, and other academic units constituted for the purpose of organizing curricula and providing instruction to students. The term research program is used to describe research activity conducted by faculty within and between academic units and within units especially designated for research (organized research units). Groupings of similar curricula, instructional, and research-field concentrations are referred to as disciplinary areas. Independent of the organizational mode in which teaching and research are performed, the level of organization below the discipline is specified as the subdiscipline, that is, the instructional or research field of specialization.

Critical mass in instruction at the academic unit level is defined as that portion of the curriculum essential to performance of both instructional and research missions-- the minimum curriculum and research activity that an academic could not reduce and still maintain a satisfactory academic program given the mission of the institution and the unit and the quality criteria employed by the faculty. Critical mass in research denotes the minimum breadth of research specializations necessary for an academic unit to support its critical mass instructional program and that research which is deemed necessary by faculty independent of instruction. Determinations of the "satisfactoriness" of curricular and research breadth and depth in the critical mass approach are made initially and principally by the faculty of an academic unit.

CRITICAL MASS RESOURCE PLANNING

In order to clarify the procedure by which critical mass disciplinary and subdisciplinary fields are defined, and to explain how these procedures fit into an overall strategy of academic resource planning and allocation, a step-by-step description of the critical mass resource planning process is provided below.

1. Academic units, including organized research units, develop goal statements within which they specify the subdisciplines they plan to initiate and terminate in the next five years. Units also identify the composition and size of their curriculum or research program in three states: minimum necessary instructional course coverage, future subdisciplinary areas and/or courses necessary to meet student demand, and future ideas and/or courses necessary to balance or augment academic unit curricular and research goals. An example of this last category would be a new subdiscipline that faculty wish to add to keep the academic unit up-to-date with development of the discipline, regardless of student demand, and course offerings. These states are identified initially as unconstrained by institutional financial or faculty position projections or constraints. In drafting these statements, academic units may be assisted by academic planning, institutional research, or other academic support offices to gather data and draft statements of objectives. In these statements, one format must be established. This format is determined by institutional academic executives in consultation with representatives from appropriate committees of the academic senate, faculty advisory committees, and institutional

planning and research staff. The format is selected on the basis of experience gained in selected pilot applications in academic units conducted prior to full-scale implementation.

2. Academic-unit goal statements are reviewed throughout the academic organizational hierarchy, with the flow of this activity coordinated by campus academic program executives and staff and a designated academic senate committee in order to ensure that reasonable timetables for analysis and review are established and maintained.

3. Once academic unit goal statements are completed, institutional budget planning and research staff, working with academic unit faculty and staff, assemble academic program data profiles on each academic unit. Profiles include information on enrollments, instructional course load, faculty workload, plus other performance-related indexes arranged by the subdisciplinary areas defined by academic units. (More on the content of these profiles is specified later in the chapter.) Profiles are prepared and returned to units for verification of accuracy. Once approved by the faculty of the unit, these profiles become a part of academic unit goal statements and plans; they also become the basis upon which resources are negotiated in the budget process.

4. The relationships between academic unit goals and performance by subdisciplinary area are analyzed by academic units, committees of the academic senate, and the campus academic executive and staff to gain better understanding of how and why resources are used as they are within and across units and disciplines. This review may occur as a part of the existing budget process, or it may be incorporated as a budget and planning process is developed.

5. The budget committee of the academic senate, assisted by the campus academic executives and staff and other academic advisory committees, where appropriate, determines priorities for future allocation of faculty and support resources. Allocation plans require setting the priority of institutional program preferences at this point, a task involving considerable deliberation, consultation, and negotiation. Also at this point, planning for future resource allocations over a five-year span is performed, informed by the use of faculty renewal statistical modeling to aid in predicting the number of academic appointments

by level available for reallocation across units through attrition, independent of funding to create positions or make available other new financial resources. Decisions at this phase comprise the heart of the budget-planning process. In essence, this phase represents the development of a multiyear steady-state academic resource plan, assuming only that the budget will be augmented to keep pace with inflation. In fact, this assumption may not be accurate. To prepare for different levels of resource availability, two additional alternative resource level plans are prepared at this point: one that anticipates moderate growth and the other to prepare for financial reduction. The levels of augmentation or reduction are determined by university administration based upon revenue and expenditure projections made at university, systemwide, and state government levels. Thus, the program priorities established in the critical mass process are used to allocate new faculty positions and other resources should they become available, to reallocate existing positions, or to reduce positions and academic support if necessary. The multiyear budget has three iterations: steady state, augmentation above the rate of anticipated inflation of factor input costs, and reduction.

6. Academic unit plans and resource priorities, as well as university resource planning priorities, are routinely reviewed about every third year using the process outlined to ensure that plans are up-to-date and that university priorities comprehend academic unit priorities accurately. It must be emphasized that even though university priorities are intended to be developed and reviewed at the institutional level, these priorities may be affected by systemwide and/or state academic resource decisions. The critical mass approach is based, however, on a bottom-up versus a top-down approach to resource planning and decision making.

7. During the two-year period in which resource plans and priorities are in place, objective statements and critical mass data profiles are used in the ongoing budget and academic program review process. Use of these data is intended to reduce the ad hoc data collection typical in academic budgeting and planning.

The critical mass model is not based on the assumption that quantitative comparisons between academic units be used exclusively in resource planning and decision making, nor the view that academic programs can best be understood through the use of quantitative information. Most importantly, the model is not exclusively or even primarily student enrollment driven. Indeed, the principal thrust of the process is to capture qualitative strengths and weaknesses in disciplinary coverage at both the academic unit and campus levels, where these dimensions are defined initially by faculty to justify the allocation of resources necessary to sustain desired disciplinary coverage in instruction and research. This is particularly necessary in a period of stable or declining student enrollments and financial resource availability. The critical mass approach to resource planning and decision making assumes that institutional faculty themselves should define the curricula necessary to fulfill the missions of academic units and of the institution more generally, somewhat but not exclusively independent of student demand changes. It is expected that quantitative data collected in the critical mass modeling process would be used in analysis of existing academic programs, new program initiatives, or program reduction proposals to improve the quality of decisions, with the objective of sustaining academic program vitality and continuing the provision of financial rewards to successful academic units and faculty in such a way as to strengthen the university during periods of financial stress.

CORE RESOURCES FOR BUDGETING

Up to this point, definition of the critical mass model has emphasized planning the academic program composition of an institution, that is, setting minimum curricular and research breadth. However, budgeting is a process that includes decision making and implementation in addition to planning, proposal, and negotiation. Thus, it is necessary to define more clearly the methods used in the critical mass approach for translating academic program priorities into resource allocation. Once critical mass disciplinary plans have been established, in order to guide budgetary decision making and allocation it is necessary to define the levels of resources required to support critical mass instructional and research programs. Resources in this context are defined as faculty and academic unit support positions, student-teaching and research assistance positions, financial resources, physical plant, and other tangible assets necessary for operation of academic programs.

To accomplish this translation, the concept of core resource requirements is applied. The definition of core program resources is based upon the critical mass resource planning and decision-making process outlined above. Core resources are those needed to fund critical mass academic programs. Thus, academic staff required to teach a critical mass program may be defined as the core faculty. Core faculty may be identified according to their principal research and teaching subdisciplinary specializations as a means of translating program planning into faculty resource planning. Similarly, core teaching assistance support may be defined in relation to the number of core courses requiring teaching assistants within the critical mass curriculum. Other core program resources, such as administrative support, may be defined utilizing this methodology. The two keys to definition of core resources are the way in which (1) academic units define their critical mass and (2) the resource allocation-academic performance budgetary ratios are defined at the institutional level.

To translate academic program needs into resource needs, the critical mass and core budgeting approach requires comparison of information on academic unit instructional activity as a means of aiding academic decision makers in understanding how academic units utilize staff and support resources. The critical mass curriculum, defined by disciplinary subspecialization, and the core faculty of an academic unit can be related to academic program performance indexes through the construction of instructional program performance matrices. As shown in Tables 3.1, 3.2, and 3.3, critical mass curricula by subdiscipline can be cross-referenced to the following six instructional variables: (1) course offerings, (2) student enrollments (further subdivided by student majors versus service load), (3) average course enrollment size, (4) frequency of course offerings, (5) predominant course type (lab, lecture, seminar), and (6) faculty teaching workload, for example, number of courses or student credit units taught per term or per year. The critical mass and core budgeting approach also permits evaluation of academic unit performance relative to qualitative performance statements rendered by academic units, a process facilitated by

TABLE 3.1

Sample One-Page Summary of Department Core Modeling Data Format (Field of Specialization Profile, Three-Quarter Summary for the Department of _____, Academic Year 19XX-XX)

Instructional Field of Specialization	Course Number F,W,S	Offered	Not offered	Deficiet	Instructional Mode					Student Enrollment Level				Faculty Rank	Faculty FTE			Faculty Instructional Field of Specialization	Comments
					Lecture	Seminar	Indep.	Lab	Other	LD	UD	G	T		Budget	Actual	Temp.		

Source: Prepared by author.

TABLE 3.2
Example of Data Profile for a Department of Economics (Core Modeling Field of Specialization Profile, Three-Quarter Summary for Academic Year 19XX-XX)

Instructional Field of Specialization	Course Number F,W,S	Offered	Not Offered	Deficient	Class Type					Enrollment				% Maj.
					Lecture	Seminar	Indep.	Lab	Other	LD	UD	G	T	
Economic Theory	101A w	x			x					3	16	5	24	8
	101B s	x			x					3	16	4	23	52
	201A f	x			x					0	3	76	79	37
	202B w	x				x				0	1	6	7	57
	202C		x											
Econometrics	140 s	x			x					6	70	0	76	81
	241B w	x				x						23	23	70
Econ. History	112B w	x			x					7	47	2	56	46
	211 w	x				x						6	6	83
Other	299 w	x					x					5	5	80
	299 s	x					x					3	3	67

Comments: 202C not offered 19XX-XX by Instructor choice--(no deficiency).
Source: Compiled by author.

| Faculty Name | Faculty Rank | Faculty FTE | | | Faculty Instructional Field of Specialization | FOS FTE | Course Topic Area |
		Budget	Actual	Temp.			
Smith	Asst. Prof.	1.00	1.00	0	Econometrics	1.00	Econ.Analysis
Brown	Assoc. Prof.	1.00	1.00	0	Monetary Thy.	.50	Econ.Analysis
					Econ.Devel. &		
					Planning	.50	
Taylor	Asst. Prof.	1.00	1.00	0	Econometrics	.50	Econ. Theory
					Indus. Org.	.50	
Jones	Prof.	1.00	1.00	0	Econ. Theory	.33	Theory of
					Econometrics	.33	Competitive
					Math. Econ.	.33	& Part.Equil.
							Adv.Macro Thy.
Wall	Asst. Prof.	1.00	1.00	0	Econometrics	1.00	Econ.Stat. &
							Econometrics
Sell	Assoc. Prof.	1.00	1.00	0	Econ. Theory	.50	Econometrics
					Econometrics	.50	
Rule	Asst. Prof.	1.00	1.00	0	Econ. History	1.00	Econ. History
							of Europe
Rule	Asst. Prof.	1.00	1.00	0	Econ. History	1.00	Econ. History
							Seminar
Steel	Asst. Prof.	1.00	1.00	0	Econ. History	.50	Indep. Study
					Monetary Thy.		
					& Policy	.50	
Brook	Prof.	1.00	1.00	0	Public Fin.	.00	Indep. Study

TABLE 3.3

Department Core Modeling: Summary Profile for the Department of Economics, F.W.S. Quarters 19XX-XX

Departmental Indicators	Field of Specialization								
	Econ. Theory	Econometrics	Math. Econ.	Econ. Hist.	Compara-tive Econ. Systems	Hist. of Econ. Thought	Aggre-gate Econ.	Monetary Theory & Policy	Labor Econ.
Number of courses:									
In catalog	13	5	4	8	7	4	4	5	7
Taught 19XX-XX	11	5	4	7	3	4	4	3	6
Avg. class size: LD	0	0	0	0	0	0	0	0	0
UD	37	76	0	126	36	68	24	90	60
Grad.	40	31	6		6	9	9	8	13
Faculty headcount (H.C.)	5	5	3	5	2	2	2	2	2
Faculty FTE: Perm. budget	2.66	3.33	1.33	4.00	1.50	1.00	0.83	1.00	1.33
Temp. funds	0	0	0	0	0	0	0	0	0
Total faculty FTE									
# Catalog crs./Faculty FTE	4.9	1.5	3.00	1.97	4.66	4.0	4.8	5.0	4.5
/Faculty H.C.	2.6	1.0	1.33	1.6	3.5	2.0	2.0	2.5	3.5
# Crs. taught/Faculty FTE	4.1	1.5	3.00	1.72	2.0	4.0	4.8	3.0	4.5
/Faculty H.C.	2.2	1.0	1.33	1.4	1.5	2.0	2.0	1.5	3.0
Graduate student enrollment	[Only totals applicable]								
Grad. student/Faculty FTE									
U.D. majors/Faculty FTE									
Instr. service load: UD	66.1	18.4	0	70.8	44.4	49.3	31.9	88.9	37.9
Grad.	51.8	34.4	78.3	17.5	9.1	17.6	11.8	17.6	21.6
Deficiencies: Faculty		1.00				1.00			1.00
Courses		1				1			
Students									
Future programs required: To balance dept. offerings		Econometrics				Marxist Econ.			
To meet student demands		Econometrics							Labor Econ.

| | | Field of Specialization | | | | | | Total | Comments |
Departmental Indicators	Urban Econ.	Public Finance	Indust. Org. Econ.	Econ. Develop. & Planning	Interna- ional/Trade Econ.	Other	or Average	from Department
Number of courses:								
In catalog	3	6	6	8	6	23	109	79 percent of classes offered were taught in 19XX-XX
Taught 19XX-XX	3	6	5	5	3	17	86	
Avg. class size: LD	0	0	0	0	0	403	403	Econ. 1A & 1B only LD offerings
UD	39	66	83	70	65	19	43	Indep. Stdy reduces avg.
Grad.	N/A	10	8	5	13	4.5	10	Faculty listed in multiple FOS
Faculty headcount (H.C.)	3	3	3	3	3	0	28	
Faculty FTE: Perm budget	1.50	2.50	2.00	1.50	2.50	0	28.5	Includes 2 Act. Asst. & 1 Visit. Assoc. Prof.
Temp funds	1.00	0	0	0	0	0	1.06	
Total faculty FTE							29.56	Total FTEF
# Catalog crs/Faculty FTE	1.2	2.4	3.0	5.33	2.4	0	3.7:1	
/Faculty H.C.	1.00	2.0	2.0	2.66	2.0	0	3.9:1	
# Crs. taught/Faculty FTE	1.2	2.4	2.5	3.33	1.2	0	2.9:1	
/Faculty H.C.	1.0	2.0	1.66	1.66	1.0	0	3.1:1	
Graduate student enrollment	[Only totals applicable]						124	Three quarter avg.
Grad. student/Faculty FTE							4.2:1	
Upper-Division majors							309	Three quarter avg., incl. 16 double majors
UD majors/Faculty FTE							10.5:1	
Instr. service load: UD	35.8	34.9	23.5	0	27.7	77.5	60.36	BA, PhD (MA not offered) Total service load: 45.41
Grad.	0	35.3	44.0	45.0	7.7	15.0	35.92	
Deficiencies: Faculty					1.0	Econ. Demog- raphy	4.00	Faculty needed for Econ. 191H: Women in the Labor Force and others as noted
Courses					2	1	5	
Future programs Students required:								
To balance dept. offerings					Intl. & Trade Econ.			
To meet student demand							2	

Source: Compiled by author.

the availability of quantitative indicators of performance to validate qualitative assumptions and proposals. It should be stressed that Tables 3.1 and 3.2 are intended only as examples of one approach for display of critical mass data. Other approaches will be defined by individual users.

The most important decision points in the critical mass resource allocation process that occur outside the academic unit are determination of institutional program priorities, as noted above, and the definition of the ratios of fiscal resources to academic program attributes and performance activity. The critical mass and core modeling approach provides information so that resource utilization ratios may be applied uniformly or differentially across academic units. Decisions on how resources are to be allocated result from application of university program priorities determined in the context of the critical mass process. However, these decisions are not presumed to result simply from having more and better information on academic unit performance. Better information enables decisions on program priorities to be made with greater certainty and improves the translation of priorities into the budget allocation process. It also enables budgets to be controlled more effectively once they are allocated. Still, the critical mass approach will not remove the heavy responsibility of setting and implementing institutional academic program development strategy from institutional decision makers. In fact, the system improves accountability for decisions by more clearly identifying relationships between resource inputs and programmatic outcomes. Improved accountability is likely to reward good decision performance. However, it may also penalize decision makers where mistakes are made. Additional aspects of budgeting with critical mass data are discussed subsequently in this chapter and in Chapter Eight.

TEST APPLICATION OF THE CRITICAL MASS AND CORE RESOURCE MODEL

In order to illustrate the characteristics of the critical mass and core resource approach, a test application was performed for four departments located at two major research-oriented public universities, the Universities of California at Berkeley and San Diego. Data for the pilot implementation were collected and analyzed for a period of ten years using historical departmental statistics.

The critical mass and core resource data matrices shown in Tables 3.1, 3.2, and 3.3 assume that the process of data collection, interviews, integration of departmental feedback, and specification of program goals and objectives outlined previously has been completed satisfactorily, resulting in definitions of critical mass by instructional fields of specialization. For illustrative purposes, the tables show how the model may be applied to a department of economics for one academic year. For faculty, the instructional fields of specialization covered are identified through the use of core program profiles. Profiles are represented in the sample matrices that array instructional fields of specialization, faculty, courses, and other data against various indexes of instructional performance, for example, student enrollment by level, student credit hours, instructor hours, student and classroom hours, service load, and other variables. Additional faculty requested by instructional field of specialization to augment the core instructional program and subdisciplinary areas where existing faculty depth is lacking may be determined, along with instructional fields of specialization least important to departmental critical mass mission.

Under instructional mode, patterns of instruction are identified at both the undergraduate and graduate level; the number of primary lectures, number of secondary sections, partial assemblies, number of labs, and number of seminars, with average class size and service load for each course offered, are specified. In addition, for graduate instruction, the average number of second-level graduate students supervised per faculty and the imposed class-size limitations are identified. Course offerings by program may identify courses offered during the year, number of courses required for the major, number of additional courses required for service responsibilities, number of remedial courses offered (by level of student), and average course workload per faculty. Computerization of this data base is essential for full-scale implementation of critical mass procedures.

Using the profiles, it becomes possible to estimate
and summarize faculty and student capacity for the core
instructional programs given a specified student-faculty
ratio, the number of graduate students supervised, the
relationship of faculty to numbers of courses offered by
level, and the service load by field of specialization.
Tables 3.2 and 3.3 are examples of formats that integrate
some of the data referred to above by subdisciplinary
specialization.

An analysis of the results from critical mass and
core modeling of four departments in three distinct disciplines at two public research universities produced the
following conclusions:

1.   The ability to compare curricular offering
within and between institutions could typically be much
improved through the implementation of critical mass core
modeling.   Instruction field of specializaton resource modeling allows a greater degree of comparability between
institutional offerings than does standard department or
decree-titled-oriented planning by identifying important
similarities and differences in academic programs.   Policy
directives, for example, that every academic field of endeavor should be offered on at least one campus within a
multicampus university system, would be difficult to implement under a scheme of department or degree-title resource
planning.   However, under core modeling at the subdiscipline level, comparisons may be made within and between
campuses to determine what fields of academic endeavor
are offered, regardless of the particular academic unit
organization employed at individual institutions.

2.   Sound academic resource planning must include
statements of individual program goal that clearly represent the thinking and strategies of department heads and
faculty.   These statements should be drafted after careful
review of core resource utilization profiles displaying
various department performance indexes by instructional
field of specializaton.   The format for academic resource
planning statements should be uniform and data elements
clearly specified.   As examples, Table 3.1 displays data
for instructional fields of specialization for a department
of economics and Table 3.3 summarizes some of the data
useful for analysis by department faculty in determining
critical mass plans.   Data displayed in the profiles were
found to be useful for resource planning in that they

revealed information about departments not previously known or confirmed and weighted assumptions about the manner in which departments utilize their resources.

A major advantage of a fully implemented critical mass core model that draws together data for all university academic units is clarification of program priorities and identification of program interrelationships. It improves the ability of campus administrators to estimate the multiunit effects of adding new programs (for example, a graduate school of public administration or environmental planning) to existing campus programs, analyze resource requests and allocate the additional resources required for the operation of the new program, and estimate the effects of budgetary reductions on existing programs.

3. Core modeling points out differences between large and small departments in the same academic discipline relative to how the subdisciplines are defined and how resources are used; for example, the subdisciplines for a small department may be much broader than the subdisciplines for a large department with a more specific instructional focus. Such was found to be the case in analysis of departments of economics at the University of California, Berkeley, and the University of California, San Diego. Also, several subdisciplines in a smaller department may be much more narrowly defined because of the existence of a particular program (for example, a medical school) that places instructional demand on an academic unit. Critical mass is unlikely to be defined in the same way for large and small departments, or for departments of equal size on two different campuses. However, by grouping instructional fields of specialization for large departments and making extrapolations of fields for small departments into interrelated subdisciplines or "nests," reasonable common denominators can be seen to exist.

Modeling of the economics departments at the University of California, San Diego and at Berkeley provided the opportunity to test the adaptability of the model to departments offering instruction in the same discipline where size, age (of unit), breadth of specialization, teaching emphasis, and developmental missions are different. The economics department at Berkeley has a large faculty who teach in more fields of specialization than at San Diego. The size and age of the department, and differences in faculty specializations, enable instruction in a number of separate and well-defined instructional fields of specialization aligned into seven groups or nests of interrelated specializations at Berkeley, compared to four more generalized fields comprising San Diego's program. Service load data by field of specialization showing the demand placed on departmental workload by field of specialization by other instructional programs revealed that as the size of the campus and the number of instructional programs are increased, the service demand for instruction in specialized subdisciplinary fields increases differentially. While this is hardly an earth-shaking revelation, the core modeling approach allows the measurement of service load demand by field of specialization rather than across the department as is the case with most induced course-load forecasting systems. Modeling by instructional field of specialization also lends itself to identification of course offerings on different campuses that are similar enough to allow joint-program offerings between institutions where feasible.

4. Differences in departmental instructional emphasis and its relationship to institutional mission is clarified through subdisciplinary analysis. In the period analyzed, San Diego was growing rapidly and, consistent with this objective, the department of economics was attempting to expand undergraduate course offerings to meet student demand. Core modeling data was useful to the department to plan for potential demand from a new college, which was to begin admitting students in the fall quarter of the following year. In addition, with the planned growth of San Diego's political science department, the service demand on economics was to increase. The faculty indicated that core modeling facilitated planning for the accommodation of new service demand by indicating instructional fields of specialization needed to match the curricula of the new college and expansion of political science.

At Berkeley, economics was attempting to concentrate on doctoral instruction and service to other departments at the graduate level consistent with the overall emphasis on graduate education at the institution. Berkeley's faculty-graduate student ratio of 4.2:1, compared to 3.4:1 at San Diego, and an overall graduate service load of 36 percent were indicative of the heavy graduate emphasis, especially in the fields of mathematical economics, industrial organization, and economic development and planning. The service load pressure was substantial enough for Berkeley's economics department to consider offering a master's program for students enrolled in Ph.D. programs in other departments.

5. The model highlighted the extent to which alternative funding methodologies are employed to finance programs on the two campuses. At Berkeley, headcount and permanently budgeted faculty were nearly the same. At San Diego, more core faculty (nontenured) were financed on temporary and outside funds, for example, National Science Foundation development grants. Because the discontinuation of special grants affects program stability, the conclusion was drawn that if extramural funding is used to support instructional programs, it should be used only for temporary faculty and in noncore areas.

6. The importance of understanding the "life cycle" of a department was pointed out by an analysis of economics at Berkeley. For example, through the loss of one or several faculty members, a department may have gone past its peak in productivity and prestige in an area of instructional specialization where it was once a national leader. This necessitates a reevaluation of subdiscipline instructional specializations because it is often impossible to recruit qualified faculty to fill vacated specializations or it is undesirable to recruit in the same subfield due to changes in the discipline. Reevaluation may change the recruitment, hiring, and future instructional and research strategy of a department by articulating the need for development of a new or existing but only moderately strong subdiscipline through recruitment or by shifting the instructional responsibilities of existing tenured faculty, where feasible.

These insights would be very important in a period of financial restraint where allocation of scarce faculty resources is required. Student demand for instruction in new subdisciplines is another factor that can stimulate reevaluation of instructional fields of specialization, within or across academic units. In some instances, faculty may be teaching in one area but are qualified and interested in teaching in a developing specialization. Where this occurs, critical mass core modeling can indicate some of the costs and benefits of reallocating faculty instructional responsibilities.

7. Evaluation of academic unit disciplinary strategies is intended to be integrated into the university resource

planning process through application of the critical mass core modeling procedure, thus increasing the sensitivity and "real-worldness" of resource planning data and decision making. As noted above, an example of this at Berkeley was the economics department's plan to begin offering a master's degree program designed for doctoral students in other departments. Given the assumption that academic units should evaluate their specializations continually as disciplines and student demand shift, and further that under budget restraint units may be forced to set priorities for reduction of nontenured and, in some cases, tenured positions, core modeling may be employed to indicate to university decision makers where new positions should be allocated, where existing positions may be reallocated, or where existing positions might be reduced with the least significant impact on critical mass. Under many university resource planning systems there are little or no data on field-of-specialization emphasis to guide institutional resource allocation decision making. Instead, budgetary decisions are typically made on the base, with adjustments reflecting projected enrollment change. The critical mass and core modeling approach is intended to increase certainty in resource allocation or reallocation so decisions may be explained and defended on grounds other than enrollment or reputational variables that are often difficult to interpret and compare. These data may also be out-of-date. More specific service load data, combined with the communication and understanding of program disposition developed in the core modeling process, increase the likelihood that new curricula and degree programs will be approved rather than rejected by institutional or state officials attempting to check unwarranted degree proliferation, or where budgetary restraint threatens the approval of any new program initiatives.

8. The data required for critical mass core modeling may be difficult to collect at some institutions because of the absence of existing information systems. However, with the availability of aggregate instructional data by academic unit, and supplementary data relating faculty by level and instructor hours per week to course by level to student credit hours by level, the data-gathering effort can be reduced significantly. Once these systems are developed, the costs of maintaining them are small in part due to the low opportunity costs associated with using slack clerical and support resources that are present in

many academic units. However, system development costs
are relatively high where no such information systems exist. During the pilot application of the critical mass
model at Berkeley and San Diego, it was estimated that
had existing instructional information and budget systems
not been in place, the direct short-term system development
costs would have exceeded $600,000 over the first three
years of implementation. In 1985 dollars this would have
resulted in expenditures on the order of $250,000 per year
for three years at an institution the size of the University
of California, Berkeley, given carefully specified, managed,
and controlled implementation. Systems development costs
include development of computer software for critical mass
and core modeling, but no hardware costs.

     9. Critical mass application facilitates resource
planning in conjunction with enforcement of enrollment
limits or other constraints applied to control program size.
In application, the model served to familiarize academic
decision makers with some of the concepts and vocabulary
of disciplines in a manner that improves resource reallocation. Institutional administrators expressed satisfaction
at understanding more clearly how academic units actually
use their resources. This satisfaction was also evidenced
at departmental, school, and college levels.

     10. The formats provided in Tables 3.1, 3.2, and
3.3 depict critical mass and core modeling as an instructional information system based upon faculty instructional
and research expertise and interests. These formats are
useful for translating critical mass and core planning into
budgets at academic unit and institutional levels in the
following way. Academic units request budget augmentations based upon subdisciplinary priorities and the core
resources (faculty and support) needed to fulfill them.
Instructional performance data collected and displayed in
the critical mass formats support budget requests. Institutional budget staff and academic program decision makers
review all academic unit budgets, aggregated to the school
and college level, in allocating additional budget appropriations (or reductions under retrenchment). This analysis
is based upon a campuswide ranking of critical mass subdisciplinary priorities, with data on instructional performance reviewed and compared in the formats as provided
in Tables 3.1, 3.2, and 3.3. Performance data can be
analyzed against indexes of support such as FTEF, student
credit hours and FTEs, and a number of other measures

that may be derived from the instructional data available by subdiscipline. This approach improves budget analysis and clarifies budget decision making. More on critical mass budgeting is provided in Chapter Eight.

Although the application of the critical mass resource allocation in several departments on two campuses cannot be presented as conclusive evidence that the benefits of the model will be worth its costs, the test application did indicate that benefits from implementation would be achieved, and would be distributed across various levels of organizational decision making in universities. From one view, the costs of implementing this model are essentially the opportunity costs of not investing in another system. This assumes that institutions will recognize the need for better information systems to improve academic resource decison making, particularly where budgetary constraints are present. Many such systems already exist in universities that have invested in academic resource decision information improvements.

As noted, disaggregation of costs by fields of specialization expresses core resources so as to enable application of critical mass program priorities to the augmentation, reduction, or reallocation of existing budgets. However, significant barriers to resource reallocation are present in most academic departments and institutions, as they are in most complex organizations. Some of these constraints are explored in greater detail in Chapter Four.

CRITICAL MASS FOR ORGANIZED RESEARCH UNITS

The critical mass approach for instructional academic units, as outlined above, encompasses research resource planning integrated with instructional responsibilities and goals. Critical mass may also be used for organized research unit resource planning. Often it is difficult for university decision makers to define the complimentarity or overlap of research activity in organized research units with the rest of an institution's research and instructional activity. Applying the critical mass concept to organized research units enables resource allocation planning to occur typically where little coordination exists. Care must be taken to avoid the implication that applying critical mass techniques to organized research units would result in excessive guidance of substantive research planning. This would be contrary to arguments in favor of relatively unconstrained sponsored research in universities. However, it is assumed that better definition of research strengths and weaknesses will enable institutional identification of comparative advantage so as to improve the use of resources in attempting to secure external research funding.

With this understanding, identification of critical mass composition and core resources in research units is useful to relate organized research unit efforts to campus missions as articulated in academic plans and budgets, identify the extent of integration of instructional specializations and research efforts, suggest areas of instruction not presently served by organized research units, and illuminate areas in which organized research efforts are weak or inappropriate. Relating subdisciplinary areas of research to instructional subdisciplinary fields and areas of faculty expertise will also clarify criteria employed in the selection and promotion of faculty. Further, it can highlight the development of academic unit strategies for reorganization of research efforts. In turn, this may have an important impact on future faculty hiring and promotion decisions.

Research program critical mass may be defined by identifying the sub-areas of a discipline in which research is engaged. Initially, this information can be obtained from organized research mission statements, research project profiles, annual reports, and other documents on research programs. Areas of research deemed vital to the maintenance and development of the discipline unit and institution are established by intra- and interunit analysis and negotiation in the same manner employed for definition of instructional unit critical mass. Research unit profiles may be prepared by research units themselves, with the process coordinated by academic senate committees on research assisted by institutional administrative staff experienced in preparation of instructional unit critical mass and core resource profiles.

Using the critical mass approach in organized research units makes it possible to coordinate organized research resource planning on and between campuses within a multiinstitution university. Critical mass modeling of existing research efforts, because of its subdisciplinary concentration, facilitates the identification of similarities and differences in independent research efforts. Creation of a critical mass research program inventory, supplemented by cross-indexes of faculty and other resources allocated by area of specialization, permits core resource identification and coordination of resource allocation and acquisition strategies.

ASSUMPTIONS SUPPORTING THE CRITICAL MASS APPROACH

Although critical mass and core resource concepts should be applied to define the minimum financial and other resources necessary to sustain critical mass academic program breadth, it is important to note the differences between critical mass as an external budgetary strategy and critical mass as an internal academic planning and budgeting methodology that attempts to inform decision makers about institutional academic activity. The emphasis of the critical mass approach is on establishing the latter so that the former may be accomplished with greater effect. The critical mass approach to academic resource allocation is intended to enable establishment of academic program priorities so that institutional budgetary strategies may be developed and executed effectively in short- and long-range resource acquisition plans for single institution and also for a multicampus university. Most importantly, the comparison of program priorities is intended to enable university decision makers to plan more effectively for the establishment of different resource allocation standards for different types of programs. Where such plans are integrated into budgetary strategy for public institutions, they will guide the development of annual budget proposals to state government. As such, critical mass is intended to play an important role in resisting state government budgetary retrenchment efforts.

At the institutional level, critical mass assumes that sound academic resource planning and decision making must rest upon clear statements of the goals of individual academic units. Critical mass program size is generally determined by faculty review and negotiation within academic units. Academic unit critical mass plans represent the strategies of faculty department chairpersons, deans, and other academic administrators. The critical mass resource planning approach may thus be viewed as equitable and participative in placing the responsibility for judging what ought to be taught and researched jointly in the hands of faculty and institutional academic decision makers rather than with multicampus or state government budgeteers and planners.[7] The use of critical mass and core resource performance measurement techniques in instruction is intended to provide decision makers with information so that they may plan how to supply the highest quality instruction and most comprehensive curricula to students. The process intends that faculty, students, and other members of the university community participate in the resource planning process consistent with the "open systems" planning approach advocated in planning theory.[8] Further, it is assumed that in budget execution, cost center control will be exercised using critical mass criteria to guide these efforts. It also is assumed that budgetary and cost control may be exercised best in academic units and within institutions rather than by state higher-education budgeteers.

With respect to identification of critical mass elements, most of what the critical mass resource planning mode attempts to accomplish rests upon existing and desired faculty research specializations. This is true simply because academic units in research-oriented universities tend to hire and promote faculty on the basis of research performance and on the "fit" of the faculty expertise into the curriculum offered or planned by an academic unit.[9] In short, the definition of what ought to be taught and researched is intended to be guided to the greatest extent by the individual and collective research interests of faculty.

EVALUATION OF THE CRITICAL MASS MODEL

In evaluating the satisfactoriness of critical mass implementation, a number of criteria may be used, including cost relative to other information and decision systems, usefulness of information provided in decision making, adequacy and comprehensiveness in describing academic programs, improvement in establishing program priorities, cohesiveness of academic program planning and budgeting, operational feasibility and flexibility, adaptability to environmental changes and constraints, applicability in short- and long-range resource acquisition strategy setting, and others.[10] It is assumed that such criteria would be applied periodically as the model was implemented; for

example, once every three or five years. However, forma-
tive evaluation would enable modification of implementation
on an ongoing basis.

The test application of the model described earlier
provided some minimal yet very positive results from implementation. In lieu of the opportunity to evaluate the entire model in practice, we may develop several sets of
theoretical criteria against which the model may be evaluated. The first set of criteria has a resource and systems
planning orientation, as follows:

1. Resource plans should be realistic in setting operational goals for the organization that are feasible,
   given political constraints and the financial and human resources available to the organization.
2. Resource plans should anticipate alternative funding
   levels and alternative program priorities as accurately
   as possible.
3. Systems to implement programs and policies should
   comprehend, to the fullest extent possible, the goals,
   values, and expectations of faculty, students, administrators, decision makers, and general public beneficiaries of higher educaton.
4. Choice among program alternatives should result from
   open bargaining between competing service providers,
   that is, academic units.

The second set of criteria employed to evaluate the critical mass approach is drawn from analysis of organizational behavior and theory, based upon the work of
James D. Thompson.[11] This analysis provides a framework
and vocabulary that may be used to test the model relative
to criteria that are sensitive to changes in internal organization reflecting external environmental conditions.
Initially, the critical mass resource planning model will
be evaluated against the four resource and systems planning criteria listed above.

Goal Clarity and System/Resource Feasibility

Resource plans should be realistic in setting operational goals for the organization that are feasible, given
political constraints and the financial and human resources
available to the organization.

In employing the critical mass resource planning approach, academic unit, university, and multicampus system academic program goals should be determined principally by faculty. In defining critical mass in academic unit plans, faculty identify minimum-necessary curriculum coverage, future subdisciplinary curricula or course offerings needed to meet anticipated or actual student demand, and curricula or course offerings needed to balance or augment the academic program. Thus, goals are categorized initially according to student demand forecasts, and also according to curricular feasibility. Screening of academic unit proposals by the academic administrative hierarchy provides additional checks to determine whether goals are realistic and compatible financially and programmatically with overall organization mission and objectives.

A third level of judgment incorporated into the critical mass approach occurs when key academic senate committees and the president or chancellor of the university, assisted by his or her academic and budget staff, establish priorities for allocation of faculty positions and support resource. Under the critical mass approach, decisions reached at this level should comprehend institutional mission and responsibilities, academic program development plans, and financial resource projections. Academic unit critical mass plans and priorities are used to argue externally for new resources, or to reduce the threat of budget cuts, and would guide allocation of budgets once approved by state governments and/or systemwide offices in multi-institutional systems.

The most important judgments with regard to how the institution intends to meet the political, economic, cultural, and environmental needs of society are to be accomplished by individual faculty in critical mass academic unit resource plans. Whether institutional academic decision makers reviewing critical mass plans and proposals comprehend faculty views on what ought to be done in their disciplines is dependent upon a number of factors. The most important of these are the adequacy of critical mass goal statements and supporting data and the flow of information on disciplinary and academic development priorities within the university. As noted by Wilensky, for information to be used effectively to influence organizational policy and strategy, it must be clear (understandable by those who must use it), timely (available when decisions are made), reliable (factually accurate and

reflective of the diversity of opinion in the organization),
valid (conforms to reality in concept and as tested against
accepted standards, and also has high predictive value),
adequate (covers all relevant aspects of the problem or
issue), and comprehensive (all major alternatives are
presented).[12] Organizational failure to use what Wilensky
termed high-quality intelligence, as represented in academic unit critical mass plans, could result from inadequate articulation of goals and policy priorities, poor
systems design, weak information search, storage, and
retrieval procedures, uninformed and ill-conceived critical
mass definition and analysis, and bad communication
practices.

Regarding the use of high-quality intelligence
where it exists, Wilensky noted that "the more complex
the structure [of the organization], the more use of ex-
perts . . . the larger the size . . . the more intense
is the problem of internal control, and the more resources
. . . [that should be] available for the intelligence function."[13] This view would appear to argue for allocation of university resources to academic budget and planning staff. However, the critical mass approach is designed to use academic unit faculty to provide the information that comprises the model. The role of administrative staff in this process is to design the system according
to the procedures presented in this chapter and then to
act as consultants to academic units where communication
or assistance is desired. As such, the critical mass approach seeks to use existing academic administrative staff
effectively, rather than to expand more financial resources
on academic administration and institutional research.

Alternative Funding and Priorities

• Resource plans should anticipate alternative funding
levels and program priorities.

The critical mass methodology is designed to articulate academic unit priorities so that they may be applied
in decision making where financial resources are increasing, stable, or declining. The system is flexible in antic-
ipating alternative funding levels by virtue of the way
critical mass is used to define core resources. Core resources needed to maintain critical mass research and
instructional programs represent the bottom line below

which funding cannot fall if program quality and service output is to be held to existing levels. Critical mass defines the external budgetary strategy most useful to the academic unit under alternative states of resource availability. Additionally, critical mass indicates how budgets are to be allocated if approved at levels requested, increased, or reduced. Finally, the critical mass core model translates the academic program by subdisciplinary area into instructional performance standards and indexes to improve budgetary control. It also provides the methodology for allocation faculty workload and identifying areas where the instructional curriculum may be under- or over-funded relative to student demand and academic program goals. However, the performance standards in the critical mass system emerge from analysis of how existing resources are utilized, rather than as a result of imposition from central academic administrators or state government budgeteers.

While no performance standards for research are provided by critical mass definition, the model indicates how future resources, including faculty positions, ought to be filled, and also what arguments might be successful in proposing the allocation of new faculty positions or reallocation of existing positions. Further, the critical mass approach is intended to be used as a budgetary strategy by academic units, by institutions, and by multicampus university systems to resist budget cuts based upon student enrollment loss. Thus, it is multidimensional in its resource generation objectives, allowing academic institutions to use the disciplinary attributes of the system in resource acquisition and in allocation and control.

Use of the critical mass approach in defending proposed budgets to state government is one of the major reasons for adopting the critical mass mode of resource planning. As student enrollments decline, it is likely that the university will need to defend itself against efforts to reduce its overall state budget allocation, threats to reduce funding for specific programs, and a more resistant climate for new-program approval.

It is assumed here that if the university has accomplished critical mass definition, accompanied by appropriate supportive data, and has translated these definitions into resource requirements as described earlier in this chapter, then it will be better equipped to argue for resources to enable selective academic program development as well as to defend itself against outright reduction of budgets and faculty positions during periods of resource scarcity.

System Sensitivity to Social Needs and Academic Values

• Systems to implement programs and policies should comprehend the goals, values, and expectations of organizational members and constituents.

As faculty state how they would prefer to develop their academic programs under prevailing resource constraints and also as relatively unconstrained by resource input expectations, their judgments will attempt to anticipate university and social needs to the greatest extent possible. Theoretically, this is one of the major advantages of decentralized, open-system, bottom-up resource planning versus planning guided by central institutional or state budgets and master plans conceived and written at the top of the state or university educational hierarchy and disseminated to lower levels for implementation. By the very nature of their purpose, critical mass statements attempt to anticipate the values and expectations of the process participants, particularly those of faculty and students, while acknowledging limitations in university resources.

Whether and how well faculty critical mass models integrate the values and expectations of students as beneficiaries is of crucial concern. The critical mass approach invests the essential responsibility for resource planning in faculty committees and academic unit heads and, secondarily, in institutional administrators. Responsibility for incorporating the values and expectations of students lies with the faculty. A trend toward greater student participation in academic unit planning and governance is evident over the past decade. The critical mass approach would not alter the incentives for students to continue pressing for full participation in resource planning and governance decision making.

The critical mass approach is based upon the notion that clients (faculty and other institutional decision makers), planners (faculty and nonfaculty planners), implementors (faculty and nonacademic support staff), and beneficiaries (students, interest groups, and citizens of the state and nation) should be involved or represented in some manner in definition of academic resource plans and priorities. The critical mass process is based not just on

the expectation of faculty, involvement in representing academic values, but on the faculty's direction of resource
planning and decision making, so that the resource definition process is sensitive to the most critical knowledge
production and communication attributes of the institution.
The critical mass approach is consistent with the mission
of universities to discover and communicate new knowledge
or to interpret existing knowledge to solve social, economic,
and other problems. The subdisciplinary composition of
academic units represents, as closely as is feasible for
resource decision making, the diverse knowledge production
activities of universities.

Open Negotiation of Program Priorities and Resources

• Choice among program alternatives should result
from open bargaining between competing service providers,
that is, academic units.
Open bargaining of program priorities is provided
in the critical mass approach in that the process for
assembling information on academic unit plans and performance is accomplished within an integrated planning and
decision-making system that is decentralized and based in
academic units and in that setting priorities for faculty
and support allocations would require substantial discussion by academic unit faculty, committees of academic
senates, and institutional academic executives and staff.
That final program priorities will be established by key
committees of the academic senate and by university academic executives, as is typically the case, is a result of
the fact that in any organization, critical resource allocation decisions must eventually be made by a designated
unit or individual. Under the critical mass approach,
resource acquisition and allocation plans and decisions
are intended to be strongly influenced by academic senate
committees. For this reason, the critical mass approach,
as it fits into the existing mode of governance employed
at many institutions, meets the criterion of open process
planning and decision making. However, implementation
of critical mass core modeling will do little on its own to
ensure that decision making will be more open and participative. Academic administrators and academic senate budget and planning committees must maintain a commitment to
participative decision making in order for it to occur.

As noted previously, the critical mass model is intended to be employed strategically in resource generation and justification. Definition of universitywide critical mass size and academic program development plans to implement the model anticipates that within an institution, and certainly within a multiuniversity system, strategies will develop in competition for the establishment and continuation of academic programs. To manage competition between individual institutions within a multicampus system, systemwide academic senates could act as the coordinative bodies to provide leadership in negotiating differential academic program development, temporary or permanent faculty exchange between instructional and research programs, and other aspects of cooperation between institutions. However, an assertive and well-organized systemwide senate is necessary to approach this task realistically.

ORGANIZATIONAL THEORY CRITERIA FOR EVALUATION

The second set of organizational behavior and theory criteria to be used in an ex ante evaluation of the critical mass model is adopted from the work of James D. Thompson. Thompson analyzes organizations as means for achieving goals subject to constraints imposed by the larger social systems within which they operate. His contingency adaptation theory of organizations, rendered in a series of propositions on organizational power and behavior, describes how organizations adapt differentially to various challenges posed by the environment. The theory also emphasizes the principle of resource interdependence, that is, that organizations and organizational units are dependent upon each other and upon particular domains of their environment for critical resources.

Thompson's work focuses on organizations as problem-solving entities. Borrowing from Simon's bounded rationality concept, Thompson views organizations as means for achieving goals, the principle of which is survival, subject to constraints of rationality and resources. His thesis is that the design, structure, and behavior of organizations will vary according to the "task" environment in which they exist, especially relative to the technology of the "task" environment. The "task" environment is defined as "those parts of the environment which are relevant or potentially relevant to goal setting and goal attainment."[14]

The ways in which various organizations seek survival, self-control, and goal achievement differ according to their design and structure, which in turn are determined largely by the nature of their environments. Organizations and their components are viewed to have domains or spheres of both power and dependence in their external environments. Organizations and their components can seek strategies for cooperation and defense relative to their domains and dependence.

Nonhierarchical organizations such as universities are analyzed as superior problem-solving entities in some types of environments. Hierarchical organizations are too often overmanaged, biased to seek too much certainty, characterized by lack of knowledge, and, in certain circumstances, do not evolve secure inner circles of decision makers and advisors to guide problem solving.[15] The theory posits that in many nonhierarchical organizations, it is easier for technical core staff to receive and work on problems and then to communicate solutions to the dominant coalition of executives, than in hierarchical organizations. At times in hierarchical organizations, executive decision making breaks down because decisions become too complex, executives are flooded with too much information, and contingencies are faced on too many fronts. When this occurs, dominant coalitions, led by an inner circle, take control.

Thompson designed the matrix shown in Table 3.4 to explain decision-making strategies with respect to outcome preference (horizontal axis of the matrix) and beliefs about cause-and-effect relationship (vertical axis). The matrix is used to illustrate how organizations seek self-control.

TABLE 3.4
Decision Strategies

Preferences regarding possible outcomes

		Certain	Uncertain
Beliefs about cause-effect relationship	Certain	Computation	Compromise
	Uncertain	Judgment	Inspiration

Source: Compiled by author from J. D. Thompson, _Organizations in Action_ (New York: McGraw-Hill, 1967).

Table 3.4 shows the variables of decision making arrayed
on a certainty-uncertainty continuum to illustrate four
types of decision strategies: computation, compromise,
judgment, and inspiration. When preferences of outcomes
and beliefs about cause and effect are certain, strategy
setting is computational. Simon characterizes this type of
decision as "programmed."[16] When preferences are uncertain but cause-and-effect beliefs are certain, strategies
are likely to involve compromise; that is, decisions on
policy issues in this circumstance are likely to involve
compromise because decision makers' preferences are not
fixed and compromise is thus facilitated. When preferences
are known but cause-and-effect relationships are uncertain,
policy analysis is needed to inform choice regarding the
possible consequences of alternative decisions. Decision
makers will want to have information upon which to judge
alternative outcomes. When preferences and cause-and-
effect beliefs are uncertain, Thompson describes decision
making as inspirational, a term that is a bit humorous
because it describes the way in which many decisions appear to be made in the real world.

The theory concludes that coalignment of strategic
variables--technology, task environment with a viable do-
main, and organization design and structure appropriate to
that domain--is the essence of organizational administration,
that is, "Shooting at a target of coalignment."[17] Administration is thus a dynamic process of coordination characterized by a continual search for flexibility to permit
mobilization of various resources to solve recurring and
new problems.[18] The ability to provide discretion and
flexibility to solve problems under conditions of uncertainty
is the basis for power in the administrative process.
Further, the tighter the norms of rationality in administration, the more energy the organization will spend on
attempting to achieve certainty, which is expensive. As
will be noted, the critical mass approach attempts to minimize costs of achieving certainty while maintaining information quality controls.

Accepting Thompson's theory that dealing with uncertainty is the largest task of an organization, combined
with the proposition that technology and the environments
are the main sources of uncertainty, it is understandable
that these elements are important determinants of organization structure and behavior. According to the theory,
organizations employ two types of "rational" strategies to

deal with uncertainty. Technical rationality seeks to protect the technical core from environmental influences. Organizational rationality seeks to achieve and maintain a balance in such a way that internal units manage external forces by use of techniques such as buffering technological cores with input and output units, stockpiling, smoothing input and output transactions, adaptation, rationing, and other responses.

A summary of this analysis of relationships between technical and organizational rationality may be made along five dimensions: (1) power, (2) structure, (3) organizational assessment, (4) human behavior, and (5) control. These dimensions may then be related to characteristics of critical mass resource planning and decision making.

Power

Organizations try to achieve power by maintaining alternatives, seeking prestige, and gaining control over elements upon which they are most dependent. Strategies of contracting, coopting, and coalescing are used to gain power. Under the critical mass model, power-seeking behavior results foremost from academic unit disciplinary aspirations rather than from outside academic units.

Structure

Organizations structure themselves to minimize the cost of coordination. The type of interdependence evidenced by an organization affects the costs of coordination, as shown in Figure 3.1.

FIGURE 3.1
Interdependence, Coordination, and Costs

Type of Interdependence	Means of Coordination	Cost
Pooled, Generalized	Standardization	Low
Sequential	Planning	Medium
Reciprocal	Mutual Adjustment	High

As indicated in Figure 3.1, three types of interdependence exist: pooled, where each part of the organization renders a discrete contribution to the whole and each is supported by the whole; sequential, where one part of the organization is dependent upon the previous output of another part, yet both are interdependent for production of organizational outputs; reciprocal, where the outputs of each or many parts of the organization become inputs for other parts.

The contingency adaptation theory notes that complex organizations evidence all three types of interdependence to varying degrees, and that organizations attempt to coordinate their activities in different ways. It identifies the methods of coordination as standardization of rules and expectations, that is, coordination through standard operating procedures, coordination by planning, and coordination by mutual adjustment. The theory then relates the types of coordination and types of interdependence to indicate that coordination costs are the result of the ways in which the various parts of the organization relate to each other. For example, where interdependence is reciprocal, costs of achieving coordination through mutual adjustment are likely to be high. Mutual adjustment of reciprocal interdependence of the type that characterizes universities requires considerable negotiation between organizational parts, negotiations which often have to be coordinated and mediated by some party in the organization. The costs of coordination in this circumstance can be considerable, both in terms of the time and effort of mediators and organizational-unit representatives, and the potential conflict that may be generated between units and between units and mediators.[19] The implications of these observations for critical mass modeling will be discussed subsequently.

The nature of the external task environment thus has much to do with organizational response to environmental change. For example, the environment may be characterized as either homogeneous or heterogeneous, stable or shifting, unified or segmental.[20] The task of achieving internal organization coordination is higher when the environment is heterogeneous, shifting, and segmented. Importantly, combinations of these environmental states should cause decentralization of decision making in order to gather and use information effectively in deciding how the organization should adapt differentially to change.

This understanding is important in helping to justify the critical mass approach to resource planning and decision making.

Assessment of Organizations

The nature of the assessment of organizations depends upon beliefs about knowledge of cause and effect (complete/incomplete) and the character of the desirable standards (crystallized/ambiguous). If the knowledge to use objective evaluation techniques is lacking, social tests are often used, that is, group norms, satisficing norms, internal historical comparisons, and comparison to other organizations. If these criteria fail, organizations try to shift the ground rules for assessment in their favor. The critical mass approach would attempt to prevent such shifts by establishing clear standards for evaluation.

Human Behavior

Human behavior is conditioned by culture and by choice of occupations into more or less homogeneous behavior patterns. These patterns are reinforced by inducement/contribution "contracts" between individuals and organizations. As long as individuals see the possibility of upward mobility, they will identify with the goals of the organization. When individuals view themselves as stationary, control mechanisms and job security become important. The critical mass process is intended to stimulate faculty motivation by giving faculty the key role in determining how academic unit and university program priorities are established.

Control

Complex organizations depend on coalition management to achieve political control while relying on standardization, coordination, and mutual adjustment to achieve organizational control. This is true in part because it is virtually impossible for central decision makers to handle well all the information and decision variables presented by complex problems. Decision making is dynamic; that is, the actors and scenarios are constantly changing. The strategic decision matrix (Table 3.4) indicates under what conditions different types of decision strategies are likely to be used. The critical mass approach attempts to accommodate high degrees of organizational diversity and environmental complexity in that it gathers information on adaptive behavior from throughout the organization, rather than only from the top of the administrative hierarchy.

CONTINGENCY ADAPTATION THEORY

The series of propositions rendered in the contingency adaptation theory summarized above indicates that the total costs of implementing a comprehensive resource planning and decision system like the critical mass approach would be high and, further, that these costs would be distributed throughout the organization. Management of interdependence in universities would appear to require coordination by planning and by mutual adjustment. High costs of coordination may be viewed as necessary where the environmental constraint of budgetary retrenchment is present. This is because the loss of faculty and university productivity under such conditions is likely to be considerable as a result of uncertainty and conflict over how expenditure reduction criteria are developed and implemented. The cost of making incorrect decisions in executing budget cuts may be viewed as greater in the aggregate in terms of reduced research and instructional and public service performance than the costs of obtaining more and better information for decision, coordination, and mutual adjustment through critical mass resource modeling.

The contingency adaptation theory may be applied to universities generally, and to academic units using the critical mass model in particular, to indicate how and why they perform as they do under varying conditions. Universities are supposed to satisfy social goals for discovery and communication of knowledge and for problem solving. Universities are constrained by and dependent upon their environments. They are dependent upon student demand for instruction and social demand for research performance, and they also depend on outside entities for financial and political support. As organizations, universities are constantly attempting to understand and adapt to environmental change through individual faculty research efforts and in collective development of instructional curricula. Institutions within a multiuniversity system are to some extent mutually dependent, but they also compete for students within domains defined by geography, student academic abilities and preferences, and other variables. Universities employ technical core staff in their faculties, plus other teaching staff and researchers, to devise and implement strategies intended to achieve the goals of discovery and communication of knowledge. In some cases where resources are threatened, goals may be limited to mere survival.

The contingency adaptation theory prescribes the task of administration under uncertainty as "providing boundaries within which organizational rationality becomes possible."[21] In addition, it notes that the ability to provide flexibility to solve problems under conditions of uncertainty is viewed as the basis for power in the administrative process. The critical mass resource planning process is intended to provide university decision makers with a more exact understanding of the complex set of activities that takes place in a university in a manner which allows the flexible management of a relatively fixed set of resources. This is an important component of the rationale for incorporating an explicitly coordinative planning process into organizations which appear to have flourished in the past without much formal planning. However, resource abundance may explain why this has been the case. Under conditions of resource constraint, the costs of avoiding mistakes is likely to increase, as noted above.

The contingency adaptation theory divides organizational rationality in adapting to new conditions (for example, resource constraints) into technical and organizational categories. Rationality thus defined may be applied to evaluate the adequacy of the critical mass model as a means of managing resource scarcity. Technical rationality seeks to protect the technical core of an organization, the faculty and academic programs of a university, from environmental interference. The critical mass planning mode attempts to establish plans, priorities, and defensive strategies from within, rather than having these decisions imposed externally. Organizational rationality attempts to establish an equilibrium in internal production units by buffering technical core staff (faculty) with administrative staff and processes to enable adaptation

and self-defense with the minimum expenditure of defensive
effort by technical core staff. The critical mass approach
is designed to enable setting priorities in academic development plans, supplemented by information, so that small
"buffering units" of resource budgeteers, planners, and
administrators will be able to respond well to external
challenges. As such, it may be speculated that the critical mass approach will reduce the amount of data gathering within universities and allow buffering to be accomplished with fewer, but more knowledgeable, administrative
staff. However, until the critical mass approach is fully
implemented, this remains an untested hypothesis.

Contingency adaptation theory observes that efficient
problem-solving organizations retain power by maintaining
alternatives, by seeking prestige, and by attempting to
gain control over internal and external elements upon
which they are dependent. The critical mass approach
attempts to accomplish these objectives by making the academic activities of a university more understandable to
faculty and to administrative staff within the university
so that academic program decision alternatives are clearly
understood by participants in the resource planning process
and so that internal university tension generated in resource competition is reduced through consistent and stable
rules and information for setting priorities in negotiation
of resources. The contingency adaptation theory's assertion
that organizations should structure themselves to achieve
coordination through various means appears to support the
employment of a rational resource planning process such as
the critical mass approach by universities and colleges,
and also to predict its costs and to explain the purposes
served in bearing these costs.

As noted, the theory identifies three types of internal intradependence in organizations: (1) pooled,
(2) sequential, and (3) reciprocal. These variables are
related to strategies of seeking organizational coordination
and the costs of coordination. Thompson also tied these
variables to the characteristics of organizational environments; for example, when environments are heterogeneous,
shifting, and segmented, coordination costs are higher.
Universities and colleges are characterized by pooled,
sequential, and reciprocal interdependence, but especially
by pooled interdependence. This leads to the conclusion
that the appropriate coordination means would be through
standardization and that costs would be low. However,

because of the divers nature of university "production" activity (teaching and research) and "outputs" (knowledge), standardization as a means of achieving coordination has relatively low political feasibility. Rather, planning and mutual adjustment are much more likely forms by which coordination can be attempted. This implies that the costs of coordination will be higher as a direct result of production diversity and complexity, especially relative to many other public and private sector organizations that evidence pooled interdependence. In addition, because university environments are heterogeneous and segmented, the types of coordination required tend to be planning and mutual adjustment, with consequent higher costs of administration relative to standard operating procedures.[22] The key to understanding these costs in universities is that they are distributed throughout the organization rather than aggregated at the top in large administrative units. Indication of this is the goal of the critical mass approach, in part.

Shifting from coordination and resource planning to decision making, the contingency adaptation theory categorizes decision making according to outcome preferences and beliefs about cause and effect to show how organizations seek self-control (refer to Table 3.4, Decision Strategies). The four types of decision strategies indicated were (1) computational, (2) compromise, (3) judgmental, and (4) inspirational. Employment of a formalized resource planning process within a university would indicate desire on the part of faculty and administrators to have accomplished sufficient planning and information management to move toward more judgmental and computational decision-making strategies where either outcome preferences and cause-and-effect expectations are relatively certain (computational strategy) or outcome preferences are known but cause-and-effect relationships are unknown (judgmental strategy). This latter condition best fits the conditions faced by universities in the resource-restraint era. Judgmental decision making requires high-quality information. The critical mass resource planning mode intends to increase the likelihood that resource decisions are based upon clearly established priorities and well-organized, comprehensive, and accurate information, bearing in mind Wilensky's definition of quality intelligence noted earlier. Applying the contingency adaptation theory in this way indicates that application of the critical mass model will increase the quality and certainty of academic resource decision making in a period of resource uncertainty.

CONCLUSIONS ON IMPLEMENTATION OF CRITICAL MASS APPROACH

Will the employment of the critical mass model lead to greater understanding of academic unit performance and planning? If so, will this understanding be useful in university resource planning and acquisition? These are the essential questions that must be addressed before a decision is made to implement the critical mass approach. These questions are difficult to answer in the abstract. The intention of the critical mass approach is to gather better information on academic units in a more systematic manner than is presently employed in many universities and colleges and to organize this information so that resource planning and decision making can be accomplished in an efficient, equitable, and open fashion. It may be argued that presently in many institutions the quality of understanding of academic unit programs and priorities is rudimentary and fragmented. As a result, decision making, and the analysis which supports it, is ad hoc and in many cases inconsistent with academic unit or institutional interests in the long term. This inconsistency often leads to misunderstandings between institutional and state decision makers.

Analysis of pilot implementation of the critical mass approach at the University of California, Berkeley, and the University of California, San Diego, illustrates the strengths of coordinative critical mass resource planning for both faculty and administrators. Interviews with faculty and administrators conducted during the pilot implementation addressed how faculty perceived efforts to reorganize academic programs as a means of coping with reduced budgets and how they regarded the budget process in general. The interviews indicated frustration with administratively-led initiatives for academic program reorganization and the ad hoc nature of the resource planning process. However, there did not appear to be any generalized resentment about the resource planning process as a result of proposed reorganization of academic programs.

Faculty members and administrators with experience in university budgeting, administration, and governance expressed the opinion that more systematic resource planning is absolutely necessary as a means of managing scarce resources. Faculty members who had served on the academic senate budget committees were asked how faculty resistance to more systematic resource planning could be overcome. Their general response was that there was no alternative to better resource planning and decision making in difficult choices among competing and nearly equally attractive academic program initiatives in a period of limited or no growth. In addition, interviews with faculty conducted at the University of California, Berkeley, over a two-year period in preparation of the university academic plan substantiated the critical mass assumption that collection and utilization of information about academic unit planning and performance is helpful in determining campus resource allocation priorities and in stimulating faculty participation in the planning process.

Part of the reason for faculty support for the system at Berkeley was generated by the prospect of reduction and consolidation of administrative requests for information about academic units. At Berkeley, requirements for reporting had increased steadily over the previous decade. A number of systems operated routinely to require collection and display of information on academic unit activity. In addition to the normal enrollment reporting activity, data were gathered on academic unit instructional performance through a state-mandated data system for instructional resources—data on faculty and staff size, teaching workload, enrollment, teaching assistants employed, ratios of staff to enrollments, and other activities. This information was assembled annually in the Berkeley Campus Statistics and Annual Campus Statement. Data on faculty workload and performance was required in budget support documentation, as was information on faculty personal history. Once every five years, all of the above was compiled in a comprehensive university academic plan. To these reporting requirements was added data collection for reports prepared for program reviews, accreditation reviews, affirmative action reporting, federal research audits, and special studies instituted by the Berkeley chancellor, the office of institutional research, the University of California system-

wide president's office, plus various state and federal
government offices and other parties. Faculty response to
the demand for information was predictable. As one inter-
viewee noted, "Stop it! We don't have time for all this."
Given this response, organization of data collection into a
single process as proposed by the critical mass approach
would be welcomed by many faculty and academic administrators. While the participant observation and nonrandom-
ized interviews conducted at several universities in the
research project reported here do not provide completely
satisfactory evidence that critical mass implementation
would be positive and well received, the findings are certainly supportive of the concept and of the manner in
which it was developed in a pilot test.

Formal organization of the resource planning process
would provide greater understanding about academic-unit
performance to key academic senate committees and to academic decision makers and their advisors. Implicit
throughout the discussion of the critical mass approach
to resource planning and its integration into a formalized
budgeting procedure for universities and colleges is the
notion that adoption of any formalized planning procedure
must complement existing modes of campus governance in
order to be accepted by faculty, administrators, students,
and other members of the campus community. However,
conception and implementation of the resource planning
process must also conform to the ambience and pattern of
communication on a campus. The administrative "decision
styles" of university campuses are unique. Styles of leadership appropriate in some institutions are rejected in
others. Cognizance of these differences is crucial in the
development of resource planning and budgeting procedures.
Whatever the nature of institutional decision and lifestyle,
a crucial ingredient in implementation of a formalized resource planning process is likely to be the establishment
of an environment of trust between participants in the
process.

If a university or college is to function properly,
to offer a climate that encourages creativity among its citizens, it must, to the greatest extent possible, create and
maintain an internal environment evidencing security and
freedom from coercion. Individuals designated as responsible for resource management within universities, faculty
administrators and support staff alike, who collect and
organize information on academic activities, must be trusted

by academics if they are to perform the insulative and
advocative roles outlined here. Faculty trust must extend
beyond confidence in the ability of resource decision makers to understand teaching and research activities. It
must also include faith in their competence to represent
these activities outside the institution. Academic planning
and budgeting must be sensitive to the wide varieties of
activities within institutions; they must also be able to
respond well to the searching inquisitiveness of central
university system and state government resource planners
and decision makers. It must be sensitive to the institution's internal environment so as to avoid creating pressures for implementing measures that reflect exclusively the
nature and form of the dialogue and rules for budgeting
presented in the external environment, and it must be
guided by values appropriate to the intellectual climate of
universities.

In the next decade universities will need to plan
and budget so as to better utilize existing resources rather
than to depend on the continuous injection of new resources
over the existing budget base. To do this, universities
must learn more about themselves than they know at present. However, as noted in the previous chapter, this
should not necessarily imply that universities need to
tell the outside world all they learn about themselves
through the development of better resource planning and
decision systems. Further, the critical mass approach
is based upon the assumption that resource planning and
decision making should be highly process oriented. Institutional learning that results from involvement in the resource planning process comprises at least half the reason
for engaging in critical mass implementation. The other
reasons are related simply to survival and to the continued
promotion of intellectual and personal vitality in our universities and colleges.

It is intended that the critical mass approach will
enable universities to employ data on resource utilization,
programmatic attributes, and other program and knowledge
production characteristics strategically in resource negotiations with state governments that appropriate the major
share of funding for higher-education institutions. The
most important elements of the critical mass approach are
the systemization of internal university priority-setting in
resource allocation, and the consequent ability to better
argue for state appropriations using either a student

demand-enrollment strategy or nonenrollment-based critical mass programmatic approach. In fact, these strategies may be used differentially relative to student demand conditions, or in combination, to argue for resource augmentation over a budget base determined exclusively by student enrollment forecasts. The critical mass approach is designed specifically to defend against budget reduction where student enrollment is stable or falling. Use of the model thus expands the strategic opportunities available to universities in competition for financial resources.

NOTES

1. W. Bergquist and W. Shoemaker, "Facilitating Comprehensive Institutional Development," in A Comprehensive Approach to Institutional Development (San Francisco: Jossey-Bass, 1976).

2. The term critical mass was applied by Professor Raymond G. Bressler, Jr., Assistant Chancellor Errol W. Mauchlan, Institutional Research Director Sidney Suslow, and other members of the faculty and administration involved in academic resource planning at the University of California, Berkeley, in the mid-1960s. The multicampus research team that applied the critical mass concept to academic resource definition in University of California systemwide master planning for the 1980s consisted of Sandra Archibald, L. R. Jones, Errol Mauchlan (chairperson), and G. A. Sasek.

3. See, for example, V. Stadtman, Centennial Record of the University of California (Berkeley, Calif.: University of California, 1967).

4. C. Kerr, The Uses of the University (Cambridge, Mass.: Harvard University Press, 1963).

5. Observations on recognition of the need for improved resource planning and allocation procedures made by the author are based in part on field-research interviews conducted at the University of California, Berkeley, and in the multicampus University of California system.

6. Observations made by Assistant Chancellor Errol W. Mauchlan, University of California, Berkeley, April 18, 1977.

7. M. Trow, "The Public and Private Lives of Higher Education," Daedalus 104 (Winter 1975):113-27.

8. See, for example, D. Michael, On Learning to Plan--And Planning to Learn (San Francisco: Jossey-Bass, 1973); W. Bennis, Changing Organizations (New York: McGraw-Hill, 1966); G. Benveniste, Bureaucracy (Berkeley, Calif.: Glendessary Press, 1977); F. Patterson, "Institutional Planning in the Context of Change," Planning for Higher Education 6 (August 1977):1-8; F. Znaniecki, The Social Role of the Man of Knowledge (New York: Columbia University Press, 1940).

9. D. Brown, The Mobile Professors (New York: Wiley, 1965); T. Caplow and R. McGee, The Academic Marketplace (New York: Wiley, 1958).

10. R. Cope, "Qualitative Approaches to College and University Planning." Paper presented to the California Association for Institutional Research, February 1978; S. Dresch, "A Critique of Planning Models for Postsecondary Education," The Journal of Higher Education 46 (May/June 1975):245-86; Patterson, "Institutional Planning."

11. J. D. Thompson, Organizations in Action (New York: McGraw-Hill, 1967).

12. H. Wilensky, Organizational Intelligence (New York: Basic Books, 1957), 141.

13. Ibid.

14. Thompson, Organizations in Action, 27.

15. Ibid., 10.

16. H. Simon, Administrative Behavior (New York: Macmillan, 1945), 143.

17. Thompson, Organizations in Action, 134.

18. Ibid., 160-61.

19. Ibid., 134-38.

20. Ibid. These variables of environmental condition were adapted from the work of W. Dill. See W. Dill, T. Hilton, and W. Reitman, The New Managers (Englewood Cliffs, N.J.: Prentice-Hall, 1962).

21. Thompson, Organizations in Action, 162.

22. Ibid., 55-82.

Four
Recognition and Management of Financial Stress in Universities

Over the past decade, and particularly since 1978, there has been some measure of public pressure to reduce the size and scope of government. State government expenditures for higher education and other services have been limited by various factors, including an economic recession that reduced revenues for state and local governments, passage of property and other tax or spending limitation measures, and reductions in federal transfer payments and social program outlays.

This chapter provides an analysis of the manner in which universities recognize and attempt to manage financial crises and prolonged financial stress. It presents some cutback management options and provides an approach for assessing the severity of financial crises and strategies. Among the issues and management approaches analyzed are program reduction and termination costs and benefits; planning, evaluation, and participation; centralization of decision making; and improving university marketing. Among the general conclusions drawn are that (1) greater investment in market research and marketing is needed in most institutions, (2) financial crises must be adjusted to and managed cognizant of the rigidities and constraints that characterize universities as bureaucratic organizations, and (3) inability to adapt to environmental change and new social conditions reduces the probability of program survival and financial health for public universities.

The dilemma in facing cutback in the public sector generally and in universities in particular results in large part from the fact that over the past 30 years our society and economy have become accustomed to and dependent upon growth in government. We are not at all accustomed to the prospect of expenditure reduction or program termination in the public sector. Growth fits well with both the motives of political decision makers seeking support on the basis of providing jobs, public works projects, and welfare assistance, and of citizens desiring the benefits of political expenditure decisions. However, the retrenchment game does not appear particularly attractive to politicians no longer able to reward constituents, to public managers desiring to preserve their programs and jobs, or to citizens benefiting from the provision of transfer payments and services by government. It is little wonder that we avoid thinking about retrenchment, given that its outcomes are likely to displease great numbers of citizens and political actors. Aversion to change from a comfortable, munificent, and stable state to a painful, tight-fisted, and uncertain state is quite understandable.

Among the issues that must be addressed generally when governments have fewer revenues to spend are the following: Should the scope of public policies, programs, and organizations be reduced? Why do government policies become immune to review, modification, and termination? How can we tell which policies and programs should survive and which should be modified, reduced, or terminated? How should decision makers attempt to reduce or terminate public policy programs or organizations where this appears desirable?

Public managers in universities and elsewhere are facing the necessity of setting priorities for reducing and modifying programs. However, few public managers have much experience in cutback management. This chapter is intended to provide university administrators with information on·methods for improving the management of retrenchment and reallocation.

RESTRAINT MANAGEMENT OPTIONS

Financial restraint and program retrenchment in universities may be analyzed according to the causes of financial crisis, the methods for managing financial crises, the issues and dilemmas faced by administrators in attempting to manage retrenchment, and the methods to both achieve and avoid academic program termination. The second of these topic areas, the methods for managing financial crisis, typically is the subject of most immediate concern to university administrators.

The range of nonmutually exclusive cutback and re-allocation management alternatives includes the following five: (1) doing nothing, which is likely to work only for a short time if the financial crisis persists; (2) increasing revenues; (3) reducing expenditures; (4) increasing employee and organizational productivity; and (5) developing a set of more innovative responses that are productivity related. The fifth category of productivity-related responses includes a broad range of options: interinstitutional cooperation; cooptation of other universities, programs, and student constituencies; program or mission reorganization and merger. On the business management side of university operations, productivity may be increased by joint purchase and service agreements with other universities or local and state governments, contracting, privatization, and others.[1]

Before developing strategic plans and options to manage under conditions of restraint, prudent university administrators will attempt to define the seriousness of financial crisis in terms of length of time and degree of revenue shortfall relative to planned expenditures. A general framework to define the extent of financial crisis has been suggested by Schick.[2] A modification of this framework produces the following categories of financial crisis:

1. Relaxed scarcity, where revenues in constant dollars (C$) just equal expenditures for a period of one to five years.
2. Chronic scarcity, where revenues (C$) fall short of planned expenditures by less than 5 percent for a period of one to five years.
3. Short-term acute scarcity, where revenues (C$) fall short of planned expenditures by greater than 5 percent for one or two years.
4. Prolonged acute scarcity, where revenues (C$) fall short of planned expenditures by greater than 5 percent for more than two years.

Two additional categories may be added where they occur: (5) long-term austerity and (6) financial recovery with continuing revenue constraint. Definitions for these states are less precise than those for categories 1 through 4. Long-term austerity may be defined as a condition wherein revenues and expenditures are constrained in constant dollars relative to planned expenditures and also to previous patterns of growth for a period of five years or longer. Long-term austerity is a condition that many universities are likely to face over the next decade and perhaps beyond. Financial recovery with continued revenue constraint may be viewed as the condition in which universities have adjusted to reduced revenues through reduced expenditure, program modification, and improved financial and program management.

In this context, it may also be useful to note that the terms financial stress and financial crisis may be differentiated to indicate the former as a state in which difficulty is experienced in balancing revenues and expenditures over a long period of time, while the latter indicates a sudden event in a short period; for example, loss of a substantial portion of state or federal financial support resulting in financial exigency, program termination, and substantial employment reduction. In this chapter the term financial crisis is used to characterize both stress and crisis conditions, unless otherwise stated.

The two most prominent financial restraint management options are to increase revenues and to reduce expenditures. Included in the revenue option is the examination of existing revenue sources, with more analytical attention given to the degree of political support for alternative increase opportunities, to tuition and fee pricing policies and the elasticity of demand of student consumers, and to the equity implications of price increases. Recognition that pricing policy is of strategic importance may be a revelation to some university managers accustomed to the idea that pricing ought to concern only private sector firms. In fact, tuition price response by students should be of great concern where institutions attempt to maximize total tuition revenue. The revenue increase option also includes the search for new revenue sources, including new fees-and-services charges, expansion of efforts to stimulate research support funding, alumni donations and foundation giving, and definition of what may be termed the revenue rights among state organizations competing for general fund appropriations. This latter task creates a new set of challenges in institutional and governmental relations.

Nonmutually exclusive general expenditure reduction options include across-the-board reduction (ABR), specific program reduction (SPR), and program termination and merger (PTM). Expenditure reduction typically includes careful examination of legal,, regulatory, and other inter-governmental mandates to differentiate those that may be ignored without incurring law suits and loss of revenue. Across-the-board expenditure reductions may concentrate initially on program support funds in attempts to avoid personnel reductions and typically include a number of "invisible" actions such as withdrawal of unfilled personnel positions from academic units, cuts in travel and supplies budgets, and reduction of physical plant maintenance. An across-the-board reduction is directed at all academic and support units. Specific program reduction generally in-volves reducing some programs (and positions) without completely eliminating them; that is, cuts of the type made in the across-the-board approach are directed to specific units prior or subsequent to implementation of across-the-board reductions in all units. Program termination and merger results in discontinuation of specific units and may include absorption of their responsibilities and staff by other units. Reorganization under the PTM approach, along with across-the-board reduction, appears to be the most typical response to financial restraint.

The additional management options listed previously (increasing productivity and various others included under the rubric of innovative responses) are discussed subse-quently in presentation of a general model of phases of recognition and management of financial crisis. For those interested in studying other management options in depth, a body of work has emerged in this area in the past few years.[3] This literature draws heavily upon applied social science research conducted over the past 30 years and longer in political science, economics, political economy, public administration, sociology, organizational theory and behavior, anthropology, psychology, and other disciplines. While studies of retrenchment in public organizations in general, and in higher education specifically, produced by researchers in various fields of public policy and manage-ment have a distinctly professional and applied focus, this work has its origins in and owes a considerable debt of gratitude to traditional social science theory.

PHASES OF RECOGNITION AND MANAGEMENT
OF FINANCIAL CRISIS AND STRESS

A general sequence of events appears to characterize the recognition and management of financial crisis in public organizations, including universities. A summary of phases of recognition and management characteristic of the response of public organizations to financial crisis and prolonged stress is provided in Table 4.1. The sequence of events represented in Table 4.1 constitutes a scenario of methods of coping with financial stress over time. As a general model, it is subject to all the errors of generalization, omission, and potential inapplicability to specific cases and circumstances that pertain to models of this type. Despite these weaknesses, the model is presented as useful for identifying and understanding many of the events that appear to characterize financial crisis management in public organizations. The discussion of phases of recognition and management in this chapter generally follows the model. However, the section that follows attempts to emphasize the most significant components of the model in an integrative way, similar to the manner in which financial crisis, by necessity, is encountered and managed. Rarely if ever are financial crises or management responses ordered as neatly as Table 4.1 might suggest.

The response in the initial phase of financial crisis typically involves ignoring that a crisis exists. This is followed by short-term and ad hoc measures to reduce spending, accompanied by efforts to assign blame for the crisis. At this point there may occur a general displacement of organizational leadership attention in an attempt to avoid making hard choices over program cuts. Expenditures for "soft" positions and services are reduced first, and cuts are made in a manner that is relatively invisible to students and the public. These cuts are often demoralizing to faculty and staff employees and reduce the ability of the organization to cope with financial stress over the long haul. For example, ignoring physical plant maintenance and depreciation may lead to higher repair and replacement costs later. Similarly, where significant reductions are made in travel and support budgets, faculty research support services, or in organizational development staff education/training, an immediate cost is loss of morale. However, across-the-board reductions in expenditure may usually be made without significant political resistance.

TABLE 4.1
Phases of Recognition and Management of Financial Crisis and Stress

Timing and Degree of Scarcity	Phase	Events (Under Assumption that Revenues Continue to Be Reduced through Phase 7)
6 months	1	Ignoring that a crisis exists; moderate reduction in expenditures; crisis termed only temporary.
to	2	Short-term across-the-board expenditure cuts made and attempts to increase revenue from existing sources instituted.
2nd year Relaxed and chronic scarcity	3	Recognition that crisis may persist for longer period (more than one year); casting the blame for causes of the crisis; ad hoc "invisible" expenditure reductions (e.g., in capital plant maintenance or depreciation funding).
1st year	4	Broader across-the-board expenditure reduction; salary and hiring freezes imposed; governmental revenue assistance sought; new sources of revenue defined; efficiency-oriented program cost studies instituted; workload cost measures improved; "softer" nonessential services reduced; mandated or high-value programs examined for reduction; reexamination of tuition and fee policies.
to 3rd year	5	Across-the-board reductions continued, accompanied by additional reductions in specific programs; some employee layoffs occur; improvements sought in revenue forecasting; program and policy evaluation undertaken more seriously; unions and employee organizations resist further cuts in salary; "hit lists" of programs for possible termination are developed based upon traditional organizational criteria; the rumor mill picks up steam and employee tension increases; research support and employee training and development, staff services, and nonessential services reduced further or eliminated; adaptive capability weakened.
Chronic to short-term acute scarcity	6	Across-the-board and specific program reductions cause more employee layoffs and some job terminations; specific programs terminated, with some functions absorbed by other units; some employees transfer to other units; employee morale and

Timing and Degree of Scarcity	Phase	Events (Under Assumption that Revenues Continue to Be Reduced through Phase 7)
		productivity drop; some skilled and highly valued employees seek jobs outside the organization; negotiations held over trade-offs between salary reductions versus more employee layoffs and terminations; organization heads recognize need for better and more comparable program information; user fees increased or instituted.
	7	Further program terminations implemented; university administrator and leaders recognize need for longer-term strategic planning to integrate program and financial strategies; need for restoring some expenditures recognized (physical plant maintenance and capital investment, employee development and training); program priorities and reduction decision criteria reexamined; revenue base and structure analysis conducted; organizational leaders use political contacts and leverage in attempt to gain revenues or avoid further reductions; budgeting and planning processes developed
Prolonged acute scarcity		to improve employee participation, instructional and public service planning and evaluation; fees, charges, and other discretionary service prices increased; organizational leadership may change in response to political or administrative demands.
3rd year	8	Development and implementation of long-term program and financial planning; organizational missions and objectives renegotiated; new revenues balance budget at reduced expenditure level; employee layoffs and terminations discontinued; organization invests in market analysis to complement internal program evaluation; pricing policies, service demand changes, and market segmentation studied; budgetary strategies examined and
5th year		modified; continued austerity conditions accepted; major reorganization plans considered or implemented; greater involvement of external participants in program and financial review.

Table 4.1, continued

Timing and Degree of Scarcity	Phase	Events (Under Assumption that Revenues Continue to Be Reduced through Phase 7)
Prolonged acute scarcity to long-term austerity	9	Implementation of program, financial, and market plans; reorganization of functions and responsibilities undertaken; revenues and expenditures increased significantly for one or two successive years; some service responsibilities eliminated through contracting, privatization, and other means; planning and budgeting service priorities set over long term; salary increases instituted and some new employees hired in specialized areas; attempts at marketing new organizational missions and objectives; employee productivity and morale improved; confidence in leadership strengthened.
Beyond 5th year Long-term austerity and financial recovery	10	Revenues and expenditures increased over three-or-more-year period; renewed capability for financing of new programs and innovation; some closed programs reinstituted; search for new solutions to budget problems; development and testing of "utopian" technologies and instructional approaches; reformulation of some service objectives and obligations; revenue generation capabilities negotiated and shifted; recognition that some service and revenue problems will persist; improvements made in integration of program and comprehensive financial planning; citizen support for organization improves.

Sources: This sequence is based in part on field research conducted by the author in over three dozen universities and local governments over a five-year period, and also on a number of case studies by other researchers. See for example C. Levine, Rubin, and Wolohojian, The Politics of Retrenchment (Beverly Hills, Calif.: Sage Publications, 1981); A. Pascal, Fiscal Containment of Local and State Government (Santa Monica, Calif.: Rand Corporation R-2494-FF/RC, September 1979); R. Duncan, 101 (Plus) Ways to Squeeze More out of Local Government Dollars (Upper Marlboro, Md.: Prince George County, 1981); R. Zammuto, D. Whetten, and K. Cameron, "Environmental Change, Enrollment Decline and Institutional Response," Peabody Journal of Education 60 (Spring 1983):93-106; M. Johnson and K. Mortimer, Faculty Bargaining and the Politics of Retrenchment in the Pennsylvania State Colleges, 1971-1976 (University Park: Center for the Study of Higher Education, 1977); K. Mortimer, "Procedures and Criteria for Faculty Retrenchment," in Challenges of Retrenchment, ed. J. Mingle (San Francisco: Jossey-Bass, 1981), 153-70; J. Lee, Case Studies of Institutional Decline (Washington, D.C.: ABT Associates, 1981); K. Alm, E. Ehrle, and B. Webster, "Managing Faculty Reductions," Journal of Higher Education 48 (1977):153-63.

Given that financial crisis conditions persist, the next phase involves making deeper across-the-board reduction in program support budgets, perhaps accompanied by hiring and salary freezes, salary reduction, and even short-term institutional closures, for example, ending the academic year early. Universities and other public organizations begin at this point to face the choice between reducing employee compensation and cutting employees. There is considerable disagreement among academics and practitioners over which strategy is best--across-the-board cuts versus reductions targeted to specific programs. Proponents of smoothing the impact of reduction through across-the-board cuts or more dramatic program termination and merger argue the benefits of their respective approaches. Supporters of across-the-board cuts and salary reduction allege that where union contracts and other employee compensation contractual constraints may be contravened, organizations will be better off if they reduce their budgets evenly, relying on normal employee attrition, withdrawal of vacant positions, hiring and salary increase delays or freezes, cuts in supplies and support budget and services, and physical plant maintenance deferral to reduce expenditure levels.

Advocates of program termination and reorganization argue that the across-the-board strategy weakens organizations throughout and is inequitable in that high-demand programs and high-quality personnel are cut the same amount as weaker ones. Further, they maintain that the across-the-board approach is not cost-effective in that it does not take into account public service needs and preferences. The advantage of the program termination approach is conceived to be that it enables the establishment of priorities to guide expenditure reduction with the goals of maintaining high-quality programs and services, the most valuable employees, and responsiveness to public service demand. Because program termination often involves merger and reorganization, this strategy requires advanced planning, a reasonably sophisticated information base for decision making, and considerable negotiation. Further, as argued in Chapter Three, it would be improved through definition of critical mass program operations levels, that is, resource levels below which programs cannot operate and still achieve their objectives satisfactorily.

While program termination may appear on face value to be a more cost-effective strategy, research on termination effects indicates that the long-term costs of program termination are higher than most advocates of this approach acknowledge.[4] When recruitment, training, employee replacement costs, loss of morale, employment compensation for terminated employees, and hard-to-measure personal and social instability costs caused by layoff and unemployment are considered, reduction through across-the-board cuts and attrition may be more cost-effective than program termination. Whether social costs are added to internal organizational costs is of considerable importance in comparing the cost-effectiveness of the two approaches. In addition, whether organizations evaluate these two general strategies on the basis of cost savings in the short term or cost-effectiveness and net benefit over a longer period is of crucial importance in choosing one approach over the other.

Generally, public organizations, including universities and public employees, appear to prefer the across-the-board and attrition approach, with "nonessential" services cut first and the last-hired untenured faculty and staff employees the first fired. Unfortunately, the application of length of service rather than merit criteria typically eliminates less experienced and younger staff. Further, faculty and staff employees cut in this phase often include a higher proportion of women and minorities than is represented in the total organizational workforce. There may also be an accompanying loss of highly skilled and valuable faculty and staff employees who find better-paying and less stressful employment in other universities or organizations.

Some universities and other public organizations have developed procedures to mix length of service and merit criteria in determining layoff or employment termination schedules for staff employees. Employee performance evaluation systems may be designed so that employees generate service credits for high performance ratings. These credits are then added to other credits earned through length of service and other ways, with total service credits then used to define employee layoff order and rights to "bump" other employees in the same or similar job classification elsewhere in the organization. The service credit system may also be used to set priorities for employee reassignment to new positions within the organization, either at the point where personnel cuts are made initially or after a period of layoff.

While reductions in force (RIFs) often include the provision of bumping rights across organizational units, unlimited staff bumping is stressful, disruptive, and may cause serious losses in employee morale and productivity. The "single bump within class" system that restricts movement rights to a single choice and compares the qualifications of those seeking to bump other employees with requirements for the position in question appears to be a preferable option. Union contracts may constrain the close application of qualification and requirement definitions, as may civil service rules.

One of the most important dimensions of personnel management under cutback conditions is the extent to which the organization invests in retraining, education, and placement of faculty and staff employees whose jobs have been cut. Education and retraining may be necessary to enable reassignment of employees to new positions within the organization, for example, to existing or new academic units. Similarly, investment in placement services within the organization, and assistance provided in job search outside the organization, is costly but defensible not only from the perspective of responsible management but also because it builds morale and promotes productivity to employees whose jobs remain, especially for those who face the threat of job loss in the future.

Development of criteria for faculty layoffs generally is based upon tenure, enrollment, and academic program reputational considerations. The general practice in higher education is for academic units to be reduced or terminated by academic program as identified in the university catalogue, with nontenured faculty cut first. Tenured faculty may be relocated to other units where feasible, or they may be terminated as well. Academic units with low enrollment demand usually are first to be reviewed for the "hit list." Reputational variables of the unit and its faculty, along with research and contract support revenue generation capability, are also important. High-prestige and nationally ranked programs, or programs with strong accreditation support, are less likely to be reduced than lower-prestige programs. Membership of faculty on key university committees, external research support, and size of base budget by various measures (for example, per FTEF [full-time equivalent faculty] support or budget divided by student credit hour production) are traditional indexes of power in universities indicating an ability to influence budget and program policy decisions.[5] These characteristics appear to be important in resisting program reduction as well.[6]

Definition of the rights of tenured faculty under termination are still evolving under American Association of University Professors (AAUP) guidelines and as law suits and court decisions create precedent.[7] To quote Gray, "The courts have attempted to balance the need [of universities] to cope with financial stress against the contractual right of a tenured faculty member. . . . The courts have been asked to determine (1) whether financial exigency exists, (2) whether the [faculty] dismissals were demonstrably bona fide, (3) which party has the burden of proof, (4) the appropriate remedy in the event of a 'bad faith' dismissal. There is no 'law of the land' regarding [these] issues."[8] Courts have upheld that tenure policy is part of the faculty employment contract and, therefore, that tenure status provides legal entitlement to continuous employment subject to program discontinuance and academic exigency. Due process requirements must be met in dismissal; for example, AAUP guidelines or other conventions must be met. The specific definition of financial exigency is subject to considerable difference in interpretation, and there is no clear rule that applies. In some instances it has been interpreted as legislatively mandated budget reduction; and in others, as relative to the size and length of time of expenditure cuts or operational deficits. In some cases exigency has been applied to academic units rather than institutions.[9] Thus, some precedent exists for terminating tenured faculty in specific academic units without declaring financial exigency for the entire university. Universities are able to terminate tenured faculty where they can demonstrate financial exigency. This is similar in concept to private sector employee termination practices under bankruptcy, where unionized staff have been reduced; for example, in the airline industry.

PROGRAM TERMINATION

Despite the political difficulty and productivity disadvantages of outright program termination, if financial crisis conditions persist and revenues continue to be reduced, universities may be forced to terminate programs and employees. At this phase of cutback management universities may not have program characteristics and performance data of sufficient amount, quality, and specificity to make rational program comparisons and choices. This is the dilemma that argues for implementation of critical mass and core model resource management systems. In absence of a means for setting program priorities, cuts may be made on the basis of length of tenure of the program or unit, with the newest programs the most vulnerable because of their lack of deep roots into the organization and base budget. Another factor may be that the newest units are more innovative and less like the rest of the university in mission, instructional and research focus and approach, faculty composition and background, and other ways.

Other prominent decision rules that operate in budget cutting at this point are political clout in the inner circle of university decision making and management, public support and political pressure applied by the general public and by opinion leaders from outside the university, ability to generate additional tuition and fee revenues, and the general reputation of the program within the academic hierarchy. The ability to generate additional revenue may become the operant definition of productivity and value to the university at this phase, although revenue generation capability may not outweigh other performance-related variables, for example, research productivity and funding. This proposition, among others noted here, needs to be investigated empirically to determine whether and under what conditions it applies.

The development of "hit lists" of vulnerable programs normally takes place in this phase, and their circulation causes no end of consternation and work productivity loss for employees in units listed.

A range of management styles may be employed in communicating the degree of vulnerability to termination. In some cases information intended to be restricted to only a few decision makers leaks out across the institution. Breach of secrecy may become an issue upon which institutional decision makers dwell. Academic unit heads, faculty, and staff employees may be unable to ascertain the validity of rumors. Whether program termination priorities are a closely held secret within the institution, and there appears to be some justification for this where the extent of the financial crisis is highly uncertain, or whether they are explained openly to employees appears to have an impact on employee morale and productivity. The best approach would seem to be where termination decisions can be explained openly, based upon a clearly defined set of institutional priorities and criteria for decision, and where priorities and criteria are consistent with those developed through a long-term planning process that has provided the opportunity for participation for a large number of employees. However, because financial crises often arise rapidly, this ideal approach may evolve only after several iterations of cuts have been made, and only where organizations invest in planning and participation to define priorities and decision criteria explicitly. More on this topic will be noted subsequently.

Analysis of program and policy termination has developed as a topic somewhat unto itself within the general field of public policy. Some research on termination preceded the widespread study of cutback. Studies of the factors that accompany and contribute to termination have benefited from previous research and theory on organizational survival and change dynamics on the one hand, and bankruptcy, reorganization, and merger in the private sector on the other. Case studies have produced a list of lessons for would-be terminators, or for those wishing to avoid termination, that includes "don't float trial balloons," "enlarge the policy constituency," "focus attention on the policy's harm," "inhibit compromise," "recruit an outside terminator," "avoid legislative votes," "accept short-term cost increases," and "buy off the beneficiaries."[10] Research on public organization termination indicates that demonstrating the harm done by the program or policy is crucial; simply pointing out that a program is inefficient or ineffective is seldom sufficient to terminate it. It has also been demonstrated that when programs have been discontinued, the functions they performed have usually been absorbed by other units.[11] Often this has involved absorbing some "terminated" employees as well as the former unit's mission. Whether the students served by a program are likely to be absorbed by another unit may be a criterion used in university termination decision making.

The causes of termination appear to be generalizable across the public and private sectors and include competition, inadequate marketing strategy, leadership failure, poor analysis and decision-making procedures, and obsolescence. The immediate indication of organizational failure typically is revealed in reduced consumer demand, for example, declines in student enrollment and credit hour production in academic units. However, a single demand index such as enrollment rarely reveals the factors that cause the decline in service demand. Investigation of these factors is the task of market research. Academic units and faculty wishing to precipitate or avoid termination are wise to assess the political potency of termination arguments, advocates, or allies and the basis of motivation for seeking this outcome. Termination motives may include that a program is not needed as judged by student demand; is inefficient, ineffective, or too expensive; is out-of-date relative to developments in its field and prevents implementation of new approaches to instruction and research; is ideologically unacceptable; and does not fit within the institutional mission.[12]

PLANNING, EVALUATION, AND PARTICIPATION

In the heat of battle that characterizes program termination, university decision makers may begin to recognize that to defend decisions internally and externally, there is need for more careful development of cutback criteria, priorities, and procedures. Broader faculty, staff, and public participation in expenditure-reduction decision making may appear desirable. This recognition may stimulate the deployment of program evaluators and policy analysts to measure academic unit activities and corresponding student demand characteristics. Regrettably, it is at this phase that organizations typically become aware of how much they are in need of good program activity and outcome information organized in a way that enables comparison of program costs and benefits. Capable cutback managers recognize that cuts ought not to be based exclusively upon program workload measures, ill-defined program reputational factors, age, and other informal but convenient decision rules. Productivity, program quality, adaptability, and future demand should also be considered. It may be argued that these criteria should dominate others in restraint decision making.

To cope with cutback effectively, academic decision makers may be willing to invest more resources in defining the length and severity of fiscal crisis and the development of a process for long-range resource planning and management. From the view presented in Chapter Three, at this time it is important to design and implement a resource planning process that generates accurate and reliable information to enable comparison between programs and with other organizations. Program performance data displayed in a format applicable to the varied activities of the organization are needed. The resource planning process and strategic program development or reduction plans also ought to articulate with longer-term budgetary, financial, and capital planning. Decision makers may be frustrated at this point to learn the extent to which the institution has underinvested in or simply squandered valuable planning, program evaluation, information management, budgeting, and other analytical resources in the past.

The issue of participation in cutback decision making is much debated. Arguments for broader participation are often made on the grounds of fairness, contribution to employee morale, and adherence to democratic management values. A much stronger argument for participation, and one that appears to be present in "Theory Z" organizations as described by Ouchi, is that faculty, students, and other program constituents have information that should be assessed in deciding whether and how to make cuts.[13] Many of the best suggestions on how to save money and to increase efficiency are likely to come from the academic unit level if faculty and staff are asked or required to contribute to the resource management process.

In the longer term it may be useful to employ external evaluators to assess the value and need for the programs and services provided by the institution. It may be argued that outside evaluators are less willing to be captured by the organization and, if properly trained and allowed to work without interference, are less likely to reflect the biases that inevitably are present in the minds of academic unit heads, faculty, and institutional decision makers.[14] This presumes that universities understand how to use consultants, which is often not the case. Given the constraints of managing retrenchment, decision makers may be reluctant to employ outsiders, may tend to prescribe results, without much external input, or may not be willing to use consultants over a long enough period of time to derive the benefits of the knowledge they have developed. Additionally, evaluational consultants may not be involved to any degree in implementing their recommendations even though their skills would be useful for im-

proving performance. And, for a variety of reasons including poor analysis, even where it is performed, evaluational results may be ignored entirely.[15] This may occur
even when evaluation is performed by internal faculty committees and institutional research staff.

CENTRALIZATION OF DECISION MAKING

Whether external evaluation is employed and participation opportunities are expanded, it may be expected
that some degree of centralization of decision making will
result under conditions of financial stress. The dominant
form of authority structure employed to manage organizational crises, including financial crises, appears to be
centralized decision making.[16] While this may be necessary
and useful in the short term, it is likely to be a poor
long-term response.[17] Resolution of the New York City financial crisis in the 1970s was managed initially by a few
individuals, but later it involved a great number of participants. The same appears to be true for the management
of the post-Proposition 13 fiscal crisis in California.[18]
Case studies of universities indicate centralization of decision making in the president's office.[19]

Prolonged dependence on one or a few individuals
to make cutback decisions may produce many of the bureaucratic weaknesses characteristic of the Chinese mandarin
system of management by personal influence. However, the
degree of centralization of authority in financial crisis
management may not be the most important variable in explaining successful crisis resolution.[20] Smoothing the impact of cuts, continuity of leadership, the extent to which
crisis management is politicized, form of government, ability to define and communicate organizational mission and
goals, and extent to which service priorities are established and budgeted may be more important variables. The
dilemma of centralization of decision authority versus
broader participation has been summarized as follows: "The
crux of the retrenchment problem comes down to a fundamental trade-off: Centralize and limit representative, responsive [governance] or leave authority more or less fragmented but open to access, thereby limiting the ability
. . . to prioritize and target cutbacks. Either way, something of value will have to be sacrificed."[21]

SEARCH FOR LONGER-TERM CRISIS RESOLUTION

The phases of financial crisis management that follow are not well documented because few universities or other public organizations have advanced in actual practice to the point where they provide examples for research. Hypothetically, the succeeding phases of management benefit from systematic assessment of (1) additional revenue generation opportunities, (2) the mission of the institution and its component programs, (3) program outcomes, and (4) student and public needs and preferences. The pressure of continued reduction in revenue from traditional sources and the results of internal program evaluation may cause universities and other public organizations to provide fewer services than in the past, and to refine those that are offered to better fit public preferences and demand patterns.

Where substantial reduction in state and/or federal financial support for universities or state systems has occurred, long-term financial and capital planning is needed in addition to academic planning to evaluate the revenue effects of instructional program and service changes, assess property and equipment leasing and liquidation options, develop accurate capital asset depreciation and replacement costs and schedules, improve inventory management, improve cash flow management and investment practices (and pension fund solvency where applicable), limit debt load if it exists to fit debt service capacities, and establish sufficient fund reserves to balance the budget in the event of future revenue short-fall where state law permits. Long-range financial planning may require the employment of financial management consultants and others to rebuild confidence in the financial accountability and cost-effectiveness of the enterprise. Financial planning should be integrated with academic resource planning of the type provided in the critical mass approach to ensure that the administrative and academic sides of university management are planning under the same assumptions and objectives.

To improve productivity in public universities and in public organizations generally, administrators may discover that as is the case for private organizations, risk capital is required for investment in new equipment, faculty and staff employee hiring and training, program analysis, and market research. Computerization of academic program re-

source planning and financial and other information systems
may demand investments that are expensive initially but
produce greater efficiency and cost savings over the long
term. Likewise a down market provides good faculty recruitment opportunities for institutions that are able to finance
efforts to hire outstanding researchers from other universities or to attract the best new doctoral degree recipients.

In the university business management area, contributions to productivity may come from facility maintenance,
and the replacement of used equipment when needed to prevent productivity losses resulting from downtime and employee frustration. Increased health and safety and reduced
legal liability should result from better risk management
and insurance procedures. In many public organizations
where across-the-board and "invisible" budget cuts have
been made over a multiyear period, equipment replacement
alone may require substantial investment of capital.

As noted earlier, one of the first areas of the budget to be reduced when revenues fall short is employee development and training. In the short term, training of
nonacademic personnel may be postponed, but elimination
of training is likely to have a serious impact on productivity, especially where new systems and equipment are
purchased. Further, reduced capability of providing faculty incentives through funding for innovative approaches
to instruction and research or for staff training and development causes employee morale to suffer. Valuable human resources may be lost to other organizations. Reductions in support for research and for opportunities to attend
professional conferences, the absence of rewards for high
instructional performance, and the loss of salary purchasing power to cost-of-living inflation combine to reduce academic and staff productivity in universities.

Under financial crisis constraints, many new solutions to organizational problems may initially appear too
radical but later prove workable. For example, the city
of Oakland, California, sold its museum to private inves-
tors but has continued to provide museum services under
lease agreement with the new owners. Similar sale and
lease-back agreements have been established in other cities
and may be workable for public universities. Such arrangements enable the reduction of maintenance and operation costs while private investment incentives help to ensure proper maintenance and care for facilities. Through
new or increased user fees, student and community users

of university facilities may be required to bear a larger proportion of costs for services they consume. Where this occurs, the equity implications of the user fee system should be considered. Careful cost accounting may provide information regarding appropriate fee levels that may be differentiated by income class or some other measure of ability-to-pay. Fee exemptions may be provided to some students and patron groups. Further, the public goods justification for the provision of university services should not be ignored in the rush to institute user fees and charges.

IMPROVED MARKETING

Operating in a long-range resource planning orientation under conditions of continued austerity, universities and other public organizations may begin to give greater attention not only to program outcome analysis and net program benefits but also to how they market services to constituents. University administrators may become more sensitive to the definition of marketing as something more than advertising and selling. For example, the importance of market research to define student attitudes and institutional/program selection behaviors may be recognized as vital for enrollment planning. Attention to the various components of what in the private sector is termed the marketing mix may result in better understanding of relationships between market research, program development, pricing, distribution, advertising, promotion, sales, and evaluation of public services and consumer behavior.[22]
The importance of research to determine student and public ability-to-pay and market segmentation variables may be recognized. Accompanying this recognition may be an awareness of differences between private and public sector marketing in terms of product-versus-service orientation, and that where indirect marketing to state government takes place in the public sector in the budget process, there is no consumer payment for services rendered. A market-planning orientation in universities recognizes that because large portions of financial support come from governments instead of directly from consumers, greater attention is needed to internal political marketing in contrast to the external consumer marketing focus of private sector organizations. Political marketing is an essential but

often misunderstood component of the public budgetary process. Most universities engage in a considerable degree
of marketing activity, although it is often poorly organized,
not coordinated between academic and administrative units,
and not well executed.

The desire on the part of decision makers for better
information on student and political constituent preferences
may stimulate universities to develop new procedures for
assessing public attitudes toward specific types of services. Definition of instructional and public service market segmentation through survey research may be a first
step in improving university responsiveness to service quality, price, distribution, and other constituent preferences.
Universities may become more willing to invest in innovative communication procedures, ranging from survey by
mail and telephone to computer-assisted, interactive tele-
vision and telephone opinion-sampling systems.

Efforts to improve market preference assessment will
create new problems, including information overload and
finding money to finance experimentation with new marketing
and communication technologies. However, better information on programs, priorities, and markets should make it
easier to defend budget decisions based upon critical mass
and equity considerations. Objection to the obligation of
universities and government in general to provide services
in part based upon financial need, and ignorance of the
public goods justifications for service provision, appear
to be implicit in some citizen-based efforts to limit university and government revenues and expenditures.

CONCLUSIONS

Some observers predict that over the next decade
public universities and other public organizations will reduce the range of services they offer, surrendering many
services now provided to citizens, nonprofit organizations,
and private institutions.[23] This view indicates that
some services may simply lapse from better to worse, for
example, research.

Some changes in university operations should be anticipated. For example, we might expect continued increases in tuition and fee revenue generation efforts. Universities may become more responsive in the instructional
and research service they offer. On the business side of

university management, there may be an increase in the already-prevalent uses of private contracting, joint lease and purchase agreements, intergovernmental credit and bonding assistance, and shared support service arrangements; for example, for campus police and fire protection. Concomitant with these changes may come a reorientation of the manner in which financial resources are allocated to and within universities, recognizing that greater financial resource flexibility is needed in an era of restraint. Approaches such as the public voucher system to provide students with money or credit to spend directly for the instructional services they prefer may improve the manner in which academic program, pricing, and other service distribution policies are defined. The search for broader and more stable revenue bases for universities and other public organizations may make them better able to survive sudden and sharp reductions in one or several sources of revenue. Better resource planning and program review through critical mass model application may result in better services, higher employee and student morale, and stronger citizen support for universities. In the long term, a critical mass resource management approach combined with a new marketing orientation may result in development of better solutions to social problems through research, instruction, and public service. Some attempts at innovation may inevitably be regarded as "too utopian" due to the degree of their departure from present practices and the incorporation of new and somewhat untested instructional and research procedures and technologies. Still, experimentation must be undertaken and funded if better and more cost-effective methods are to be found.

Nonetheless, financial stress must be adjusted to and managed in universities one step at a time, cognizant of the rigidities and constraints built into our overly hierarchical public university bureaucracies. Manifestations of organizational rigidities and constraints include devotion of inordinate amounts of time to self-defense rather than to problem solving, problem avoidance through obfuscation, resistance to the implications of new information and technologies, and a fear of adaptation to new social conditions. Inability to adapt reduces probability of survival if we accept that the principles of biological evolution apply to universities and other public organizations. Recognition that these rigidities and constraints exist should cause us to devote more resources to the study of restraint and methods for managing financial crisis and organizational change.

NOTES

1. A good general text on cutback causes and management options is C. Levine, ed., Managing Fiscal Stress (Chatham, N.J.: Chatham House, 1980). See also K. Boulding, "The Management of Decline," Change 64: 8-9, plus references below. Several good sources on restraint management in higher education are included in J. Mingle, ed., Challenges of Retrenchment (San Francisco: Jossey-Bass, 1981). See especially J. Mingle and D. Norris, "Institutional Strategies for Responding to Decline," in Challenges of Retrenchment, 47-68. See also F. Bowen and L. Glenny, State Fiscal Stringency and Public Higher Education (Berkeley, Calif.: Center for Research and Development in Higher Education, 1976); S. Hanyle, ed., New Directions for Institutional Research: Coping with Faculty Reduction (San Francisco: Jossey-Bass, 1981); R. Zammuto, D. Whetten, and K. Cameron, "Environmental Change, Enrollment Decline and Institutional Response," Peabody Journal of Education 60 (Spring 1983):93-107; K. Cameron, "Strategic Responses to Conditions of Decline: Higher Education and the Private Sector," Journal of Higher Education 54 (1983):359-80; I. Rubin, "Retrenchment, Loose Structure, and Adaptability in the University," Sociology of Education 52 (Spring 1979): 211-22; D. Whetten, "Organizational Response to Scarcity: Exploring the Obstacles to Innovative Approaches to Retrenchment in Education," Educational Administration Quarterly 17 (1981):80-97; I. Rubin, "Universities in Stress: Decision Making under Conditions of Reduced Resources," Social Science Quarterly 58 (1977):242-54.

2. A. Schick, "Budgetary Adaptations to Resource Scarcity," in Fiscal Stress and Public Policy, ed. C. Levine and I. Rubin (Beverly Hills, Calif.: Sage Publications, 1980), 113-34.

3. For example, see Mingle and Norris, "Institutional Strategies," 47-68; G. Chambers, "Negotiating Mergers between Institutions," 88-108; D. Smith, "Preparing for Enrollment Decline in a State System," in Mingle, Challenges of Retrenchment, 259-72. In the general area of productivity, see H. Hatry et al., How Effective Are Your Community Sources? (Washington, D.C.: Urban Institute, 1977); H. Hatry, "Current State of the Art of State and Local Productivity Improvement," in Levine, Managing Fiscal Stress, 269-80. See also R. Bingham, B. Hawkins, and F. Hebert, The Politics of Raising State and

Local Revenue (New York: Praeger, 1978).   Much recent
work in alternative service delivery draws on earlier research such as R. Bish, The Public Economy of Metropolitan
Areas (Chicago: Markham, 1971); R. Bish and E. Ostrom,
Understanding Urban Government (Washington, D.C.: American Enterprise Institute, 1973); E. Savas, ed., Alternatives
for Delivering Public Services (Boulder, Colo.:   Westview,
1977).
   4.   E. Dougherty, "Evaluating and Discontinuing
Programs," in Mingle, Challenges of Retrenchment, 69–87;
E. Craven, "Managing Faculty Resources," in Mingle, Challenges of Retrenchment, 109–33; K. Mortimer, "Procedures
and Criteria for Faculty Retrenchment," in Mingle, Challenges of Retrenchment, 153–70; L. Greenhalgh and R.
McKersie, "Reductions in Force: Cost Effectiveness of Alternative Strategies," in Levine, Managing Fiscal Stress,
313–26; L. Greenhalgh, A Cost–Benefit Balance Sheet for
Evaluating Layoffs as a Policy Strategy (Ithaca, N.Y.:
School of Industrial and Labor Relations, Cornell University, 1978).   On the social effects of job termination and
economic stress, see E. Weeks and S. Drengacz, "The Non-
Economic Impact of Community Economic Shock," Journal of
Health and Human Resources Administration 4 (Winter 1982):
303–18; D. Dooley and R. Catalono, "Economic Change as a
Cause of Behavioral Disorder," Psychological Bulletin 87
(1980):450–68.
   5.   J. Pfeffer and G. Salancik, "Organizational Decision Making as a Political Process: The Case of a University Budget," Administrative Science Quarterly 19 (1974):
135–51.
   6.   Mortimer, "Procedures and Criteria"; J. Lee,
Case Studies of Institutional Decline (Washington, D.C.:
ABT Associates, 1981); K. Alm, E. Ehrle, and B. Webster,
"Managing Faculty Reductions," Journal of Higher Education 48 (1977):153–63.
   7.   J. Gray, "Legal Restraints on Faculty Cutbacks,"
in Mingle, Challenges of Retrenchment, 171–93; P. Strohm,
"Faculty Responsibilities and Rights during Retrenchment,"
in Mingle, Challenges of Retrenchment, 134–52; W. Furniss,
"Retrenchment, Layoff, and Termination," Educational
Record 55 (1974):159–70; W. Furniss, "The Status of 'AAUP
Policy,'" Educational Record 59 (1978):7–29.
   8.   Gray, "Legal Restraints," 172.
   9.   Ibid., 177–78.

10. R. Behn, "How to Terminate a Public Policy: A Dozen Hints for the Would-Be Terminator," Policy Analysis 4 (Summer 1978):393–413.

11. H. Kaufman, Are Government Organizations Immortal? (Washington, D.C.: Brookings Institution, 1976).

12. E. Bardach, "Policy Termination as a Political Process," Policy Sciences 7 (June 1976):123–26.

13. W. Ouchi, Theory Z (New York: Avon, 1982).

14. L. Jones, "Termination Gamesmanship: The Strategic Uses of Evaluation, Feasibility Assessment and Marketing" (Eugene, Oreg.: Institute for Social Science Research, 1982); E. Dougherty, "Evaluating and Discontinuing Programs," in Mingle, Challenges of Retrenchment, 69–87.

15. C. Weiss, Evaluation Research (New York: Prentice-Hall, 1975), 110–28; E. Suchman, Evaluative Research (New York: Russell Sage Foundation, 1967), 152–53.

16. R. Behn, "Closing the Massachusetts Public Training Schools," Policy Sciences 7 (June 1976); C. Levine, I. Rubin, and G. Wolohojian, The Politics of Retrenchment (Beverly Hills, Calif.: Sage Publications, 1981), 197–207, 213–16.

17. Levine, Rubin, and Wolohojian, Politics of Retrenchment, 197–202.

18. On the New York fiscal crisis, see M. Shefter, "New York City's Fiscal Crisis: The Politics of Inflation and Retrenchment," The Public Interest 48 (Summer 1977): 98–127. On Proposition 13, see D. Bouchard, "Experience with Proposition 13 and Other Retrenchment Conditions," Journal of the College and University Personnel Association 31 (1980):61–65; more generally, see F. Levy, "On Understanding Proposition 13," The Public Interest 56 (Summer 1979):66–89; W. Oakland, "Proposition 13: Genesis and Consequences," National Tax Journal (Supplement, June 1979):387–409; J. McCaffery and J. Bowman, "Participatory Democracy and Budgeting: The Effects of Proposition 13," Public Administration Review (November/December 1978):530–38.

19. Mortimer, "Procedures and Criteria," 156–60; Lee, Case Studies; Alm, Ehrle, and Webster, "Managing Faculty Reductions."

20. Levine, Rubin, and Wolohojian, Politics of Retrenchment, 209–12.

21. Ibid., 216.

22. P. Kotler, Marketing for Nonprofit Organizations (Englewood Cliffs, N.J.: Prentice-Hall, 1975); C.

Lovelock and C. Weinberg, Readings in Public and Non-profit Marketing (Palo Alto, Calif.:   Scientific Press, 1978); M. Mokwa and S. Permut, Government Marketing (New York: Praeger, 1981); Zammuto, Whetten, and Cameron, "Environmental Change."

23. E. Savas, Privatizing the Public Sector (Chatham, N.J.:   Chatham House, 1982), 89-111, 124-50. Although this book has received considerable criticism, it provides a useful inventory of some of the cutback management options available to public administrators.

PART II
State Government Budgeting and Control of Universities

State government officials often view their responsibilities to include taking action to improve the responsiveness
of public higher-education institutions to the public will and
to cause universities to operate more efficiently. State policy
toward higher education in many instances appears to be guided
exclusively by a concern for short-term responsiveness and
financial accountability. The perception that pressure must
be exerted from state government to stimulate university responsiveness often justifies attempts at exertion of direct
influence and control over internal university management decision making. Through executive and legislative oversight,
informal suasion and political strategy, regulation of market
entry, supply and program content, and by means of line-item
and other types of budgetary control, state officials constrain
discretion over resource management decision making in universities.

The chapters that follow argue that while the intentions
of state officials may be laudable, many of their actions to
influence and control universities are misguided in that the
restrictions imposed on university decision making typically
result in less rather than more responsiveness and accountability, and they also cause a waste of public funds. Arguments
are advanced that state strategies to influence instructional
adaptation to social demand are (1) sometimes conceived narrowly to necessitate reduced emphasis on research in universities,
(2) that some types of budgetary controls are unnecessary, and
(3) that most direct regulation of institutional competition is

unwarranted. It is suggested that reform of state budgeting and regulation of higher education is in the public interest. Such reforms should increase rather than reduce university resource management flexibility in a period of stable but shifting student demand and financial restraint.

Five
State Government Strategies to Influence University Instructional Performance

State government executive and legislative decision makers typically view part of their responsibility in representing the public interest in higher education to include stimulating universities to respond to student demand for instruction. Through executive and legislative oversight, and particularly in the budget process, state decision makers and their staffs often attempt to influence university instructional planning and performance. While university administrators and faculty skeptically view these attempts to alter behavior as an erosion of academic freedom and managerial autonomy, state officials defend their actions as necessary to ensure proper public responsiveness and accountability to public service preferences and also as a means for improving the cost-effectiveness of university operations.

We should expect no ultimate resolution of these two views. Public universities compete with other state-funded programs, including human services, health, primary and secondary education, aid to local governments, and transportation for budget appropriation, under relatively constant conditions of scarcity. This is so because state revenues seldom if ever match the total of the expenditure requests of spending agencies. This is the nature of the budget game; budgeting is inherently competitive.

Budgetary competition evidences several major dimensions. The first is interagency competition, as noted above. The second dimension is competition between the budget minimizers, or budget cutters, and the budget maximizers, or spenders. State legislative budget committees and executive budget offices play the role of the budget cutters. Executive branch budget offices normally perform the key budget control functions in budget preparation and execution. Generally, executive budget office staff attempt to minimize expenditures as guardians of the public fisc. Legislative budget committees more often alternate in their role between spending restriction and spending advocacy. The executive budget control office and legislative budget committees share the objective of using budgetary appropriations to influence spending agencies, including universities, to conform to their interpretations of state government objectives. However, typically there is conflict and competition between legislative and executive views of the priority of state government program and service objectives.

The budget process role played by universities and other spending agencies is expenditure advocacy. Their role is to seek the highest budget appropriation level possible and to spend everything they receive in the provision of services to their constituencies. While state government officials often view this behavior as spendthrift, the budget process provides signals in the form of financial incentives for agencies to increase their appropriations by spending more money to serve new or existing constituents. Agencies typically receive more money if they can attract more consumers of the services they provide or if they can persuade state government to increase service quality. And unless agencies spend their entire budget appropriation, they are unlikely to be able to lay claim to the same level of money as the base for the budget of the following year. The incentive is clearly to get the highest appropriation possible and to spend it all within the fiscal period in which the budget is appropriated.

If we understand the budget process to operate in this manner, for better or worse, it is easier to place into perspective the conflict and competition that inevitably is revealed in the annual or biennial trauma of negotiating and enacting a budget. It is important to recognize that despite the bias of service providers such as university faculty and administrators, state government officials normally view their role as necessitating the application of some degree of control over university performance, either through the use of leverage in the budget or through program service requests and mandates.

The purpose of this chapter is to explore various approaches to the use of state control to influence the instructional performance of universities. While it must be acknowledged that state governmenfs also wish to influence university research and general public service performance, in practice the lion's share of state budget appropriations provides support directly or indirectly for instructional activity. The chapter further enquires into how the state may attempt to influence universities to innovate in adaptation to changes in public preferences for instruction. This topic concerns and, indeed, often preoccupies state decisioń makers. This is so because state officials either want universities to respond to their own instructional program preferences, presumably representative of their legislative constituencies, or they want universities to innovate so that instruction is provided more cheaply on a per-unit basis; that is, state officials want to cut the budget or reduce an appropriation increment as much as possible.

The strategies explored in this chapter are not mutually exclusive, and certainly they are not the only strategies employed by state government. Further, the strategies identified are generalized models of alternative approaches. As such, the program change strategy, the salary limitation strategy, and the enrollment market strategy are hypothetical approaches that appear in various and diverse forms in the real world of state government and university relations.

PUBLIC EDUCATION OBJECTIVES
AND STATE FINANCE POLICY

Can state fiscal and budgetary strategies be employed successfully to create incentives for instructional innovation in universities? In analysis of this issue, it is acknowledged that the primary responsibility for implementing new instructional methods and programs rests with institutional faculty. However, the mechanisms state decision makers utilize to finance public higher education may also be observed to affect the degree and rate of instructional experimentation in public universities. Although state budget decision makers often do not understand many of the consequences of their decisions in appropriating state funding to higher-education institutions, their actions define important conditions that affect performance in programs.

That this is true will not come as a shock to students of education finance, nor to state and institutional administrators. State decision makers have long attempted to influence behavior in public universities and colleges and are familiar with strategies for accomplishing this end. However, strategy setting by state decision makers has not received the attention it deserves, although some efforts have been made in this regard.

In his study of secondary schools, Pincus points out that rates and types of innovation in educatonal institutions are influenced strongly by pressure from the external environment. "School districts face a certain set of incentives that systematically affect their preferences for different kinds of innovations."[1] He also makes some prescriptive observations about those innovations which the state ought to stimulate: "Some federal and state subsidy . . . for innovation should not go for things that schools want to do, but rather for things that they would otherwise be reluctant to do."[2]

This chapter attempts to go one step beyond the understanding that has guided state government strategy setting to influence instructional innovation in higher education in the past.[3] It attempts to show that achievement of public education objectives could be improved through employment of a finance policy that would promote institutional resource allocation flexibility and stimulate institutions to satisfy student instructional preference. Using the California system of higher education as an example, we may speculate that both state and institutional decision makers would be better off employing a different higher-education resource appropriation methodology than that which is employed presently in many states. State budget and program controls now in use may constitute a major impediment to increasing the responsiveness of universities to the preferences and interests of students.

THE PUBLIC INTEREST IN INNOVATION

Implicit in this discussion is the assumption that society is served by a higher-education establishment that provides instruction in response to student preferences.

Exponents of the "social demand" theory from which this assumption is generated maintain that this approach best achieves social goals. This notion is not universally accepted. Critics of the social demand model assert that meeting student preferences is sometimes very costly and, therefore, financial limits must be set beyond which society is unwilling to support institutional response to student demand. They point out that the number of students to be accommodated in high-cost professional degree programs such as medicine must be constrained at some point. Just how this point should be determined often is unclear.

Accepting the validity of the social demand model, given the caveats expressed above, the social objectives to be achieved through public funding of higher-education instruction may be summarized as

1. Maximization of citizen understanding and participation in the affairs of the polity in order to maintain a democratic society.
2. Acquisition and maintenance of an educated and skilled manpower pool for social problem solving.[4]

The objectives of government funding to implement these broad social goals in higher education include maximization of citizen access to instruction, provision of programs of instruction and research sufficient in quantity and quality to satisfy society's need for educated citizens and a skilled manpower, support for research to guide social problem solving, provision of information to inform students about market demand for their skills, and achievement of an optimal degree of student and social satisfaction with education at minimum cost.

While achievement of these objectives may be viewed as the primary responsibility of universities, state government officials may perceive that in some instances these objectives could be achieved more effectively through exertion of external influence and control over instruction. External stimulation of instructional innovation and adaptation may be perceived as necessary to provide new types of learning in response to changes in student preferences that reflect the nature of market demand for their skills. Experimentation with new ideas and instructional modes may increase student satisfaction in learning, or it may result in achievement of degrees or credentialization at reduced public cost. Instructional innovation may increase the geographical or intelllectual access of students to learning. State influence over instructional innovation may be perceived as necessary in order to overcome the apparent bureaucratic rigidities of academe that inhibit instructional experimentation.

The impact of state-funding decisions on instruction programs and student choice is considerable. Decisions made in state capitals typically determine how much and what kinds of postsecondary education services will be provided, where and by whom such services will be made available, who will receive the benefits, and who will pay for them. State governments spend billions of dollars each year to influence the terms and conditions upon which higher-education instruction is made available. This influence is both direct, through public provision of operating and capital budget support and student financial aid, and indirect in that state funding influences levels of local and federal government expenditures and, to some extent, private contributions to higher education. Government funding exerts strong influence on student decisions to attend higher-education institutions, on the length of time students spend in school, and on the institutions and programs they select. Government influence is exerted in appropriation of budgets that specify how much the state is willing and able to spend on higher-education instruction and research, and how and where money is to be spent.[5]

In reviewing higher-education budgets over the last decade, state government officials have become increasingly willing to make specific their influence over university instructional performance; that is, state government has a strong interest in stimulating institutions to evaluate their commitment to discovering new ways of teaching and learning. State decision makers have questioned whether change is occurring fast enough to serve student interests. This enquiry has at times been severely critical of institutional management.

STALEMATE IN THE STIMULATION
OF INSTRUCTIONAL INNOVATION

The thesis that higher education instruction should adapt to changing student needs and interests has not been and is not likely to be strongly contested by institutional faculty and administrators, except to point out that change occurs continually in colleges and universities and that not all new approaches to learning can be expected to produce the results desired. Institutional responses to state prodding for instructional change often maintain that despite resource constraints, a significant number of innovative instructional programs designed to serve emerging student interests have been mounted in the past decade. These responses point out that a considerable amount of institutional resources have been expended to stimulate instructional innovation. Institutional representatives concede that whether these efforts have been sufficient relative to student and social needs is open to question. However, they maintain that to characterize institutional efforts as insignificant is inappropriate. Universities assert that where state budgetary support has been available, faculty and students have readily devised new approaches to learning. This suggests that rapid change can be achieved if institutional administrators and state budget decision makers provide money to support innovation.6

Clearly, there is a difference of opinion over the adequacy of institutional instructional adaptation. Institutional administrators argue that they are stimulating change to the greatest extent possible, given the constraints of state-level budget and program controls. Moreover, they maintain that further institutional reallocation of existing resources would reduce the quality of current programs. State decision makers exhibit the bias that public universities are unresponsive, inefficient, and unwilling to innovate unless forced. This disagreement has resulted in a stalemate in many states. Under existing financing mechanisms and support constraints, it is unlikely that significant new instructional program efforts can be launched by most public institutions unless state decision makers are willing to provide new money to stimulate their provision. External or off-campus degree programs are a case in point.

In many states external degree programs have been proposed in the state for funding to improve educational access for nontraditional degree seeking students. Universities want to expand access to citizens who, because of employment and other responsibilities, cannot come to university campuses as full-time students. In some cases, such as California, state executives have approved funding for the program, but at a lower per-student funding rate than for the regular on-campus instructional program. In many states no state support for enrollment in off-campus programs has been provided, forcing these programs to operate on a self-supporting basis. Numerous universities have created off-campus instructional programs leading to degrees in business administration, engineering, and other professional disciplines that have been accepted enthusiastically by part-time students and members of local communities.

The University of California charged fees to external degree program students to generate funds that were combined with state appropriations to pay salaries for regular university faculty teaching and for instructional support costs. Student demand for some programs was higher than could be accommodated. Based upon the success of the program, the University of California sought continued state support. However, after several years of "pilot phase" funding, state administrators asked the university to continue the program without state support. This action was consummated through the governor's item veto of the program from the budget bill approved by the legislature. The University of California maintained that elimination of state support was unwarranted and that it could not afford to deploy its own funds to continue the program indefinitely at existing quality and quantity levels. Despite protests from the legislature, the governor refused to appropriate additional funding and, as a result, the university discontinued the program. The losers in this disagreement were students desiring high-quality, degree-oriented instruction taught off-campus.

While it can be expected that programs will be offered by other higher-education institutions to at least partially satisfy student demand in cases like this, whether these programs will meet student quality, scheduling, and degree preferences is not clear. The point here is that in many instances innovative public instructional programs designed to respond to student needs and preferences will not survive or will not be developed unless they are specially funded by the state and this support is integrated into institutional budget bases.

It is apparent that external degree programs and nondegree-oriented instruction have constituted a significant growth area for many institutions, particularly in the past five years; much of this expansion has been made

by private, rather than public, institutions. State decision makers may point to the private sector institutions as
an indication of the unresponsiveness of public universities.
However, such conclusions may overlook several important
considerations. The first is simply that it takes money to
make money. Private institutions, and some public universities as well, have invested significant amounts of money
and have incurred operating deficits to develop off-campus
programs. Endowment reserves permit risk taking for private institutions, while in contrast many public universities have been struggling to survive under fiscal constraints related to enrollment decline. University critics
argue that institutions should shift more of their instructional efforts off campus to stimulate student enrollment.

To some extent this view has merit. However, as
we shall note in Chapter Seven, state government regulation sometimes circumscribes such efforts even when they
are undertaken. Further, often there are geographical,
transportational, and other barriers to expansion of instruction in off-campus locations that are not easily or in-
expensively overcome. Interacting with these constraints
are public university instructional quality standards that
impose self-limiting discipline to prevent offering instruction in off-campus locations where quality standards cannot
be met. Public university faculty and administrators observe that in many instances it would be inappropriate to
attempt to compete with private institutions or state and
community colleges in off-campus markets. This is because
universities are not staffed or equipped technologically to
compete in providing mass education where lower-quality
and cheaper instructional performance satisfies student demand. In fact, a portion of the off-campus market demand
is for nondegree-oriented instruction.

The fundamental defense universities use against the
criticism of unresponsiveness is that the institutional support state governments provide to public universities in
regular line-item appropriations is intended to purchase
university faculty research as well as instructional performance. Consequently, officials and the public often
overestimate the amount of slack resources available in
universities to provide off-campus instruction. In fact,
university faculty often buy time off from on-campus instructional responsibilities with externally funded research
support. From the university perspective, significant increases in off-campus instructional program offerings cannot

be achieved unless financial incentives are provided to stimulate this type of innovation. As we shall observe, state and local governments have provided such incentives to community colleges to cause them to pursue a strategy of enrollment maximization. However, the property taxpayer's rebellion and state budget deficits have circumscribed these efforts in some states.

STATE STRATEGIES TO STIMULATE INSTRUCTIONAL ADAPTATION AND INNOVATION

Accepting the assumptions that state decision makers perceive they have legitimate reasons for wanting to stimulate instructional adaptation and innovation and that state financing procedures affect institutional behavior, several scenarios can be developed to indicate how state government may attempt to influence university instructional performance.

Out of a range of approaches available to state decision makers to influence the type, amount, and intensity of instructional innovation in public higher education, the following strategies are both technically, if not politically, feasible and consistent with past state control behavior.[7] In formulating these strategies, ideas have been drawn from methods used or proposed by state governments in California and in other states. Some of these methods have been employed to exert leverage on institutions beyond the realm of instructional innovation, for example, in disagreements over faculty workload policies, research overhead reimbursement procedures, institutional fund expenditure control, and faculty salary and benefit compensation policies. The strategies are drawn intentionally as archetypes and, as such, may appear unnecessarily generalized or unrealistic to some observers. However, let us not underestimate the ambitiousness of state decision makers in attempting to control university behavior.

Of the three strategies discussed below, the first two (program change and salary limitation) would apply most appropriately to public research-oriented universities and to state universities and colleges where the state provides a large portion of institutional operational expenditures through item appropriations in state budgets. These strategies would be less applicable to community colleges where operating funds are provided by the state through enrollment-driven formulas (for example, average daily attendance) and through property taxes collected and allocated by local government independent of state budgetary control. However, in states where a large proportion of community college support is provided principally by the state, and where it is provided through a line-item budget not strictly tied to enrollment levels, these first two strategies could be employed. However, the implications for research in these strategies would clearly not apply for community colleges. The third strategy explored here applies to all public higher-education segments because it involves modification of the overall procedure by which state funding would be provided to public higher education.

Discussion of these alternatives is guided by the notion that certain types of decisions may be made more effectively by state governments, while others are better made and executed by institutions. The intention is to indicate that decentralization of certain types of resource allocation decision authority from states to institutions would increase the probability of achieving state educational goals. It would also provide substantial additional benefit by increasing institutional resource allocation flexibility while maintaining existing but seriously threatened commitments to institutional autonomy and academic freedom.

Program Change Strategy

The alternative of program change would utilize the state budget and legislature or administrative guidelines to require segmental reallocation of funds from existing programs to new programs designed to increase instructional quality and breadth.

Program change strategy would involve substantial state intervention into zones of institutional authority. Control language in the state budget would require certain amounts of money to be spent on innovative instructional programs. Also, increased appropriations for teaching assistant positions or for teaching assistant training could be provided to improve instruction. Precedent for this type of action has been set through provision of funding for special instructional programs in a number of states.

This strategy would require either increased state expenditures to pay for the increase in instructional emphasis desired or a "trade-off" of funds from existing programs to new programs. The practice of trading off funds within overall budget appropriations to higher-education institutions has become commonplace in many states. To trade off is to reduce funding for an existing program and transfer the amount reduced to support a new program, often eliminating a request for new funding. This practice is typically initiated at the suggestion of budget control staffs in state departments of finance under general guidelines established by state governors. In the past, implementation of such trade-offs generally have been forced upon institutions by state decision makers.

One mechanism used in California by the Department of Finance to force trade-offs is termed the negative program change proposal (PCP). Instituted in the early 1970s, the "negative PCP" permits the governor's budget analysts to stipulate inefficiencies in institutional operations and deduct the costs of these inefficiencies from the budget base. The burden of proof to reacquire funds eliminated through this procedure rests with the institution rather than the governor and his staff. Legislative budget hearings act as some check on this practice, enabling agencies to appeal decisions executed in the governor's budget before they are passed into law. However, the legislature also has used this strategy as a means of inducing trade-offs, justified through investigative studies conducted by its staff of consultants and analysts.

The trade-off mechanism, variously termed, has been used in numerous states to put teeth into special studies conducted by state auditors and program evaluation specialists whose analysis is often conducted independent of annual budget cycle activities. Prior to the use of negative PCPs in California, the Department of Finance had experienced difficulty in attempting to bring into the budget process the findings generated through special audits and program reviews. This has been the experience in other states as well.

Because of the tight state control of funding and program approval maintained over the California State University and California system, trade-offs of funds forced in their annual budgets have often achieved the specific program changes desired by state decision makers. The University of California has constitutionally guaranteed autonomy in internal budget allocation and also has substantial alternative sources of financial support. These attributes have provided the University of California considerably greater freedom in determining program and expenditure priorities. As a consequence, when its funds have been traded off in state budgets, the university at times has been able to reduce the impact of state action.

Given the high probability that the program change strategy would involve budget trade-offs, and accepting that the objective of this strategy is to increase institutional attention to instruction, one state implementation strategy would be to reduce expenditures for research to pay for increased attention to instruction. This would, in effect, raise the standard teaching load for university faculty. This change could be accomplished through budget control language specifying the relative distribution of funds within the instruction and research (I & R) component of institutional budgets to reduce appropriations for faculty research efforts while increasing instruction correspondingly. Such an action would have to be followed up by faculty workload analyses to determine whether more faculty time was being given to instruction and less time to research. A second approach would be simply to reduce I & R appropriations while holding instructional, research, public service, and other performance expectations constant. If I & R funding were not reduced, university production of student credit hours would increase in order to maintain the same level of state budget support.

While reducing state funding for research is by no means the only feasible program change strategy, reduced expenditures for research would reduce incentives for faculty to conduct research. With reduced emphasis on research, undoubtedly some faculty would attempt to find alternative employment to continue their research efforts. The intended impact on instruction would thus be twofold. It may be inferred not only that there would be less research done as a result of the shift in direct state expenditures but also that research-oriented faculty would seek employment in other institutions, leaving room for recruitment of faculty more interested in instruction. While this action would ignore research indicating that productive scholars are also good instructors, state decision makers could assume that the outcomes of their funding policy would work themselves out in the faculty labor marketplace.[8] The negative implications of this strategy in terms of institutional decision-making autonomy are obvious.

In order for this strategy to achieve its state-defined objectives, it can be assumed that a major shift in state funds for direct and indirect support of research would have to be implemented. Reductions in state support for research in public universities and colleges would attempt to shift the burden of research to institutional endowment funds and to federal and other funding sources in a period characterized by diminished constant-dollar research support available for many institutions. In addition, it can be observed that most state universities and colleges have substantially fewer alternative sources of support for research than do public and private research-oriented universities. In both cases, over time it is likely that the total amount of research would be reduced if this strategy were employed.

The program change strategy could, of course, be pursued without reducing research funding. In the past in some states, funds have been traded off from faculty position authorizations, noninstructional institutional support, and other areas to support new instructional programs. Such program trade-offs often require considerable administrative time and effort in negotiation between institutions and state budgeteers. The principal arguments against this approach for the university view are reduced funding for research, increased faculty teaching workload, and loss of institutional authority over academic program policy.

Salary Limitation Strategy

The second approach, salary limitation, would require exertion of state budgetary and administrative control over salary appropriations in the state budget and in salary-related legislation to place ceilings on institutional salary ranges.

The salary limitation alternative could be implemented in a number of forms similar to the case of the program change strategy. For example, budgetary language could be used to mandate institutional procedures for allocating faculty salary increases. The objective of this approach would be to reduce the growth of salaries at the top steps of salary ranges for tenured faculty ranks, without exercising similar controls over lower steps and for nontenured faculty. A salary limitation strategy of this type would compact faculty salary schedules and, over time, would reduce the overall amount of state money allocated to higher education for faculty salaries.   Teaching, research, public service, and other performance requirements could be held constant.

Restricting growth of higher faculty salaries while allowing lower salaries to increase would force institutions to deploy discretionary funds for faculty salaries in order to maintain salary scale structures and/or salary levels. By virtue of statutorily or constitutionally defined autonomy, some institutions such as the University of California could render this budgetary intervention ineffective unless legislation or an amendment were passed to require compaction of salary ranges.   However, many institutions have neither sufficient discretionary funds nor statutory authority to counteract this strategy.

The rationale of this approach is similar to that for the program change strategy in that reducing salaries for senior faculty would reduce the amount of research conducted because some research-oriented faculty would seek employment in other institutions.   The salary savings funds gained by the state by holding some faculty salaries constant could, under this plan, be redistributed over time and appropriated specifically to support hiring of instructors or development of innovative instructional programs. There is some precedent in community colleges for salary reallocation for this purpose.[9]

An additional consequence from reduced research support as a result of implementation of either the program change or salary limitation strategies might be reduced student demand for graduate study in public institutions. This outcome could free additional funds from budget bases to support innovative instructional efforts.   Given the wide range of public benefits believed to result from the conduct of research, and the fact that many faculty who are productive researchers also engage in more instructional or public service activities than do less research productive faculty, the high cost of these first two strategies or similar approaches is evident.[10]   Further, if we accept the social objectives for education cited earlier, reducing research activity would weaken our ability as a society to solve critical problems.   In addition, institutional autonomy and academic freedom is seriously constrained in implementation of these and similar strategies.

A more immediate cost to students, faculty, and the public would be to reduce the prestige of public colleges and universities as sources of knowledge and creativity.

Reduced prestige influences social perceptions of the worth of university and college degrees. That student choice of attendance at particular institutions is influenced heavily by prestige and its career impact is supported by the following evidence: the high prices students are willing to pay to enroll in high-prestige institutions, especially in private schools where tuition rates are not as constrained as they are in public institutions; and the continued enrollment demand at prestigious public universities and colleges. It may be speculated that reduced emphasis on research with a corresponding increase in emphasis on instruction could eventually reduce student educational demand in the aggregate. A sacrifice of social equity, in addition to level of education, could result if reduced access to higher education was accompanied by an increase in costs to students as institutions raised tuition revenues.

Enrollment Market Strategy

The third alternative to increase instruction innovation through state action, an enrollment market strategy, would provide funding to public higher education on the basis of marginal changes in student enrollments, funding these marginal enrollments at an equal rate for all types of institutions. This approach may be referred to as equimarginal enrollment funding, or per-unit marginal subsidy. Equimarginal in this context means equal at the margin and not based on marginal costs. Marginal cost funding methods and implications are discussed subsequently. Equimarginal subsidy differs from the program change and salary limitation strategies in that it would require less state-level accountability and control over specific institutional program and financial resource management decisions. However, greater attention would be given to the impact of state fiscal and budgetary policy in order to establish incentives for achievement of state higher-education objectives. While this approach would not satisfy critics of present trends toward centralization of educational authority in state capitals, it would represent a major step in decentralizing resource management control and reducing state accountability requirements.

The enrollment market alternative would in many cases require major alteration of the methods by which states appropriate funds to higher-education institutions.

For example, in place of current methods of state budget construction that establish program base, program maintenance adjustments, and program change funding somewhat independent of student enrollment changes, the market approach would appropriate new money or reduce funding on a strict per-student enrollment basis. Enrollment-funding variations for different types of public institutions and instructional workload standards would be eliminated. The only nonenrollment-related budget adjustments would be made to compensate for the impact of increases in prices of nonsalary goods and services consumed by higher-education institutions and for faculty salary cost-of-living changes. In most states, inflation and cost-of-living adjustments are made by means of state pricing memorandums or inflation guidelines issued by executive finance departments to guide agency budget preparation. These guidelines identify price increase allowance for particular types of goods and services and a general inflation allowance which is applied in cases when no specific purpose index is available. Often, inflation or price increase allowances are based upon the consumer price index, the wholesale goods price index, and other indexes; and they are sometimes modified downward by finance departments to stimulate state agencies to exploit the effects of price changes. Salary adjustments are defined by separate methodologies that vary from state to state but that generally take into account cost-of-living statistics and salary comparisons with other similar institutions.

To summarize, the equimarginal enrollment strategy would operate under two appropriation guidelines:

1. New funds would be allocated for marginal enrollment change upward or downward.
2. State appropriations for marginal students enrolled would be set at the same per-student rate for all public higher-education institutions.

As a consequence, equimarginal per-student appropriations would be expected to increase institutional competition for students, thereby achieving the state objective of increasing emphasis on instruction.[11] It is assumed, further, that institutions would be entirely free to set their own pricing policies for instruction in both on- and off-campus settings.

IMPLEMENTATION OF EQUIMARGINAL BUDGETING
WITH UNIT SUBSIDIES

A critical issue in implementing the equimarginal approach would be whether funding would move with student enrollments in both directions, so that institutions would lose funding if their enrollments declined. Although it may be assumed that state budgeteers would favor this approach, if our intention is to foster innovation, this feature might be interpreted to work in opposition to equimarginal incentive system objectives. On the other hand, movement in both directions may be justified as necessary to produce responsiveness to student demand.

Setting the marginal rate of change in subsidy at the same level for all public institutions would provide more equal institutional incentives for innovation consistent with public objectives to achieve innovation at minimum cost. However, because institutional instructional capacities and instructional program costs vary, complete equalization of incentives would not result. In fact, the prime criticism of this approach might be that it would cause institutions, particularly universities, to provide lower-quality, high-volume, and revenue-producing instruction rather than high-quality teaching. The response to this criticism is that market demand should be met as it is revealed, given appropriate price and quality trade-offs. It might also be assumed that some institutions would choose only to provide high-quality, high-cost instruction whatever the context. Because institutions would be free to set their own programs and prices, such attempts at accommodation of market characteristics is possible.

In response to institutional actions, the state is free to change the per-unit subsidy rate or to develop differential rates to encourage or discourage specific types of performance. In setting the level of the equimarginal per-unit student enrollment subsidy there appear to be no simple rules to follow unequivocally. According to the precepts of price theory, if universities behave as rational revenue maximizers under such a system of state subsidy, then they will attempt to set tuition prices at the level of their marginal costs. However, we recognize that determining true marginal costs across an entire institution is difficult, and that there are a number of other problems associated with marginal cost definition as discussed in Chapter Six.

From the perspective of state government, the most appropriate method for setting the subsidy is at the level (price) that induces institutions to perform according to state higher-education access, enrollment, and instructional adaptation objectives. The first step at the state government level is thus to determine explicitly in quantitative terms what enrollment levels and what distribution of students across institutions is preferred. State master plan goals should guide this effort, as will history, information on the existing distribution of students within public and private higher education in the state, tuition levels, parental income levels and high-school grade averages of existing and prospective students, population distribution, and other factors. The number of state students choosing to enroll outside of the state and the number of students attracted from other states and internationally may also be considered. Institutional student enrollment capacities in terms of physical plant size and optimal enrollment level plus the enrollment composition preferences of institutions (for example, undergraduate versus graduate) should inform these decisions. Other factors such as the distribution of students between public and private institutions in the state could be considered.

It has been the practice in many states to set enrollment subsidy levels by institution or by segment (community college, state college, and university) according to average cost-of-instruction figures by level of student or instruction, with average costs derived by a variety of methods. Although there is no economic or cost-accounting logic for setting subsidies in this manner because in adding or reducing enrollments it is marginal, rather than average, costs that are pertinent to institutions from an actual service cost perspective, the average cost-of-instruction approach is followed in many states. This occurs as a result of historical convention and, in part, because it is a politically acceptable decision rule that governs state and university relations. In some instances, it is likely that state and institutional representatives believe that average costs of instruction mean something in terms of the enrollment costs and management decisions faced by institutions, that is, that average costs are an accurate measure of real costs incurred by institutions in serving additonal or fewer students.

This belief ignores the concept of marginal costs for adding or subtracting $\underline{N}$ students over or under the enrollment base and fails to comprehend differences in fixed and variable costs across different programs and institutions. It also fails to comprehend the notions of economies of scale or market service response costs for attracting new students when overall enrollment demand is declining. Such conditions often produce cost step-functions that cause increasing, rather than decreasing, marginal costs for institutions, thus eliminating scale economy advantages. Despite the fact that these factors are not considered, average cost of instruction remains a convenient heuristic to simplify a complex decision.[12]

From the view of state government, as noted above the objective in establishing and modifying the equimarginal per-unit subsidy is to achieve the desired level and distribution of enrollment in higher education. Thus, the principle that should guide state decision making is to experiment in setting and then modifying the subsidy level until quantity and distribution performance objectives are achieved, that is, until the desired numbers of students are enrolled in all segments and in all institutions. As this end is approximated, state decision makers may decide how much additional or fewer student enrollments by institution, segment, or in the aggregate are worth to the state, that is, how much new money should be allocated for instructional performance in higher education. Once this dynamic is understood, there are two primary problems to be solved: The first is one of information accuracy. How accurate are the projected and actual student enrollment levels estimated by institutions and the state? What measures might be taken to improve projection and counting accuracy? The second problem is at what level should the first equimarginal unit subsidy be set when this funding system is adopted?

The answer to the first problem is primarily an information system rather than a financing issue. To resolve the second problem, one approach would be to fund initially at an enrollment-weighted average cost of instruction across all the segments of public higher education (weighted by the numbers of students enrolled in each segment) based upon the most recent agreed-upon instructional cost data and enrollment levels. However, there would be nothing magic about this number. It would not be assumed as an accurate reflection of institutional or aggregate marginal costs. Under this system existing budget base levels for all segments and institutions would

be held constant. The bases themselves would not be re-
calculated according to the enrollment unit subsidy. However, the increment or, in the case of declining enrollment,
the decrement to the base would be set at the equimarginal
per-unit subsidy level. If after the subsidy level is calculated for the first time and the effect on institutions is
estimated, or after the subsidy has been funded for one or
several years, the level could be adjusted in attempt to
affect the amount and distribution of student enrollments in
the state. In fact, it is just this type of experimentation
over a period of time that would teach both state and institutional decision makers about the competitive, distributional, and other effects of changes in the subsidy level.

Another approach to funding would be to set the
equimarginal per-unit subsidy adjustment on the basis of
estimated or actual marginal costs. However, there are
some accounting and information problems associated with
this approach in that marginal costs are difficult to estimate under any condition. (More on this is noted in
Chapter Seven.) Additionally, marginal costs across all
institutions would have to be estimated and/or verified and
then combined into one subsidy figure by weighted enrollment or by some other approach. It can be expected that
institutions would prefer to have incremental budget adjustments based upon average cost estimates and decrements
based upon marginal costs because this method would increase the size of increments but reduce decremental adjustments. State government budgeteers may prefer a reversal
of this approach to minimize increases and to capture as
much as possible of university budgets where enrollments
decline.

A decision rule that might also be applied in determining the subsidy, as is the case in many states
presently, is to set bounds within which student enrollment changes do not alter the budget, for example, 2 percent plus or minus estimated enrollment levels. This
method eliminates the need for small adjustments, but in
principle it is not consistent with the incentives intended
by the equimarginal subsidy. Under equimarginal budgeting even small changes in enrollment would be reflected in
subsidy increases or decreases to stimulate institutional
responsiveness to student market demand. From the perspective of state government, there may be objection to
small ex ante adjustments based upon revised enrollment
projections due to the administrative burden of having to

evaluate enrollment changes and adjust appropriations.
One procedure to minimize these costs would be to allow
institutions to "bank" their actual enrollment adjustments
over a period of time, for example, two years, with marginal subsidy changes made in the subsequent budget year.

It is assumed here that subsidy adjustments under
the equimarginal system would best be made ex post actual
enrollment changes and not based upon enrollment projections. However, the subsidy could be adjusted based upon
annual enrollment projections. This would allow institutions to take some risks in enrollment estimation to generate funds needed to implement new and innovative instructional programs. However, if projected enrollments failed
to result, institutions would face the necessity of reducing
the budgets of ongoing academic programs to repay the
state for the net risk capital loss resulting from the differences between projected and actual enrollments. Because
equimarginal funding would apply to enrollments in all
programs, cross-subsidization between programs could occur;
that is, institutions could make up for underenrollment in
new programs relative to funded projections with enrollment
increases in existing programs, or vice versa.

While a policy of subsidy experimentation might
strike some observers as irresponsible, similar funding
policy experimentation takes place presently in many if not
most states, although it is not recognized explicitly as
such. Where state governments adjust higher-education
budgets relative to enrollment changes and fiscal crises, or
for other reasons, marginal subsidy policy is pursued in
that institutions and higher-education segments are provided
incentives to enroll more or fewer students, to establish
new programs to attract students, or to reduce programs
and students through establishment of quotas or some other
restrictive mechanism. The equimarginal subsidy approach
makes such decisions explicit and simplifies state funding
rules for the benefit of both the state and institutions.

Under such a system state government has a better
and simpler tool for achieving state objectives, thus reducing the need for most budgetary, regulatory, and
program review controls currently employed by states. At
the same time, institutions receive clear signals and incentives with regard to what is expected of them. Where
funding incentives are clearer, institutions may choose
among strategies that either maximize revenue or maximize
revenue subject to program, distribution, and quality

preference.   Further, they may compete freely for students
in a relatively unconstrained manner.

As pointed out in Chapter Six, a distinct benefit for
institutions would be the ability to operate free from state
budgetary controls over how to spend state appropriations.
Under the per-unit subsidy system few of the traditional
ex ante or ex post budget controls typically enforced by
state executive budget offices would be needed.   Further,
institutions would be free to set their own tuition price
schedules, thus encouraging differential tuition experimentation.   In addition, differential faculty salary levels
could be an important element in institutional strategy
setting.   Institutions would be able to manage their state
appropriations much more flexibly than is typically the
case.   For example, they could choose to maximize income
from instruction and channel earnings from tuition and the
state subsidy into new institutional program development or
into support for research.   From the state perspective,
appropriations would be made exclusively based upon enrollment changes.   Appropriations for research or special
programs would be unnecessary unless the state wanted to
establish a new program with a specific price attached to
it.   Simplified state financial control and institutional
resource management flexibility would be the objectives of
such a system.

The market strategy assumes to some extent that
creating greater incentives for institutions to compete for
students will result in greater breadth of course offerings.
It recognizes that a prominent state goal is to maximize
student participation in postsecondary education, and that
the state should be willing to subsidize this participation
up to politically defined limits of fiscal prudence.   It also
assumes that public institutions could accommodate additional students without reducing the quality of instruction
provided at present.   This last assumption rests on the
expectation that state support for public higher education
would be maintained at least at current real-dollar levels.

The assumption that increased competition for students would result from equimarginal enrollment funding is
based on the observation that in the past in California
and elsewhere, public institutions have operated as revenue
maximizers.   As enrollment demand began to weaken in the
1970s, public institutions whose resources were constrained
by enrollment shortfall began to compete more aggressively
for students.   This has occurred over a wide range of

institutions, including high-prestige schools. For example, as demand weakened for certain undergraduate programs at the University of California, Berkeley, in the early 1970s, grade point average admission requirements for community college transfer students were reduced. Similar policies have been employed by many other public colleges and universities. However, some states have responded differently. In Oregon, when enrollment demand weakened in the period 1981-83, admission requirements and tuition levels were increased.

Additional support for the revenue maximization hypothesis may be found in California and elsewhere through investigation of the attributes of community college funding policies that have stimulated enrollment competition for adult and continuing education.[13] In general, the effect of formulas that rewarded institutions financially for enrolling additional students has been to stimulate community colleges to offer a vast array of continuing education programs not offered previously. As enrollment demand declined, many public and private four-year institutions have responded with instructional programs for continuing education.

As observed earlier in this chapter, merely changing existing programs or offering the same programs to different types of students does not necessarily constitute innovation. However, as institutional decision makers perceive that they will gain additional funding by enrolling more students, especially given their understanding of the effects of steady-state population demographics, it is reasonable to expect that they will be more likely to take greater risks in supporting proposals for innovative programs that might attract new students.

Critics of the enrollment market strategy can be expected to charge that the mechanism would penalize institutions which had established policies to curtail growth. In response to this criticism, it can be pointed out that while multicampus institutions might establish such policies for several campuses that typically experience high student demand, objectives to increase enrollments on other campuses within the multicampus system could be maintained and the net effect of the strategy would be to increase aggregate enrollments over time. Equimarginal funding would provide institutions with motives and rationale to reallocate funds from existing low-demand programs to new programs to attract students. If equimarginal state funding were applied by individual institutions rather than across entire multicampus systems, even stronger incentives to innovate would be offered. Certainly it cannot be expected that institutional academic decision makers within a multi-campus system would be likely to support innovations designed to increase enrollments if the revenues gained through these actions were not largely allocated to their institutions.

In addition, if in implementation of equimarginal enrollment funding the state were to eliminate budgetary distinctions between on-campus and off-campus degree programs, any institution would be able to take advantage of the market regardless of on-campus enrollment limitation policies and physical plant capacity limitations. In analysis of this issue in California, it has been argued that the state should support off-campus degree programs as long as on-campus institutional quality control standards are maintained.[14]

An issue particularly germane to state subsidy definition is whether total subsidy ceilings would be set or whether the state would be at all willing to subsidize enrollment increases in particular types of institutional programs, for example, recreational, crafts, or other entertainment-oriented courses. Under the approach defined here, the state would retain the authority to withdraw subsidy for some types of instructional programs. In fact, whether this is desirable is a moot point; state governments would retain such power under any financing reform. However, as intended here, state government decision makers would restrain themselves from regulating student enrollment markets. The use of a differential subsidy applied equimarginally across all public postsecondary institutions to fund enrollments in the "entertainment" category might be employed or, as has occurred in California and elsewhere, the state could mandate that such instructional programs be funded exclusively by student tuition revenues. However, if the equimarginal approach is pursued as intended here, state government would not engage in price control; that is, it would not attempt to stipulate or mandate institutional tuition and fee pricing policies. The unit subsidy approach could not be applied correctly if such constraints over competition were maintained. Subsidy levels would be subject to change, but such changes would apply to all institutions and would not be accompanied by direct regulatory controls over price or market entry.   More on this is provided in Chapter Seven.

Based upon the analysis in Chapter Two, it can be expected that critics of the enrollment market strategy would claim that equal per-student funding would cause homogenization of higher education instruction because it would encourage regression toward mean quality and breadth standards.[15]   This would appear more likely to occur if equimarginal funding were implemented through zero-based budgeting because under such a procedure institutions would have to justify all resources presently obtained on the basis of enrollments and not just marginal funding changes.   However, zero-based budgeting is not proposed as an element of this strategy.   The feasibility of gaining political approval of equimarginal enrollment funding would be severely reduced if it were accompanied by zero-based budgeting, the value of which remains seriously in doubt because of its high administrative costs and questionable benefits.

The fear of homogenization ignores to some extent the different missions and activities that are assigned to public higher education institutions in state master plans, definitions which would not be altered by equimarginal enrollment funding.   It also neglects the specialization of academic programs and faculty interests, which would continue to differentiate segments and institutions as a result of institutional specialization and delineation of function. As noted, the enrollment market strategy would not affect the budget bases presently obtained by institutions.   Equimarginal funding would be applied only to determine new (marginal) budget appropriations.   While it may be argued that such an approach would favor institutions funded presently at higher per-student rates, the objection ignores that in many states where master plans designate different responsibilities to the segments of higher education, state funding mechanisms have responded to institutional demands for differential support supposedly based upon the costs of satisfying these missions.

The equimarginal strategy can be viewed as consistent with institutional preferences for greater resource management flexibility.   The market alternative could be employed to eliminate specific state allocations to institutions for institutional support, student services, and even for faculty salaries, permitting segments to determine where and how much to spend from their total budget allocations in competition for students. Increased resource allocation flexibility has been described in Chapter Four and elsewhere as essential for maintenance of institutional equilibrium in the steady state.[16] An advantage of the market strategy would thus be reduced state and institutional budget preparation, justification, and review costs.

An additional element of this approach could be employed in states that provide public funding for private higher education institutions. The equimarginal budget incentive could be extended to increase competition between public and private institutions, including proprietary institutions that presently do not receive state support. Also, such an incentive could be accompanied by student vouchers to provide income and educational benefits to low- and moderate-income students.

The purpose for outlining alternatives for increasing institutional instructional responsiveness and innovation is to indicate that achievement of such an effect can be attempted by different means and that each method has associated costs and benefits. In the following section, an attempt is made to assess the likelihood of increasing institutional responsiveness to student demand by means of changes in state financing policy of the type described in "Enrollment Market Strategy."

INSTITUTIONAL RESPONSIVENESS TO STUDENT DEMAND

In analysis of public financing of universities, James Buchanan and Nicos Develetoglou have severely criticized the present system of allocating resources in public higher education. They argue that institutions are unresponsive, inefficient, and backward because in this "industry" consumers (students) do not buy, producers (institutions) do not sell, and suppliers of resources (the taxpaying public) have little influence over the production process.[17] As a solution, they proposed a radical shift in university and college finance: full-cost student tuition accompanied by government grants and guaranteed loans to students in place of direct institutional support. Their proposal is intended to enable students to exert greater financial pressure on course-offering decisions at public institutions and to increase institutional competition for students.

Despite economic logic and continuing interest in voucher and entitlement plans, such major changes in higher education financing are not likely to be implemented in most states in the near future. Therefore, it is legitimate to enquire whether existing systems of direct institutional support can be made to respond more effectively to student and market demand through incremental changes in state policy. The program change, salary limitation, and enrollment market strategies are plausible incremental changes arrayed in a continuum from the less radical alteration of status quo efforts to influence institutional behavior (program change strategy) to the more radical (salary limitation and enrollment market strategies). The simple criterion used here to assess the magnitude of change implied in these strategies is the extent to which proposals vary from methods used presently.

The essential feature of the enrollment market proposal is the subsidy based upon enrollment. The proposal is hardly revolutionary, given that this mechanism is now used to allocate public funds to community colleges and some universities in many states. However, extension of the procedure to resource decision making for universities and state universities and colleges represents a considerable change for many states and institutions. Because the enrollment market strategy is now operational to some degree for many community colleges, we should enquire further about the extent to which it has influenced instructional innovation.

Evaluations of instructional innovation in community colleges indicate that substantial changes in attitudes toward the offering of programs and services to students have occurred in the last 15 years. As summarized in one study:

> Criticisms of the rigidity of faculties notwithstanding, the most dramatic changes in the Community Colleges have taken place in the classroom. Faculty, faced daily with growing student diversity and the problems of reorienting "slow" learners, have shown an undeniable willingness to experiment with new methods of instruction. . . . Perhaps the most persuasive evidence of change in the Community College is that, while none of the innovations was used by even a majority of

the colleges sampled in 1970, half were used
by two-thirds or more of the colleges sampled in 1974.[18]

Additional evidence on the acceleration of instructional responsiveness in community colleges is provided
from studies reporting a vast array of instructional experimentation ranging from cooperative work-study education to computer-programmed instruction, audio-tutorial
teaching, and simulation game learning.   One study concluded that "the Junior college is the most . . . dynamic
unit in American Education. . . .   The junior college
dream is clearly coming true in terms of the numbers of
our youth and adult citizens served."[19]

The importance of external sources to stimulate
higher education institutions to respond to student demand
has been identified by critics of educational reform.   For
example,

> Evidence about the importance of external
> sources of reform comes from administrators
> and faculty members . . . who, while
> they primarily see themselves as the ini-
> tiators of change, see outsiders proportion-
> ally more often stimulating major organiza-
> tional changes.   Support for this view that
> extensive educational reform is unlikely
> without some external intervention comes
> from the statistical analysis of curricular
> change at a sample of 110 colleges and
> universities.   The most dynamic institutions
> in this sample tended to be those that were
> most dependent on attracting students. . . .
> In short, we conclude that while the re-
> sponsiveness of an institution to change
> can be significantly affected by internal
> factors, the institution will seldom alter
> its functions without external influence.[20]

That the type of state budgeting mechanisms used affect the
degree and quality of innovation in institutions has been
analyzed as follows:

> There is a strong correlation between free-
> dom to use funds as professional wisdom

dictates and the academic results attained. One can identify many colleges whose records are mediocre and which are hamstrung by control devices. The line–item budget imposed by a state or city constitutes just this type of handicap.[21]

Community colleges in many states have increased student enrollments by providing services that increase the benefit or reduce the cost to the prospective student for enrolling in a program or course. Among such services provided are more courses or degree and certificate programs, better job training, better preparation for transition to four–year institutions, more stimulating instruction in the classroom, smaller classes, more locations at which courses and degree programs are offered, better marketing of information on program availability to prospective students, and better counseling to assist students in matching their talents to institutional program offerings. While many of these same services are available to many students in public research–oriented universities and state universities and colleges, often these institutions do not operate under the budget incentives that stimulate the community colleges to innovate in instruction. Public four–year universities and colleges have the capacity to influence their enrollment levels but are not always assured that revenues will be increased as a consequence, particularly in providing instruction to nontraditional students in off–campus programs.

For example, time–series and trend analysis of University of California and California State University and Colleges budgets have shown very weak relationships between changes in enrollment and changes in state-appropriated revenue, despite the widely held belief that budgets are enrollment generated.[22] To an extent, this reflects the practice of budgeting on the base and the concern in the budget process given objects of expenditures rather than program demand. In a number of states there is little direct incentive for many universities to allocate resources in such a way as to maximize satisfaction of student preferences. Furthermore, the existence of institutional, program, and course enrollment ceilings and policies that restrict more flexible pricing policies constrains student access to institutional services. The innovative instructional achievements of many public universities and colleges are impressive, given the degree to which state budget and administrative processes are inimical to innovation and the extent to which institutions are prevented from implementing differential tuition schedules.

THE ENROLLMENT MARKET STRATEGY
AND BUDGETARY CONTROL

Several additional issues must be addressed in evaluating the enrollment market budget strategy. If it were applied to high-prestige public research-oriented universities as well as to state universities and colleges and did result in greater responsiveness to student preferences, what effect would enrollment market strategy have on overall state higher education expenditures? Under the enrollment market strategy, state fiscal obligations would be limited by student preferences and by revenue schedules established by state government decision makers. By changing per-student subsidy levels, states could exercise the same type of fiscal control employed at present without having to exert any specific influence over academic program content. State degree program approval or efforts to reduce duplication of programs between institutions would be unnecessary.

The degree of state influence advocated here for equimarginal enrollment funding is limited strictly to the institutional or multicampus system rather than the program level. It is assumed, further, that the social demand approach to higher education planning and financing is generally superior to manpower planning approaches that rely heavily on state-defined enrollment controls. The argument is essentially that increasing the market sensitivity of higher education institutions would serve the public interest in achieving objectives of responsiveness, quality control, efficiency, and innovation without the necessity for direct state control over institutions. Thus it can be argued that a high degree of accountability and control could be combined with a high degree of flexibility in institutional management of resources.

In assessment of the fiscal impact to state governments of equimarginal enrollment based budgeting, it may be observed that the overall level of expenditure on higher education could be as easily controlled under the proposed system as it is at present. It would appear that state

accountability and control objectives could be achieved at
reduced costs and the fiscal consequences of decisions
made at the state level could be predicted more accurately
under an equimarginal enrollment based methodology.
These assumptions are evaluated in greater depth in Chapter Seven.

Several additional assumptions about enrollment-
based financing systems must be noted. Any funding
mechanism based upon enrollments requires considerable
attention to the development, monitoring, and auditing of
student enrollment accounting systems. Computerized enrollment accounting systems are utilized presently for
planning and for resource justification and allocation in
many public institutions. The fixed costs of administering
these systems are considerable and certainly would not be
reduced through implementation of equimarginal enrollment
budgeting. If the enrollment market strategy works as
intended, institutional and state support for research would
increase rather than decline in institutions that responded
to student demand through better research and better
planned and executed marketing strategies. Through the
implementation of programs to take better advantage of
scale economies, differential pricing, flexibility in hiring
or contracting for instructors without research responsibilities, and other cost-saving actions such as integration of
computer technology into instruction, institutions would
maintain or increase discretionary research support funds.
Further, as noted, an additional advantage of the equimarginal approach for institutions experiencing enrollment
decline would result from the determination of decrements
to the budget on a marginal cost basis.

Finally, it may be expected that some universities
will object to the control implications of state equimarginal
funding. As noted in Part I of this book in discussing
the critical mass academic resource management approach,
institutions have an incentive to argue for resources based
on program quality and minimum-size criteria in periods
of enrollment decline and steady state. As such, adoption
of equimarginal budgeting might be resisted by many institutions despite the advantages of reduced state program
control. Still, there is nothing about the equimarginal
market strategy that would prevent institutions from implementing the critical mass approach to improve internal
budgeting and resource management. In fact, this action
would improve institutional capacities to adapt and to

improve their performance under the equimarginal funding system. Of course, all this assumes that state governments perceive the wisdom of eliminating such controls as they implement an equimarginal funding methodology. As argued in Chapter Seven, state regulatory control over academic programs appears to be less necessary in the 1970s under any circumstances, although there remains a rationale for minimal state regulation to prevent unfair competitive practices such as untruthful advertising, degree sales, and outright fraud.

In conclusion, it should be noted that the benefits of the enrollment market approach would be increased by providing student consumers with clear and honest information about academic programs and the job market so that their enrollment choices would most closely match their preferences and, one hopes, long-term needs. Ultimately, enrollment-based budget mechanisms will produce worthwhile instructional innovation only to the extent that student choice is accurately informed.

NOTES

1. J. Pincus, "Incentives for Innovation in Public Schools," in Social Program Implementation, ed. F. Williams and R. Elmore (New York: Academic Press, 1976), 55.

2. Ibid.

3. This discussion distinguishes between the terms innovation and change. Instructional innovation may be defined as the attempt to teach an idea or concept to use a method which has not been tried previously, or to employ an instructional mode which has not been attempted previously in the same context. Change in instruction may be defined as teaching in a mode which differs from methods currently employed in a particular context. Thus, innovation requires change, but change is not necessarily innovative. Change in an instructional program may involve nothing more than returning to methods used previously in the same context. An innovation in instruction not only differs from the status quo but has not been implemented before in the same context. The emphasis on context is intended to indicate, for example, that employing a method or an idea in one discipline that has been used exclusively in another discipline is innovative. While these definitions may seem somewhat ambiguous, they are

sufficient for exposition in this study because the focus here is not on instructional innovation per se, but on state policies that stimulate or inhibit innovation.

4. E. Gross, "University as Organizations: A Study of Goals," in Academic Governance, ed. J. Baldridge (Berkeley, Calif.: McCutchan, 1971), 22-57; J. Keller, Higher Education Objectives: Measures of Performance and Effectiveness Ford Foundation Research Paper P-7 (Berkeley, Calif.: University of California Press, 1971); M. Trow, "The Public and Private Lives of Higher Education," Daedalus 104 (Winter 1975):113-27.

5. J. Pfeffer and G. Salancik, "Organizational Decision Making as a Political Process: The Case of a University Budget," Administrative Science Quarterly 19 (June 1974):135-51.

6. J. Hefferlin, Dynamics of Academic Reform (San Francisco: Jossey-Bass, 1971); J. Stone, et al., And Gladly Teche (Berkeley, Calif.: University of California Press, 1975).

7. On the issue of state government strategies see D. Breneman, "Strategies for the 1980s," in Challenges of Retrenchment, ed. J. Mingle (San Francisco: Jossey-Bass, 1981), 16-31; D. Spence and G. Weathersby, "Changing Patterns of State Funding," in Mingle, Challenges of Retrenchment, 226-42. On past state budget and other control behavior see Spence and Weathersby, "Changing Patterns"; L. Glenny, State Budgeting for Higher Education: Data Digest (Berkeley, Calif.: Center for Research and Development in Higher Education, University of California, 1975); F. Bowen and L. Glenny, State Budgeting for Higher Education (Berkeley, Calif.: Center for Research and Development in Higher Education, University of California, 1976); more generally, see A. Schick, "Control Patterns in State Budget Execution," Public Administration Review 24 (June 1964):97-106; A. Schick, Budget Innovation in the States (Washington, D.C.: Brookings Institution, 1971).

8. O. Fulton and M. Trow, "Research Activity in American Higher Education," in Teachers and Students, ed. M. Trow (San Francisco: McGraw-Hill, 1975).

9. L. Johnson, Islands of Innovation Expanding (Los Angeles: Glencoe Press, 1969), 277.

10. M. Trow, Teachers and Students (San Francisco: McGraw-Hill, 1975).

11. It may be observed that during periods of moderate to high unemployment, as student opportunity

costs for college attendance drop, the amount of revenue
stimulation necessary to increase enrollments is less than
it is in periods of low unemployment. This is due to the
fact that students have fewer income-producing alternatives
to education available in such periods.

12. On the issue of costs, see H. Bowen, The Costs
of Higher Education (San Francisco: Jossey-Bass, 1977);
F. Bowen and L. Glenny, "Enrollment Management," in
Mingle, Challenges of Retrenchment, 210; Spence and
Weathersby, "Changing Patterns" (see especially the dis-
cussion of marginal cost funding, pp. 227-31). On the
use of formulas in state budgeting for higher education,
see R. Meisinger, State Budgeting for Higher Education:
The Use of Formulas (Berkeley, Calif.: Center for Re-
search and Development in Higher Education, University of
California, 1976). See also Spence and Weathersby,
"Changing Patterns."

13. California Postsecondary Education Commission,
Financial Support for the California Community Colleges
(Sacramento, Calif.: State of California, June 1977); D.
Cothran, "Program Flexibility and Budget Growth in Com-
munity Colleges," Western Political Quarterly 34 (December
1981):593-610.

14. California Postsecondary Education Commission,
Analysis of Segmental Budget Change Proposals for 1977-78
(Sacramento, Calif.: State of California, 1976).

15. Trow, "Public and Private Lives."

16. E. Lee and F. Bowen, Managing Multi-Campus
Systems: Effective Administration in an Unsteady State,
Carnegie Council for Policy Studies in Higher Education
(San Francisco: Jossey-Bass, 1975); L. Mayhew, Surviving
the Eighties: Strategies for Solving Fiscal and Enrollment
Programs (San Francisco: Jossey-Bass, 1979); Spence and
Weathersby, "Changing Patterns."

17. J. Buchanan and N. Develotoglou, Academia in
Anarchy: An Economic Diagnosis (New York: Basic Books,
1970). For another analysis of higher education market
behavior, see Breneman, "Strategies for the 1980s," 25-26.

18. P. Cross, "1970 to 1974: Years of Change in
Community Colleges," Findings, Educational Testing Service
11 (1975):9-11.

19. Johnson, Islands of Innovation, 327.

20. Hefferlin, Dynamics of Academic Reform, 144-
46.

21. A. Henderson, The Innovative Spirit (San Francisco: Jossey-Bass, 1971), 288.

22, See Meisinger, State Budgeting; and Spence and Weathersby, "Changing Patterns," to support the point that institutional budgets are not entirely enrollment driven. It is common practice in many states to fund part of budgetary appropriations based upon enrollments and part on faculty salary and library, physical plant, programmatic, and other factors independent of enrollment levels. Research conducted by the California Postsecondary Education Commission (CPEC) indicates that over a period of ten years, from 1965 to 1975, about half the increase in operating expenditures in California higher education can be explained by increased workload (enrollment). See CPEC, Five Year Plan for Postsecondary Education in California: 1976-81, Appendix B; for another indication that budgets have not been strictly enrollment driven see the University of California, Summary of Budgets for Current Operations 1976-77 1, Systemwide Administration (September 1975), A-1-A-3, and subsequent University of California operations budget proposals through 1984.

Six
Misapplications of
State Government Control

This chapter attempts to develop an understanding of state government budget control in higher education.[1] It does not question the desirability of some types of control. The exercise of control is integral to budget preparation and execution. However, it does question the methods used by state budget officials, and it explains some of the perverse consequences that result from strict application of _ex ante_ controls and the misuse of _ex post_ controls where public universities, or public and private institutions, compete for students. State budget officials usually try to meet the objective of accountability by limiting university spending flexibility. Under most circumstances restrictions limiting the flexibility of universities to make fund transfers, to fill positions, or to execute other budget transactions result in considerable inefficiency. Restrictions on the duplication of instruction and other services may be viewed to fall into this category also. Such controls discourage competitive service supply arrangements that might better satisfy public needs.

BALANCING THE BUDGET AND THE APPLICATION OF EXPENDITURE CONTROLS

Budget execution typically receives less attention than the more visible processes and politics of budget formulation and enactment. This observation notwithstanding, criticism of budget execution in general and the control function in particular has increased. For example, critics have pointed out that control is imposed in the name of accountability at the expense of analysis.[2] Some controls appear to be wasteful of government money and time, to cause undue frustration for universities and other public service agencies, and to inhibit initiative and innovation. Further, central budget offices seem to misunderstand the purpose and use of alternative instruments of control. Among other things, this failing causes the collection of too much of the wrong kinds of information and the consequent misuse of data by the executive and legislators--hence the conclusion that government is overcontrolled.

Paradoxically, these criticisms of budget execution and controls have been paralleled by a growing realization that government spending is out of control and by a desire on the part of many to reestablish traditional expenditure limits.[3] Dissatisfaction with expenditure growth, higher taxes, and deficits or surpluses has resulted in the imposition of constraints on government power to tax and to spend, for example, in California and Massachusetts. Where these constraints are absent, reformers demand changes in the political process, with the expectation that these changes will affect spending outcomes. Some wish to deny government the power to spend--through balanced budget requirements, for example. Others would transfer spending power from the legislature to the executive, using the line-item veto or greater delegation of impoundment authority. Many reformers also call for an increase in party discipline to reduce the incentives that lead legislators to buy votes and trade favors on behalf of constituent interests at the expense of majority party and public interests in expenditure control and economy efficiency.

This apparent paradox, the claim that government is simultaneously overcontrolled and out of control, suggests that in budgeting, use of the term control refers to different things. It is, therefore, necessary to clarify the ways in which the term control is defined. In the first place, it is used as both a verb and a noun. Thus, one controls (that is, implements a policy such as balancing the budget) through the application of various controls--administrative rules specifying when, for what, and by whom public money may be spent. Hence, in this instance what the critics are saying is that there are too many administrative rules and not enough of, or the wrong kind of, policy direction.

In this chapter, controls refers to the means or tools used to achieve control. To clarify this usage, the phrase managerial controls is employed. Furthermore, two kinds of managerial controls are defined: ex ante and ex post controls. Ex ante controls are executed before spending decisions are implemented, in this instance before public money is obligated. Ex ante controls almost necessarily take the form of commands specifying what a manager or spending agency may do, must do, or must not do. Examples of ex ante controls include the formal reporting requirements imposed on spending agencies, allotments and apportionments that limit the timing and rate of expenditure, detailed line-item budgets together with fund or account controls that restrict transfer authority, position controls governing the absolute number of employees that may be hired by government agencies, and rules requiring competitive bidding. Indeed, binding rules requiring a balanced budget in state government are self-imposed ex ante controls that prohibit a legislature from spending more money than it has available in revenues.

Ex post controls are executed during or after the period in which public money is spent. Since costs cannot be avoided after they have been incurred, these controls work by influencing operating managers to make "responsible" (that is, efficiency-oriented) decisions in executing budgets. Ex post budget controls, therefore, involve the design and execution of incentives—rewards and sanctions. They focus on performance and typically are implemented through program and policy evaluation. As such, these controls are critically dependent upon the elaboration of well-defined objectives, accurate and timely reporting of performance in terms of those objectives, and careful matching of spending authority and responsibility.

Finally, the execution of managerial controls may be internalized or externalized. Thus, the subject of managerial controls may be an individual in a government agency directly subordinate to the organization and budget controller or it may be a free-standing entity such as a university or university system (an entire organization rather than an individual). The example given at the start of this chapter, a rule prohibiting public or private universities from competing for students by offering the same or similar specialized academic programs, is an example of an external ex ante control exerted over a free-standing entity. Such prohibitions are widespread and presumed to serve the public interest but, as argued below, often they appear to be misconceived. Indeed, it appears that ex post controls generally are superior to ex ante controls despite the extensive use of ex ante restrictions in contemporary budgeting. The simplest and, where feasible, best external ex post control is where a buyer purchases a discrete service from the competitive supplier offering the service at the lowest price, and then government evaluates consumer satisfaction after service is rendered. Further, ex post controls may best be applied where accountability is vested in an organization as a whole rather than in an individual (such as a college president). As explained in the previous chapter, equimarginal budgeting would establish accountability incentives to influence organizational decision making and behavior rather than just the behavior of individual decision makers.

This chapter argues that ex ante controls to restrict university flexibility are generally unnecessary where the state is able to fund on the basis of per-unit subsidies and to evaluate the effects of such subsidies. Analysis can then indicate how subsidies should be adjusted to achieve state higher education instructional, student access, and other objectives.[4] Unfortunately, the use of control in higher education budgeting is severely limited by an unwillingness on the part of state officials to experiment with ex post controls. Further, it is argued that attempts to apply tight ex post workload or instructional performance standards are a waste of time and lead to serious misallocation of resources despite that such controls are commonplace in state government budgeting for universities.

To develop these themes, the chapter is organized into the following sections:

1. an analysis of the behavioral incentives faced by budgeteers and institutions
2. an evaluation of problems associated with ex ante controls
3. an explanation of the resistance of budgeteers to experimentation with ex post control alternatives
4. conclusions on the appropriate uses of management controls in budgeting

OUTCOMES OF ROLE DEFINITION IN BUDGETING

Defenders of ex ante controls claim that oversight inherent in budget execution results in greater efficiency in universities, inducing institutions to eliminate wasteful activities or programs and to make trade-offs between policy and program objectives and spending priorities. These claims are valid from one perspective: reliance on ex ante controls shifts the responsibility for achieving program objectives and managing costs from the university to the budgeteer. If budgeteers are even minimally competent, they should be able to enforce some economies and efficiency. A key question is why budgeteers should want this authority and the responsibility that goes with it.

In order to explain the preferences of budgeteers it is necessary to understand that their main objective is to minimize agency expenditures. This objective is stressed at every phase of the budget process, including in preparation of estimates, in negotiation with spending agencies and legislative committees, in executive enactment, in making allotments and monitoring expenditures, in ex post audit, and in evaluation where it is undertaken. Budgeteer monomania for cost minimization is thought to be a purposeful force against the spenders' inclination to get all the funds they can and to spend all they receive. In the absence of effective competition among suppliers in general, and in academic institutions in particular, spenders are not forced to be efficient. Therefore, the budgeteer seeks to enforce efficiency.

There is a second and perhaps more important reason for the obsession of budgeteers to minimize expenditures. Flexibility is valuable to budget controllers as well as to spenders. In both cases, unallocated reserves are necessary to adapt to changing environmental conditions; they are a hedge against uncertainty. Budgeteers appear to operate predictably so as to avoid uncertainty. In part this may be explained by the fact that budgeteers are directly responsible to politicians who generally want to spend as much money as they can in order to provide benefits to constituents and supporters. Federal and state expenditures increase because people collectively want more rather than fewer programs and services, and elected officials reap their reward of reelection by meeting public expectations.

Most governments, the federal government a notable exception, have found it necessary to impose upon themselves a requirement that the budget be balanced. This results in expectations that actual expenditures will be equal to or less than the authorized budget amount and that program performance and revenues will be equal to or greater than budget forecasts. The budget office is held accountable for meeting these expectations, especially for avoiding deficits. This accounts for the priority budgeteers give to certainty. As Wildavsky has observed with respect to municipal budget control agencies:

> The concept of control has many meanings when applied to budgetary behavior. It can mean cut the estimates because there is no money, reduce estimated expenditures in the process of budget execution, or implement the policy preferences of the person who hands out the salary raises. The city manager and his finance staff have a single motivation, however, which underlies these objectives of budgetary control; they want to balance the budget by controlling uncertainty.[5]

It may be observed that budgeted performance levels designed to be obtained most of the time are likely to be low.[6] Consequently, the budgeteer's obsession with certainty both ensures the existence of slack in the budget and provides a powerful incentive to find it and specify its use.

The need for certainty by budgeteers also underlies a sometimes excessive and unreasonable demand for ever more and better information from spenders. Such information can help them do their jobs while they bear few of the costs of producing it. Since spenders have an interest in avoiding full disclosure, but do not have the authority to deny the budgeteer's demands, they may be forced to avoid collecting information useful for their own purposes as well. The only sure defense against demands for potentially damaging information is an inability to produce it. Hence, the need for certainty by budgeteers may increase both their and the spender's ignorance. The need for caution by universities to avoid revealing information subject to misinterpretation by state decision makers was noted in Chapter Two.

Finally, the need for certainty appears to underlie budgeteers' objections to ex post controls. Such controls are excluded from consideration at least in part because, unlike ex ante controls, their fiscal consequences are imperfectly predictable. This is particularly the case where per-unit subsidies are concerned. Performance levels are necessarily somewhat uncertain; automatically linking expenditures to performance by means of a per-unit subsidy reduces the certainty of expenditure forecasts. As noted by Cothran,

> There is . . . an important difference between automatic . . . funding and annual budget appropriations. The latter has less potential for sudden and unintended growth than does the former. . . . the program-matic consequences of automatic funding are highly predictable. That is, if you increase the contingent reward for certain behavior, you will probably get more of that behavior, such as services by an agency. The fiscal consequences, on the other hand, are considerably less predictable. That is, you can be relatively confident that more of the behavior will be forthcoming, but you cannot predict exactly how much more. Which budgeting method will be used will depend, therefore, on the value that is more important to the policy-maker—controlling agency behavior or controlling agency expenditure.[7]

Therefore, it seems that per-unit subsidies conflict with the budgeteer's most important objectives of minimizing expenditures and uncertainty. It is hardly surprising that, in most cases, this conflict is decided against per-unit subsidies.

Finally, the need for certainty may lead budgeteers to focus on the management of total expenditures. It is not unreasonable to infer that budgeteers might prefer a solution to the budget and output problem wherein spenders accept a less than optimal budget and output combination in return for a smaller budget containing greater slack or "fat." If so, budgeteer preferences for monopoly supply and opposition to ex post controls, especially per-unit subsidies, may be explained by the need to preserve an implicit trade-off bargain. Reliance on per-unit subsidies could lead to an increase in the number of service suppliers, threatening any such tacit bargain that might exist.

Recognition that the need for certainty may result in some perverse behavior on the part of both budgeteers and spending agencies such as universities does not mean that governments ought to release themselves from the obligation to balance budgets. The plight of New York City in the mid-1970s, other deficit-plagued municipalities, and the federal government reminds us of the unhappy consequences that may be expected when politicians are freed of the self-imposed discipline of budget balancing. It would seem a poor exchange to trade the certain benefits of fiscal self-discipline for an uncertain promise of more efficient fiscal and program management. However, it does suggest that greater attention should be given to structuring service supply arrangements so that the budgeteers have less incentive and opportunity to behave perversely. It appears advisable as well to restructure the incentives faced by budget controllers so as to motivate them to make decisions that are more consistent with public preferences.[8]

EVALUATING EX ANTE CONTROLS

Modification of the incentives faced by budget controllers may, unfortunately, not be sufficient to ensure greater reliance on competition, on per-unit subsidies, or even less reliance on ex ante controls. The fact is that reliance on ex ante controls is not wholly attributable to the budgeteer's need for certainty. Controls also serve a political function. Frequently, legislators appear to be as interested in how and where public money is spent as they are in what the money buys. Ex ante controls may not promote efficiency, but they can ensure compliance with legislative preferences for particular suppliers of specific types of services (and in specific geographical locations). Efficiency is primarily concerned with output of goods and services—it is often blind to how and where they are produced and who produces them. Legislative preferences are not blind. Legislators employ budgets, in effect, to buy support for reelection from service suppliers and jobs for their constituents.

Budget execution may be viewed, therefore, to serve at least three distinct purposes: (1) efficiency, or the management purpose; (2) certainty, or the expenditure-limiting purpose; and (3) assurance of compliance with legislative intent, or the political purpose. These purposes are both complementary and competitive. This is an important point because insofar as loss of managerial control is the price paid to secure political objectives or expenditure certainty, one can do no more than clearly specify the trade-offs and hope that the choice between them is wise. Nevertheless, for the reasons noted above, if the choice is left to the budgeteers, they are unlikely to choose wisely, particularly with respect to the relative importance of expenditure certainty. Legislators could be more receptive to the benefits of per-unit subsidies than budgeteers. Frequently, legislators choose to build their relationships with service-providing agencies, including universities, on the basis of self-denying ordinances, creating and funding public agencies but retaining only limited powers of prior review or control. As a group, legislators appear to have a healthy regard for the role of fiscal incentives in accomplishing public purposes. The claim that legislators want to maintain ex ante controls over the activities of government agencies as an end in itself may be the result of the selective attention that budget controllers are required to give to a few key members of fiscal committees. While these committee members may have served for many years and have considerable influence, often they have learned budget control from budgeteers. Their concerns, including the emphasis given to certainty and compliance, often appear to reflect and reinforce the concerns of the budget office. Consequently, an important question is when are legislative preferences for specifying spending to aid constituents and for ex ante budget controls most likely to conflict?

AN INCREASING COST CRITERION FOR COMPETITIVE MARKET SUPPLY

Whether service supply costs are increasing or whether service outputs are homogeneous may seem unrelated

to this issue. In fact, these considerations are central
to understanding how managerial controls can be used to
promote efficiency in budgeting. In economics, the suppliers of specific goods or services are called an industry.
An industry can be made up of one or more public and
private suppliers, as is the case in higher education.
The normative question "what is the optimal number of
suppliers in any industry?" can be answered by reference
to the cost behavior of the most efficient supplier. If
costs decrease as output increases, opportunities for
achieving efficiency through economies of scale result in
the conclusion that there should be only one supplier.
Furthermore, if that normative judgment is enforced by
government, it also will be necessary to exercise careful
oversight of supplier performance. In theory, oversight
may be achieved through careful design and execution of
ex post controls, for example, program evaluation. In
practice, ex ante controls have been found easier to apply
and more reliable. On the other hand, if costs are increasing, then more than one supplier is optimal because
under a market arrangement efficiency will result from
competition. Determining the optimal number of suppliers
resolves to a question of cost behavior under this economic
logic. But where there is only one buyer and suppliers
are not-for-profit entities, cost behavior is not so simple.

     A theory of bureaucratic supply and public demand
based upon the utility-maximizing assumptions of micro-
economics explains government behavior.9 Within this
theory a nominally subordinate agency such as a university sells its services to a superior unit, that is, state
government. The government is a monosonist (the only
buyer) and typically, but not always, buys a given service only from a single agency (monopoly supplier). In
this model, demand behavior is assumed to be conven-
tional--the quantity of service demanded by government
will vary inversely with price. However, in this market
the services are provided by an agency for a period of
time in exchange for a budget, rather than purchased at
a specific per-unit price as is the case in most markets.
The government in this market is assumed to be concerned
with maximizing net benefit in terms of satisfying citizen
preferences for services.

     On the supply side, the model makes the following
assumptions: (1) Agencies will seek to maximize their
budgets. (2) They will avoid both profit and loss (average

revenue or price will equal average cost or expenditure).
As noted earlier, suppliers will try to get all the money
they can and spend everything they can get. Under certain conditions this implies an additional set of economic
assumptions: (3) The supplier will operate on a production
frontier; that is, the supplier will produce the maximum
output of services possible for each feasible combination of
resource inputs. (4) The supplier will choose the least-
cost resource input combination for each level of output.

Since this model assumes that the production of most
services is characterized by increasing marginal and average costs (increased costs are necessary to attract additional consumers), its main policy prescription is to permit
several agencies to produce the same service and compete
for government budget appropriations. As noted, public
utility theory in economics tells us that increasing cost
conditions imply the desirability of competitive supply arrangements. Competition is supposed to provide the service
producer with the incentive to "least-cost" operation; that
is, revenue maximization will be consistent with cost minimization. Therefore, in applying this theory to the public sector given the assumptions above, the government or
its fiscal agent, the budget office, need only establish a
per-unit price. This price is the average expenditure
from the standpoint of the state and the average revenue
from the standpoint of the service-producing agency. This
price, or subsidy, equates the government's marginal expenditure with its judgment of marginal benefit to be received by the public from service provision. This is the
notion of government budget offices operating as "good
purchasing agents."[10] In the absence of interagency
competition, however, this conclusion is moot; competitive
pressure for efficiency and responsiveness to public demand
are necessary to make the system work.

It should be noted that under some circumstances
competitive supply would not be appropriate. As several
critics have observed, conversion of government agencies
to competitive suppliers in some cases misses the whole
point of government to provide public goods.[11] Some of
the services that are publicly financed and produced by
government agencies are characterized by decreasing average marginal costs. Therefore, it would be incorrect to
propose that in every case universities and other agencies
should be induced to compete against other institutions for
government budget appropriations. Decreasing supplier

costs to the limits imposed by the market size imply that
supply should be monopolized. In addition, despite the
apparent benefits of converting increasing-cost agencies to
competitive suppliers, there are a number of practical
considerations arising out of technical problems of cost
analysis, on one hand, and the structural characteristics
of the budget process, on the other, that limit the applicability of competition to certain cases. Some of these
problems and characteristics must be analyzed more
thoroughly.

SPECIFICATION OF COST FUNCTIONS

Knowledge about the nature of costs faced by universities and other public agencies is the key to efficient
structural organization of the provision of public services.
However, statistical supply and cost analysis has not
yielded unambiguous conclusions in the private sector, and
it is unlikely to yield clear conclusions with regard to
the supply of public services. [12]   (The research on cost
functions in higher education is reviewed in more detail
in Chapter Seven.)   One might try to derive cost functions
deductively in a manner similar to the method used in
conventional price theory. [13]   This approach can be no
better than the assumptions on which it is based.   A more
promising avenue may be found in a careful program of
experimentation with budget subsidies and agency program
output levels.

It appears feasible that standard budgetary practices could be modified to obtain the information sought
from this experiment, and that it could be carried out in
such a way as to avoid the risk that budgets would expand without limit.   To start, it may be assumed generally
that a single institution provides services at a single location in a given area and is granted a lump-sum budget
in return for a promise to provide a given level of service
output.   The budget is usually composed of a base, reflecting the previous year's budget appropriation and
service output level, and an increment for price increases
and workload changes.   Under conditions of declining
service output the base may be reduced, although in most
instances the decrement is achieved by holding the budget
constant or relatively constant as prices increase with the
rate of inflation.   Most of the key features of the normal

budgetary system need not be modified to obtain the information needed for the test. The budget base can be
retained, as can the practice of awarding a budget to a
single university or system in an area. However, the base
would be augmented by a per-unit subsidy based upon increments (or decrements) of output over the base-year
level and the university would be free to offer services at
additional locations, including locations in areas served
by other public and private higher education institutions.
The per-unit subsidy would be set well below the university's average expenditure per-unit of output (that is, to
approximate marginal costs) but would be large enough to
be taken seriously by university managers. In addition,
limits could be established on the maximum increase in
service output permitted at service-providing sites and on
the total expansion permitted in a given year.

Assuming the above conditions, if the institution is
operating above its least-cost schedule and if marginal
cost does not dwarf the subsidy, output should increase
modestly. If higher education is an increasing-cost under-
taking, the bulk of the increase in output might occur at
new locations as university managers take advantage of
lower unit costs at a relatively small scale of operations.
This outcome would justify further experimentation in the
direction of competitive supply. On the other hand, substantial expansion of the service output level at existing
locations or plans for very large expansion in the scale
of operations would imply decreasing costs, the suitability
of monopoly supply arrangements, and no automatic justification for an increase in subsidy (holding programs offered
and quality constant).

RESISTANCE OF BUDGETEERS TO EXPERIMENTATION
WITH SERVICE OPTIONS

Even a cautious experiment such as the one proposed here is likely to meet with state government and
institutional resistance. As noted, budgeteers typically
do not welcome greater competition. More extensive reliance upon ex post controls, especially per-unit subsidies,
would make the task of budgetary planning more difficult.
The thesis is that if budgeteers were receptive to the benefits of market and quasi-market mechanisms, the problems
they face in coping with expenditure uncertainty would be

reduced considerably. Even if budgeteers were to become more appreciative of the potential benefits of per-unit subsidies, expenditure uncertainty, as explained previously, would remain a barrier to their use. To believe otherwise would be to underestimate greatly the intensity of the budgeteer's commitment to solving the problem of balancing expenditures against revenues. Solving this problem is frequently the key to budget planning, since inaccurate expenditure forecasts may mean embarrassing budget surpluses or illegal and politically unpalatable deficits. Budgeting on the base makes the expenditure forecasts included in the budget document certain.[14] Linking expenditures to output necessarily reduces the certainty of expenditure forecasting. Per-unit subsidies conflict with budgeteers' perceptions of their most important objectives and responsibilities. In most cases, this conflict is likely to be decided against per-unit subsidies for reasons of uncertainty and unfamiliarity. Similarly, institutions resist uncertainty in budgeting. Therefore, unless the uncertainty associated with per-unit subsidies can be reduced, this approach is unlikely to be employed.

The kind of experimentation described requires a level of economic sophistication both in design and in interpretation that many professional budgeteers lack, although this may be changing. Insofar as budgeteers and other participants in the budget process lack the skills needed to make appropriate subsidy proposals and adjustments, they might be forced to accept assistance from policy analysts or management auditors trained in cost analysis and economics. This also could cause resistance as budgeteers are generally quite protective of their turfs and, in some cases, are opposed to the use of policy, economic, or evaluative analysis in budgeting. It is doubtful that budgeteers, or institutional decision makers for that matter, will easily abandon what they know in order to embrace what they don't, especially given a politically reinforced aversion to uncertainty.

Budgeteers are familiar with negotiation, bargaining, trading off, and strategic misrepresentation. Traditional ex ante controls provide ample opportunity for the exercise of negotiating and bargaining skills. Bargaining power may be viewed as the power to misrepresent or bluff. Therefore, the relative bargaining power of budgeteers versus universities and other spending agencies in most situations depends upon the quantity and quality of

information available to each. The fundamental information required by state government controllers in order to
obtain their preferred budget (where they do not rely on
price search through the unit subsidy approach) is information about institutional cost ór supply schedules.
This information is required to overcome university misrepresentation aimed at getting the best budget for itself
and to persuade the budgeteer that the best budget is the
institution's minimum offer. The bargaining tactics employed are familiar to the budgeteer, for example, the
"Washington monument" tactic in which an agency claims
that failure to provide the desired budget will mean the
sacrifice of the most valued services produced by the
agency, or the "coercive deficiency" approach where the
agency exhausts its annual budgetary allowance early in
the fiscal year so that the need for supplemental funds is
urgent.[15]

Left to their own devices universities and other
agencies are likely to devote more resources to strategic
misrepresentation than are available to the budget office,
which has many agency budgets to oversee. The budget
office may not be able to counter all the distortions of
fact, threats, and promises of unconstrained agencies.
Furthermore, the budgeteer is disadvantaged by the need
to reach an agreement on schedule to meet the requirements
of budget cycle timing. However, agencies are seldom left
to their own devices. Antidistortion devices are available
to the budgeteer, at a substantial cost, in the form of ex
ante controls augmented by requests for high-quality and
expensive information from suppliers.

MISAPPLICATION OF INTERNALIZED EX POST CONTROLS

Internalized ex post controls are based upon the
principles of managerial accounting, that is, responsibility centers and cost accounting. The organizing concept
of cost accounting is the idea of a responsibility center in
which discrete outputs are associated with standard ratios
of resource inputs and costs. In a fully developed cost-
accounting system, all costs are identified with a specific
center by output, or activity, and by program, or function.
This is accomplished employing the measurement and calcu-
lation techniques of contemporary accounting and management science.

Using the results of cost-accounting analysis, the purposes of performance budgeting are identification of repetitive activities, determination of their lowest feasible cost, and enforcement of unit-cost standards through the budget process. Considerable effort is devoted to identifying standard costs and norms based upon workload analysis and historical and interprogram comparisons. Budget controllers use these standards internally to project spending levels and to evaluate the performance of the responsibility center manager, for example, the president or provost of a university. Agency managers must report their expenditures and activities regularly. The budget office audits these reports to determine whether actual expenditures and performance are at variance with budget estimates that establish performance norms, and agency managers are rewarded or sanctioned accordingly. Benefit from using cost and performance standards in this way to provide a stable basis for analysis of variances from budget estimates derives from management control held over nominal subordinates (the chief university budget officer) to equal or exceed budgeted performance projections. One problem resulting from such an accountability arrangement is failure to influence organizational decision incentives.

Further problems arise when cost standards determined through ex post analysis are treated as ex ante controls externalized to agencies, and agency behavior is compelled to conform to budget estimates. Consequently, central budget control offices specify how, when, and where resource inputs are to be employed. Typically, this is done by treating cost or expenditure standards as maximum input levels per output. Of course, universities and other government agencies tend to treat these standards as minimum input levels. Cost or expenditure standards often become fixed points with lives of their own in the ongoing bargaining process between the agency and the budget office that encompasses the period of budget execution as well as that of budget preparation. Input measures such as student enrollments (FTE) may be regarded as satisfactory measures of output and performance. Also, when such standards are treated as ex ante controls, variances that save money may be included automatically by state government budgeteers in the adjusted agency budget base; that is, the base is reduced. An example of this is found in ex ante reductions from agency budgets where funding from a previous year is unexpended. Variances that cost more money are treated like any other new expenditure proposal and must be justified by agencies accordingly in order to be included in future budgets. The point is that where such standards are applied as ex ante controls this reduces or eliminates agency incentives to innovate, compete, or even to be efficient.

The logic behind this strategy on the part of state budgeteers seems to be unshakable, given the relationships that exist between budget control offices and program agencies such as universities that have been described in this chapter. From the budget controller's view, if this strategy were not pursued with vigor, agencies could overstate budgetary requirements in high-demand areas to generate resources that could be used elsewhere, creating a precedent for a higher level of support in other and less-valued (by the controller) activity areas. However, as noted in Chapter Five, ex ante controls thus employed have the unfortunate consequence of eliminating incentive for educational improvement and innovation. This occurs, in part, because universities frequently cannot save money where it is being less effectively employed without bearing the burdens and risks of seeking a legislatively sanctioned reallocation. Consequently, when budget standards are based on existing activities, and efficiencies or inefficiencies are enforced through cost accounting standards, productive opportunities lost are the chief cost of tightly administered ex ante controls.

Another major cost of the inappropriate use of controls occurs in the collection of extensive and detailed programmatic information in budgeting. Schick has observed, "Controls cannot be exercised unless an accurate and current reporting system is in use."[16] Such reporting systems are generally expensive to create and maintain for universities and other agencies. When central budget office and university information-gathering, analysis, and control costs are added to university budgets, the price paid for educational services is considerably higher than it would be if the same quantity of services was supplied at an institution's actual supply cost. Alternatively, for the same amount of money universities could supply a larger or higher-quality output of services. However, neither of these attractive options is a real choice, given tightly controlled and government-enforced monopoly supply on the part of the institution. Ex ante information collection and

budget control costs must be borne to avoid even more un-
satisfactory outcomes (less budget) threatened by state
controllers and decision makers.   Information costs are,
therefore, an effective argument against ex ante controls
where a superior alternative is considered, that is, market
or quasi-market solutions to the problem of resource allocation where feasible and justified as proposed in Chapters
Five and Eight.

CONCLUSIONS

        Under circumstances where increasing-cost functions
appear to obtain, and given the other caveats noted, it
appears that legislators and executive decision makers in
government ought to resist the monopoly biases of budgeteers and lend their support to experiments with competitive service supply and per-unit subsidy arrangements in
higher education and elsewhere.   Employing the definitions
developed in this chapter, the unit subsidy approach to
budgeting may be classified as a performance-oriented ex
post control in which unit subsidies are based upon observed relationships between resource inputs and performance outputs.   However, subsidy levels would not be
derived using average costs, as is typically the case in
the use of cost controls in budgeting.   This form of budgeting appears better suited to obtaining both state and institutional educational goals than approaches to budgeting
employed presently by many state governments.   This improvement results from the budgetary incentives created for
universities to be efficient while attempting to meet consumer educational preferences.   Profound reservations must
be expressed about the applicability of cost standards,
performance budgeting, and close managerial controls where
competitive market arrangements are possible and preferable, as is the case under certain conditions in higher
education as explained in the next chapter.   At best such
controls are a waste of money.   They also lead to misallocation of resources and excessive control and information
costs.
        Under the equimarginal subsidy system, highly spe-
cific proposals to use budget appropriations for different
purposes would not have to be made to state budget offices.
State budget appropriations would be modified only as a

result of output performance changes by universities or shifts in output quality preferences in response to public demand.17 Manipulation of the subsidy level constitutes a powerful tool to cause institutions to use delegated freedom from ex ante controls judiciously. In addition, under the equimarginal subsidy system, state government is free to limit the total size of the appropriation made to higher education and to institutions. The ability to set ceilings on appropriations and to change per-unit subsidy levels gives state government sufficient control over expenditures so that it ought to be willing to relax ex ante controls and abandon inappropriate ex post controls. In addition, such controls should intend to influence institutional decision incentives and not just those faced by individual university budget decision makers. Institutional change and responsiveness is the goal of reform. However, before these changes can take place, state governors, directors of finance, and legislative fiscal committee leaders will have to inform state budget office controllers and higher education regulatory agencies that reform in budgetary and program policy is in order. It is to the issue of regulatory reform that we turn in Chapter Seven.

NOTES

1. Appreciative acknowledgement is given to Professors Fred Thompson, Columbia University, and William Zumeta, University of California, Los Angeles, for their assistance in drafting earlier versions of this chapter.

2. A. Schick, "Control Patterns in State Budget Execution," Public Administration Review 24 (June 1964): 97–106.

3. A. Wildavsky, How to Limit Government Spending (Berkeley, Calif.: University of California Press, 1980).

4. Some might object that responding to student preferences would cause institutional and other service quality standards to fall. However, much of the funding for higher education is provided currently on an enrollment basis, and no such outcome has resulted universally. Rather, institutions chose between various price, program

quality, and enrollment mixes. Still, it must be reiter-
ated that most state government funding approaches for
public universities are not strictly enrollment based.
Some funds are appropriated for purposes not directly
related to student enrollments, or even instruction for
that matter. Another key difference between the status
quo and the system presented here is that state funding
presently is seldom if ever set equimarginally across all
public institutions.

5. A. Wildavsky, Budgeting: A Comparative
Theory of the Budgetary Process (Boston: Little, Brown,
1975), 118–19.

6. A. Stedry, Budget Control and Cost Behavior
(Englewood Cliffs, N.J.: Prentice-Hall, 1960).

7. D. Cothran, "Program Flexibility and Budget
Growth in Community Colleges," Western Political Quarterly
34 (December 1981):610.

8. F. Thompson and W. Zumeta, "Control and
Controls: A Reexamination of Control Patterns in Budget
Execution," Policy Sciences 13 (1981):25–50. The following section of the chapter draws on material from this
article, with permission from the authors.

9. W. Niskanen, Bureaucracy and Representative
Government (Chicago: Aldine-Atherton, 1971).

10. R. Bish, The Public Economy of Metropolitan
Areas (Chicago: Markham, 1971); R. Bish and E. Ostrom,
Understanding Urban Government (Washington, D.C.:
American Enterprise Institute, 1973).

11. E. Thompson, "Book Review," Journal of Economic Literature 11 (1973):950–53.

12. J. Burkhead and J. Miner, Public Expenditure (Chicago: Aldine-Atherton, 1971); H. Bowen, The
Costs of Higher Education (San Francisco: Jossey-Bass,
1977).

13. C. Shoup, Public Finance (Chicago: Aldine-
Atherton, 1969).

14. A. Wildavsky, "A Budget for All Seasons: Why
the Traditional Budget Lasts," Public Administration Review 38 (1978):501–9.

15. A. Smithies, The Budgetary Process in the
United States (New York: McGraw-Hill, 1955); C. Levine,
"Organizational Decline and Cutback Management," Public
Administration Review 38 (1978):316–25.

16. Schick, "Control Patterns," 104. See also, A. Wildavsky and A. Hamann, "Comprehensive versus Incremental Budgeting in the Department of Agriculture," Administrative Science Quarterly 10 (1965):321–46.

17. Such preferences would be anticipated and articulated by legislative supporters of higher education under a reformed budgeting system, as is presently the case.

Seven
Fear and Loathing over Institutional Competition and State Regulation

The extent of competition between postsecondary education institutions is typically regulated by state coordinative and planning agencies as well as by postsecondary education boards and institutions. In some instances competition between institutions for new segments of the student market is discouraged by state regulation because offering more than one program in the same geographical area is thought to be wasteful of educational resources.

This chapter employs an industrial organization regulatory perspective to inquire under what enrollment and other conditions a more relaxed versus an active state government regulatory posture is likely to satisfy public preferences for postsecondary education services. A case study of state regulation of competition among institutions in Oregon illustrates the argument.

COMPETITION AND CONFLICT

Although experience differs from state to state, there is at present considerable grumbling and gnashing of teeth over increased institutional competition in postsecondary education. Competition for traditional college-age students has increased markedly over the last decade. Competition for nontraditional students, particularly for employed adult students seeking to attend courses in locations away from university campuses, appears to provide considerable potential for conflict between institutions in an era of limited resources.

Whether this grumbling escalates into fear, loathing, and open hostility between institutions appears to depend on a number of factors, including the extent to which state higher education governing procedures encourage, discourage, or ignore increased competition; institutional proclivities to cooperate, coordinate, compete, coopt, adjust mutually, or use other strategies in managing increased competition; institutional tradition; experiences and inclinations of various postsecondary education policy makers; state funding procedures for postsecondary education; and state policies toward private higher education.

Given these assumptions, it is useful to investigate further the attitudes of institutional and state-level postsecondary education leaders toward competition between institutions. The section that follows presents a case study of state regulation of institutional competition and an analytical framework for addressing the case and postsecondary education competition more generally.

CONTROL AS A RESPONSE TO FEAR AND LOATHING

In the past in many states competition in postsecondary education has been regarded dubiously at best. Competition has been interpreted as duplication of services and, consequently, as a misuse of public resources. Also, the notion has persisted that increased competition in education would reduce the quality of educational offerings; quality standards would be lowered in accommodating some student preferences. In addition, competition between public and private institutions has been discouraged as unfair to private institutions that operate without large government financial support for instruction. Further, in an era of growth, arguments for increased competition were not compelling. There were plenty of students and enough growth opportunities for everyone.

The logic supporting these assumptions appears challengeable on several grounds. If one subscribes to the economic theory of competition, and we assume that Americans believe in at least a few of the tenets upon which the mixed capitalist economy of most of the Western world is based, then one might expect increased competition to result in market segmentation and adjustment on the part of competitors rather than prolonged duplication of services. One might expect that competition would, therefore, result in a broader range of educational options available to student consumers. In addition, we might expect some new courses and programs offered under competition to be of lower quality than programs offered under the status quo (for example, as measured by the quality and amount of work required to earn three credits), while other options would be of the same or higher quality than existing courses and programs. We might also expect the quality of services offered to be reflected in differential prices charged to students, with more price-quality trade-off options available to student consumers over time. Finally, supply-and-demand forces might be expected to cause an eventual adjustment to a state of equilibrium in the market over time on the part of institutions and consumers. These effects might be anticipated for both on-campus and off-campus educational programs. Despite these assumptions, for many of the reasons noted previously we should not expect public administrators in general, and especially those in postsecondary education, to readily accept market principles.

To illustrate these points we may review as a case recent events in Oregon where the University of Oregon attempted to offer a public affairs master's degree program in Salem, the state capital, located approximately 70 miles to the north of the University of Oregon campus in Eugene. The program to be offered was the same master's degree in public affairs offered on-campus, to be taught by regular university faculty and adjunct faculty hired specifically for the program. On-campus curricula, degree requirements, admission criteria, and advising and other administrative procedures were to be employed in the off-campus program. Most importantly, the program was to be offered on a self-supporting basis, with student tuition providing support for faculty salaries, for release time for regular faculty teaching off-campus, and for compensation to the on-campus program for support resources employed. A small amount of institutional budgetary support was to be provided for start-up costs for two years. The program was not intended to generate additional state aid for new students attracted by the University of Oregon program.

Testing the water with an initial proposal to offer the program produced considerable opposition to implementation on the part of public and private higher education institutions despite the fact that, at the time, only one private institution offered even a marginally comparable

master's degree program in the capital (generic adminis-
tration--public and private sector emphasis). Opposition
was based in part on the belief that closer examination of
the proposed program's impact on other institutions was
needed, a point to which the university yielded in delay-
ing program implementation. Resistance from a number of
quarters, including the private institution based in the
capital, also rested upon the traditional argument of duplication of services and fears that increased competition
would work to the detriment of both the private institution
in question and the student population to be served.

While this reaction can be interpreted understandably
as a strategic competitive response, it was not viewed
wholly in this light by state-level and institutional decision makers. Rather, there is evidence that faced with
this and other instances of competition, state postsecondary
education decision makers have preferred to employ greater
government regulatory control over Oregon institutions by
restricting market entry by regional area, public versus
private institutional competition, and other aspects of relations between institutions. This approach has been taken
by the state legislature and the Oregon Educational Coordinating Commission while, at the same time, competition for
several markets (for example, Portland and Salem) from institutions located outside the state has increased.

In order to establish that demand existed for the
program it sought to provide, the University of Oregon conducted a market study of government employees in the
Salem area and found considerable unmet demand for
courses and a graduate degree program in public affairs.[1]
Although the university sought only 20 students to begin
its degree program, over 80 individuals expressed strong
interest in applying for and attending courses. Based upon
the survey response, it was estimated that the market for
graduate public affairs instruction in the Salem area exceeded 1,600 persons out of a population of approximately
18,000 state and local government and not-for-profit organization employees. In addition, the study found the Salem
market to be segmented in terms of the educational aspirations of prospective students; professional roles, occupations, and employers of prospective students; types of
programs desired; and willingness and ability to pay for
graduate education.

Based upon these findings and in response to opposition from other institutions, the university proposed to

offer pilot courses in order to assess demand, to gauge the
impact of its program on other institutions and other factors to determine whether a comprehensive program should
be provided as proposed. In part this strategy permitted
the university to assess the political feasibility of providing the program at minimum risk. While this seemed like
a reasonable market strategy, the extent of demand for a
comprehensive program delivered on-site appeared to war-
rant rapid program implementation. However, the prevailing climate of opposition to institutional competition from
state regulators and planners and other institutions, supported by fear of competition from private and public
higher education institutions, resulted in prohibition: the
university was prevented from offering its public affairs
program or courses to prospective students in Salem or in
other Oregon cities without the explicit approval of the
state postsecondary education planning and regulatory
agency.

Prohibition of the offering by the Oregon Educational
Coordinating Commission resulted in considerable resentment
at the University. University relations with other institutions worsened as a result of this action. University administrators assumed that the state regulatory and planning
agency had been lobbied effectively, but unfairly, to protect several private and public institutions from competition, despite absence of evidence that competition would
reduce enrollment demand or otherwise affect these institutions. Further, the state agency was able to persuade the
state chancellor's office to support its prohibition of competition. The systemwide office had previously resisted
the prospect of increased competition between state institutions but had done so informally in a way that had not
prevented the University of Oregon from proposing its
Salem public affairs program.

In Oregon, fear of competition produced some degree
of loathing, the effect of which was to limit access to any
off-campus educational programs offered by a public institution. State government regulatory action to limit off-
campus postsecondary education program development resulted in response to the prospect of increased competition
rather than its actual occurrence.

Additional results of an increase in postsecondary
education regulation in Oregon may be anticipated based
upon experience in other states: more staff and more resources are likely to be employed at the state level for

planning, budget monitoring, program review, and other regulatory activities; more staff and other resources will need to be hired in higher education institutions to respond to increased state-level regulatory control and control staffs; more public money will be expended in regulation and control. As a result of the decremental budgets appropriated to Oregon higher education in the period 1981-83, less money has been available for instruction, research, and public service activities in public universities and colleges.

In the past, Oregonians have been fortunate in not having to bear the costs of a high state-level regulatory posture in postsecondary education. By and large, the custom has been to settle inter- and intrainstitutional conflicts through "low-key" cooperative methods, rather than through state regulatory intervention. A high degree of state-level regulation thus represents a relatively significant change in the status quo for Oregon. While state regulation efforts have not accelerated yet, the legislature is considering legislation merging all educational planning and regulatory responsibilities under the aegis of a state "super-board" agency. These responsibilities are currently distributed among several boards and the state educational coordinating commission.

To gain further insight into the Oregon case, and to understand better the rationale for competition among institutions, it may be useful to evaluate postsecondary education regulation against the model of governmental economic regulation of the private sector. Applying an industrial organization model of competition and regulation, we may clarify state versus institutional spheres of authority in planning and delivery of educational services and state versus institutional roles in preventing and adjudicating competitive disputes between institutions.

APPLICABILITY OF THE REGULATORY MODEL TO POSTSECONDARY EDUCATION

Some notable efforts have been made recently to analyze the applicability of regulatory models to higher education. Some research in this area concludes that state-level postsecondary education coordinating agencies in many states carry out functions that fit the model of economic or direct regulation of the private sector by government. Economic or direct regulation is understood to include government control over prices, market entry, supply, or production. Among these regulatory functions applied in postsecondary education are the following:

1. control over new entry into the "instruction industry"
2. influence over the mix and distribution of instructional services provided
3. control over new service offerings by existing institutions
4. control over implementation of technological change
5. influence over how resources (inputs) and technologies are used to produce learning, student enrollments, or other "outputs"
6. de facto control over prices charged to consumers and classes of consumers
7. control over the planning assumptions (for example, enrollment forecasts) that help determine the size of the "industry"
8. other limitations, including complete prohibition of competition.[2]

As noted by Cheit[3] and others, "Observers of higher education in the U.S. have seen a kind of Parkinson's Law phenomenon at work as regulatory agency staff constantly generate requests for new information, which institutions must 'staff up' to digest . . . the more regulatory staff the more requests for information grow."[4]

The real and opportunity costs of postsecondary education regulation appear considerable. Whether the degree of regulation practiced in many states is appropriate in terms of its net benefits (benefits less costs) may be questioned. Careful scrutiny appears especially appropriate for states where a heavy regulatory commitment does not yet exist, as is the case in Oregon. Arguments for deregulation of postsecondary education may also result from this evaluation.

Government intervention through regulation in postsecondary education has been supported as necessary to prevent service duplication; exercise quality control over degree programs, curricula, and advertising by institutions; control capital planning, construction, and institutional-siting decisions; establish and maintain state and institutional master plans and planning processes; adjudicate disputes between segments and institutions; influence resource allocation decision making; influence employment practices, hiring decisions (for example, affirmative action), and the provision of special services to selected clientele groups; and for other reasons.

These arguments have supported both economic regulation--including market entry, price, resource inputs to service--and social regulation, for example, to assure affirmative action in admissions and employment, provision of services to handicapped students, and other services. The problems addressed by social regulations of this type are real; social regulation appears to be highly justifiable in its application to education, as it is to other industries and sectors of the economy. The types of regulation at issue in this study fall within the category of direct or economic regulation rather than social regulation.

Cost Functions and Regulatory Intervention

In the field of industrial organization as it pertains to regulatory theory, economic or direct regulation by government has traditionally been justified for industries facing declining marginal (average marginal) cost schedules. Declining marginal costs have been viewed to argue for monopolistic provision of services and monopsonist supply sponsorship by government to take advantage of economies of scale; that is, at the margin each unit of a service or commodity is cheaper to produce than the previous unit. This line of thinking has, for example, influenced public utility regulation. Where industries face increasing marginal costs, the traditional argument has been for provision of services by competing firms, employing competition to encourage the offering of services and commodities in different price-quality mixes in attempts to meet consumer demand within a market. The traditional argument holds that government monopsony permits one or several organizations in separate markets to take maximum advantage of scale economies. Economic regulation under these conditions is supposed to prevent abuses such as monopolistic (and unreasonably high) pricing policies, quality reduction, distribution inequities, nonresponsiveness to consumers, failure to provide services as advertised, and other perversities.

In attempting to apply industrial organization theory to the issue of regulation of postsecondary education, as

was the case in Chapter Six we are led to enquire into
the nature of production cost functions exhibited by colleges and universities. Most simply, the question is, do
postsecondary education institutions face increasing or decreasing marginal costs in providing additional educational
services to students? The concept of marginal cost employed here means the cost to the institution for enrolling
the next student beyond its current level of enrollment.
In this context we understand that even where overall
student enrollments are declining, additional institutional
costs may be incurred for enrolling one more student at
the margin, just as is the case where enrollments are increasing. To reiterate the argument, the explanation for
increasing marginal costs where overall enrollments are
declining, at least in part, is that the cost of enrolling
one more student at the margin increases due to the necessity for providing additional services to attract the additional student. More will be noted on why this occurs
subsequently.

The results of analysis of cost functions in postsecondary education are not entirely clear. Determining
the nature of cost functions in the private goods-producing
sector or in the public services-producing sector is tricky
and fraught with assumptions, data inconsistencies, and
all of the problems customarily faced in economic analysis.
Nevertheless, believing that economic and cost analysis
may provide some insights into the need for regulation, its
application to postsecondary education is assumed here to
merit some review.

With regard to the role of government control agencies in attempting to influence the behavior of postsecondary education institutions, Breton and Wintrobe note that
"the sponsor [in the form of an executive budget office
and/or regulatory] will [should] incur control expenses up
to the point at which marginal benefits . . . are equal to
marginal costs."[5] Under the circumstance of decreasing
marginal costs, this view would argue for government resource and regulatory control over market entry and how,
where, and what services should be provided by whom so
that monopolist institutions or cartels of institutions could
accommodate students at the least cost to the public. Government budgeteers and regulators would thus enhance economic efficiency in postsecondary education by encouraging
institutional monopoly or oligopoly to take advantage of
economies of scale in meeting student demand. However,

where increasing marginal costs exist, no such encourage-
ment of monopoly by government is desired. Postsecondary
education institutions would be encouraged by government
to compete, thus increasing the likelihood that additional
educational services would be offered and driving the price
for services downward to the benefit of student consumers.
In addition, absence of government intervention would reduce the cost of government regulation borne by taxpayers.
Regulatory expenditures incurred by government under the
latter circumstance of increasing marginal-average costs
would be unnecessary and probably would not increase institutional accommodation of student demand to any extent.
Regulatory expenditures would be, in fact, almost entirely
wasted and could decrease institutional responsiveness to
student preferences. Regulatory models which represent
these opposing views may be characterized as the central
planning and regulatory control model versus the competitive incentive model.[6]

Research on Cost Behavior in
Postsecondary Education

Research on production and cost functions tends to
support the proposition that under conditions of rising enrollments, postsecondary education institutions face decreasing marginal cost schedules, whereas under stable or declining enrollments, institutions face increasing marginal
costs.[7] Using a linear programming approach, Carlson
found that holding type and mix of program, level and mix
of students, public or private institutional status, and
other variables constant, institutions show increasing total
costs and decreasing average costs as student enrollments
increase.[8] Through regression analysis, Radner and Miller
found that for groups of institutions of similar status and
program, total faculty employed increases as enrollment
increases, but at a decreasing rate.[9] Employing enrollment as a proxy for student demand, both studies indicate
that decreasing-cost functions are produced as enrollments
increase. Thompson and Zumeta also found that, holding
service levels constant, institutional costs decrease as enrollment increases.[10]
In attempting to identify conditions that result in
increasing institutional marginal cost schedules, Hoenack,
Radner, and Miller, Kohn and colleagues, Thompson and

Zumeta, and Bishop have substantiated the notion that
college-student enrollment varies relative to the types and
levels of services provided (for example, location of services, breadth and type of offering, institutional prestige,
amount of money spent by level of student, and so forth).[11]
These findings are interpreted to explain student enrollment
increases in the period 1960-75 to result not merely from a
demographic bulge but also from an expansion of services
provided by institutions. Relating this conclusion to circumstances of declining student enrollment, Thompson and
Zumeta examined the experience of the California State University and Colleges, and the California Community Colleges. They found that as service levels were reduced in
the early 1970s due to budget restrictions, student enrollments decreased and average marginal institutional costs
per student increased.[12] In order to gain new enrollments
after budgets and services had been cut, new services had
to be added by institutions.[13] This result is consistent
with Bishop's findings on costs in higher education, and
with the hypotheses of Shoup, Breton and Wintrobe, Niskanen and others with regard to the cost functions exhibited by government agencies.[14]

A somewhat simplified explanation of the cost phenomenon identified is that economies of scale are experienced by institutions as they build to accommodate increasing numbers of students. Once student enrollments begin
to decline, institutions often are not sufficiently flexible
nor do they desire to cut back programs, faculty, and services commensurate with enrollment losses. Among other
reasons, institutions are inflexible in their response due
to inability to reduce faculty salary costs when enrollments
decline without taking the drastic step of terminating academic programs and tenured faculty. Enrollment decline
under this circumstance results in reduced student-faculty
ratios and increased average costs of instruction. Institutions are constrained in reducing tenured faculty and are
prevented from hiring new "lower cost" faculty by high
tenure rates in departments and across entire university
and college faculties. Institutions are further limited in
their ability to reduce instructional and nonteaching staff
by labor contracts, personnel guidelines, program mandates,
grant requirements, alumni and community expectations,
and a myriad of other factors. Such conditions can be
understood to produce increasing average costs of instruction and increasing marginal costs as well.

The explanation for increasing marginal costs is that it is necessary for institutions to offer new and in some cases different mixes of instructional services to accommodate shifts in student demand, such as those away from liberal arts and sciences to computer sciences or to professional and vocational programs. Whether this particular explanation of why increasing costs occur under declining enrollment comprises the primary explanatory variables is unclear. However, it is the case that the empirical research referenced above has found cost functions to support the relationships between enrollment demand and marginal costs hypothesized here. Further, the explanation that is intuitively satisfying has also been observed, that is, that institutional marginal costs increase through attempts to attract new students in a market where overall enrollment demand is falling.

Student Demand as a Critical Variable in the Cost Model

The most important element in cost and production function determination under the model presented here is the nature of student enrollment demand: whether demand is increasing, stable, or declining. Enrollment forecasts for the 1980s, like all forecasts, are subject to some degree of uncertainty, and this uncertainty is especially high with regard to off-campus enrollments. While it is highly probable that aggregate enrollments in the traditional college-age cohort will decline, this does not necessarily hold equally for all states, nor for all types of institutions, all colleges and universities, or all programs.

Based upon experience across states, and institutions over the past five years, off-campus enrollment levels are likely to depend considerably upon the incentives built into state funding formulas for postsecondary education institutions. It remains to be determined definitively in Oregon, and in other states, how institutions are to be compensated for student enrollments earned in off-campus settings. Several approaches are evident. In some instances off-campus enrollment tuition is earned by a continuing education agency that operates as a self-supporting university enterprise. Under this circumstance state governments do not provide institutions with per-capita enrollment payments, although some state money may be in-

vested to get the enterprise off the ground, as was proposed in Oregon. Under other approaches state governments
treat off-campus enrollments, or enrollments in particular
curricular areas, as regular state support earning FTEs.
Under this latter arrangement, institutions have a direct
incentive to increase off-campus enrollments to support
campus programs and to hold the line against steady-state
or declining state funding. Either arrangement provides
incentive for institutions to make expenditures in new areas
to attract new students in off-campus programs.

Given these concessions to enrollment uncertainty, it
seems reasonable to assume that aggregate postsecondary
education enrollments (on-campus and off-campus combined)
in the 1980s will stabilize or perhaps decline slightly,
even though some institutions may experience enrollment
increases. Enrollment levels for many institutions and
academic departments are likely to decline unless institutions exhibit greater skill and intensity in their marketing
activities.

The implications for postsecondary education program
development of the findings reviewed here on cost and enrollment relationships are that where total postsecondary
education enrollments are stable or declining, a high
state regulatory posture is inappropriate and centralized
planning, stricter accountability and control measures, and
attempts to eliminate "wasteful duplication" are not valid
objectives for postsecondary education governance. Under
the comprehensive planning model, where enrollments are
stable or declining, the costs of duplication of services
are the regulatory costs of attempting to avoid duplication,
plus the costs to students where access to programs is limited by regulation. The problem with competition in this
circumstance is not that it could occur, but to ensure that
it does occur.

An argument may still be made for some government
regulation to reduce the occurrence of nasty public disputes between postsecondary education institutions, to require some planning of services to be provided by institutions, to prevent the formation of regional cartels, to maintain reasonable quality standards, and to ensure fair advertising practices. This assumes, of course, that institutions cannot by themselves achieve an acceptable level
of control over inappropriate competitive behavior such as
false or misleading advertising or mail order degree busi-
nesses. It is difficult to understand, for example, how

the public interest is served if mail order institutions are permitted de facto to sell degrees without requiring student coursework, institutional residency, and so forth. Proponents of the competitive model might argue that institutions that sell degrees be allowed to continue in this practice because a degree thus obtained would prove to be of no value over time. The opposite view would hold that government has the obligation to assure minimum program quality standards for degree-offering postsecondary education.

The argument for some regulation appears persuasive in several areas, for example, fraudulent advertising and sale of academic degrees. This role is, however, significantly less prominent and less costly than the comprehensive planning orientation evidenced at present by postsecondary education regulatory agencies in many states. We should note that competitive supply would be appropriate only if three other conditions are met in addition to the existence of short- and long-run increasing marginal costs:

1. Services provided must be evaluated by users to their satisfaction.
2. Public subsidy mechanisms must be designed to compensate for discrepancies between the private and public benefits of the service.
3. The public interest would not be damaged by the failure of one or a few service providers to survive.[15]

Judgment as to whether the public interest would be damaged by financial failure of a college or university might be rendered by a postsecondary education regulatory agency. However, it can also be argued that interaction among legislators, governors, and other political participants would render this determination and implement it through budget subsidies as part of the normal politic of the budgetary process without assistance from a large educational regulatory structure.

Another relevant issue is, what should be done if a lower-key regulatory posture is assumed and enrollment patterns change? Would an increase in planning and program review be the appropriate regulatory response to another period of increasing enrollment demand (decreasing marginal institutional costs) as might occur in the 1990s? Experience with a high regulatory posture in many states in the 1960s and 1970s has taught us about the benefits and costs of postsecondary education regulation. Indeed, in this light the comprehensive style of planning evidenced in a succession of master plans for higher and postsecondary education in California and in other states appears to be entirely worth its costs. Under declining enrollments it seems equally reasonable that we would place ourselves in a position to learn about the costs and benefits of a lower-key regulatory posture.

These issues suggest a research agenda for scholars of postsecondary education regulation, planning, and budgeting in the 1980s. It is particularly important for future research to address the competitive behavior of institutions prior to the creation of state postsecondary education regulatory and planning agencies. Information on this behavior would improve our understanding of how institutions and/or state government regulators can act to prevent competitive abuses and unfair practices in new markets.

APPLICATION OF REGULATORY THEORY TO THE OREGON CASE

What does the theoretical perspective we have developed indicate when applied to the Oregon case discussed earlier in this study? First, it is necessary to look at enrollment data. The University of Oregon experienced a student enrollment decline of about 7 percent for the academic year 1982-83, with relatively stable enrollment in 1983-84. The Oregon state system of higher education experienced a 5 percent to 6 percent enrollment decline for this year. University and state system enrollments were projected to decline moderately or stabilize through the remainder of the 1980s. Second, cost data for the proposed off-campus program must be reviewed. Cost estimates for the University of Oregon public affairs curriculum in Salem indicated that increases in departmental and institutional expenditures would be needed to attract students to take the new off-campus program in the state capital. It was projected that increasing average marginal costs would be encountered in the initial five years of program implementation even though the program was to be self-supporting within two years according to official university pronouncements. Also, it was expected that additional increases in expenditure from state and program-generated funds would be needed to draw students if other institutions entered the same geographical market with a similar service, for example, a public administration/affairs master's degree program. In addition, the university expected increased marginal per-student costs in attempting to provide an undergraduate public affairs degree program subsequently in Salem.

If we apply our cost assumptions to the Oregon case, it appears that the state regulatory agency erred in two ways in precluding program delivery. First, competition between institutions would appear to be an appropriate mode for introducing a new curriculum as long as the university was willing to avoid false advertising, make its offerings known widely to potential consumers, ensure that students entering the program would be able to complete their degrees in the off-campus setting should the university terminate the program, and ensure that state money to support the program would be eliminated after a suitable start-up period. The university was willing to meet these criteria, but the offering was prohibited without consideration of these factors.

Second, by preventing the delivery of the program, a number of citizens were denied the right to choose between a moderately priced graduate public affairs program offered by a public institution and an expensive generic administration program offered by a private institution. Citizens lost the opportunity for access to a public university curriculum developed to meet the needs of adult learners employed in the public sector. Based upon the initial response to program advertisements, it may be estimated that the program would have enrolled 30 students in the degree program and 80 students for coursework only in its first academic term, and perhaps 60 or more degree-seeking students in the first academic year. Further, a university survey indicated the size of the potential market for a public affairs program at 18,000 persons in the greater Salem area. Given these numbers, it would appear that to prospective students the cost in lost opportunity from the regulatory decision to prohibit the program was substantial. This is even more apparent when it is noted that no convenient substitute service was available in the market. The nearest graduate public administration offering was a two-hour drive away, either in Portland or at the University of Oregon campus in Eugene.

Analysis of the case indicates that state postsecondary education objectives were not served well by regulation to restrict market entry. Subsequent to its ruling on the university public affairs program, the state regulatory and planning agency prohibited other public institutions from competition in offering undergraduate programs in several disciplines in off-campus locations. Additionally, the state board of higher education announced its own plans to restrict and ration market entry by dividing the state into regional sectors. The plan would give only designated public institutions the right to offer off-campus courses in these sectors.

Consistent with long-standing practice, competition between postsecondary institutions continues to be discouraged in Oregon. The university has not attempted to resurrect its plan to offer the graduate public affairs degree in the state capital. In addition, no other Oregon public college or university has entered the market with a similar program, although other educational services such as undergraduate professional degree curricula have been offered by new private institution market entrants. Survey data compiled by the state system of higher education chancellor's office indicated that sizable off-campus markets are not served presently by state institutions, despite the fact that many of these institutions are suffering the financial and programmatic consequences of loss of state per-capita budget support due to declining enrollments.

CONCLUSIONS ON REGULATION AND COMPETITION

Arguments for economic regulation of market entry, prices, resource inputs, and program quality, and requirements for comprehensive planning, appear to be far less compelling in postsecondary education in the 1980s than in the previous several decades. Justification for regulation appears to be particularly weak during a period of resource scarcity where the trade-off for adding an additional regulator or planner at the state level may be the loss of faculty positions in public universities and colleges. The addition of one state-level analyst may require institutions to employ several administrative staff to respond to state information requests and regulatory demands. Of even greater importance is that state regulation of postsecondary education may constrain competition between institutions, reducing incentives for development of special programs for working students in new geographical areas.

Under conditions of stable or declining enrollment, the opportunity costs of regulation in the form of foregone benefits for students are likely to be greater than the savings
achieved by attempts to reduce institutional duplication of
services.

In a period of stable or declining student enrollment
demand, we should question whether any efforts to reduce
duplication of educational service offerings are in the public interest. Based upon cost and other perspectives presented in this study, competition between institutions in a
period of declining enrollment demand would serve the public interest by increasing access and student choice. We
should examine the purported benefits of state postsecondary education regulation relative to its costs more closely
in the 1980s.

Over the next decade in Oregon, as in other states,
budget analysts in executive budget agencies and legislative fiscal offices will scrutinize postsecondary education
expenditure requests to find ways to cut, trim, and squeeze
resources. At the same time, budget analysts will be
searching for means to reduce budgets in other areas of
government, including regulatory agencies. The squeeze
on regulatory agencies may occur for a number of reasons,
including public and private sector pressure to reduce the
burden of regulatory administrative and compliance costs,
and belief that most direct economic regulatory control is
economically inefficient. Competition for resources and
criticism of regulation in general may combine with cost
and other arguments advanced in this study to cause state
government to question the utility of a high and costly
state regulatory posture in postsecondary education.

This chapter was written in part to address the issue of whether postsecondary education institutions are
meeting the educational needs or service preferences of
"in-service" students.[16] The answer is that such preferences are being met rather poorly in Oregon, and perhaps
poorly elsewhere, due to overregulation by state government. The extent to which adult continuing education
student preferences will be met depends to a considerable
extent on the incentives provided to institutions to meet
latent demand. A realistic view of the likelihood that incentives will be provided under the throes of fiscal stress
in state government is to think less about positive incentives and more about the removal of barriers to service
supply. The removal of regulatory disincentives for insti-

tutions to offer programs intended to meet consumer demand
in competition with other colleges and universities is a
task that ought to be considered by state executives and
legislators.

The argument for deregulation to permit competitive
supply of educational services is perhaps most compelling
from the view of the consumer, for example, working professionals who want to increase their competence and
career mobility.   It should be noted that this category of
student includes a high proportion of professional women.
In Oregon and elsewhere, the educational choice presently
afforded off-campus students is narrow.   Under a competitive arrangement, institutions would have budgetary and
other incentives to increase the range of services available
to working students in off-campus locations.   Institutions
would profit financially from meeting new demand and
could also be advantaged by increased visibility and public contact.   In terms of grass-roots political appeal, arguments for increased consumer choice in postsecondary education would appear to be nearly as marketable as those for
reduced government regulation.

While there may be considerable fear over the prospect of increased competition in postsecondary education,
especially in off-campus settings, loathing and destructive
conflict between institutions should be avoided.   One way
to avoid the type of fear and loathing that can produce
open hostility among competing colleges and universities is
to depend upon state government to regulate and adjudicate
disputes among institutions.   A second approach would be
for institutions to acknowledge the benefits, as well as
costs, of increased competition and to depend more on each
other to set the boundaries of ethical competitive behavior.
This chapter concludes that under conditions of stable or
declining student enrollment, the most efficient use of
scarce state financial resources will result from application
of the second approach.

NOTES

1.   L. R. Jones, "Salem Area Public Affairs Education Preference Assessment," Wallace School of Community
Service and Public Affairs, University of Oregon, February
1980.

2. F. Thompson and W. Zumeta, "A Regulatory Model of Governmental Coordinating Activities in the Higher Education Sector," Economics of Education Review 1 (November 1980) 74–87. On higher education regulation generally, see W. Hobbs, ed., Government Regulation of Higher Education (Cambridge, Mass.: Ballinger, 1978).

3. E. Cheit, "What Price Accountability?" Change 7 (November 1975):30–34, 60.

4. Thompson and Zumeta, "Regulatory Model." On how regulation leads to more regulation, see F. Thompson and L. R. Jones, Regulatory Policy and Practices (New York: Praeger, 1982).

5. A. Breton and R. Wintrobe, "The Equilibrium Size of a Budget Maximizing Bureau," Journal of Political Economy 8 (1975):95–101. Breton and Wintrobe explain that in many cases government budget and regulatory agencies operate as monopsonists as purchasers of services on behalf of the public from monopolies consisting of government and/or private agencies that are the sole suppliers of specific types of services in particular markets.

6. For another treatment of these models relative to state influence on institutional behavior, see L. R. Jones, "Fiscal Strategies to Stimulate Instructional Innovation and Change," Journal of Higher Education 49 (1978): 588–607; D. Breneman, "Strategies for the 1980s," in Challenges of Retrenchment, ed. J. Mingle (San Francisco: Jossey-Bass, 1981):16–31.

7. For example, see D. Carlson, The Production and Cost Behavior of Higher Education, Ford Foundation Research Paper P-36 (Berkeley: University of California, 1972); R. Radner and L. Miller, "Demand and Supply in U.S. Higher Education: A Progress Report," American Economic Review 60 (May 1970):326–34; C. Adams and R. Hankins, The Literature of Costs and Cost Analysis in Higher Education, American Council of Education (Minneapolis: Graduate School of Business Administration, University of Minnesota, 1977); S. Hoenack, "The Efficient Allocation of Subsidies to College Students," American Economic Review (June 1971):302–11; Thompson and Zumeta, "Regulatory Model."

8. Carlson, Production and Cost Behavior.

9. Radner and Miller, "Demand and Supply."

10. Thompson and Zumeta, "Regulatory Model."

11. Hoenack, "Efficient Allocation of Subsidies"; Radner and Miller, "Demand and Supply"; M. Kohn, C. Manski, and D. Mundel, "An Empirical Analysis of Factors Which Influence College-Going Behavior," Annals of Economic

and Social Measurement 5 (1976):285–307; Thompson and Zumeta, "Regulatory Model"; F. Thompson and W. Zumeta, "Control and Controls: A Reexamination of Control Patterns in Budget Execution," Policy Sciences 13 (1981):25–50; J. Bishop, "The Effect of Public Policies on the Demand for Higher Education," The Journal of Human Resources 3 (Fall 1977):385–407. See also G. Jackson and G. Weathersby, "Individual Demand for Higher Education," Journal of Higher Education 46 (November–December 1975):623–52.

    12. Thompson and Zumeta, "Regulatory Model."

    13. To quote Thompson and Zumeta, "Regulatory Model," "Where students' demand schedules are held constant, enrollment can only be increased by reducing the cost or increasing the benefit to the student of enrolling in college. Here, the law of diminishing returns should apply . . . [therefore] an institution's marginal cost increases as enrollment increases. This proposition follows from the observation that, under the given conditions, an institution can increase enrollments only by offering more course titles or degree programs, better training, more stimulating interaction in the classroom or class laboratory, smaller class size . . . or better counseling to assist the student in matching his or her interests to the offerings of the institution. These additional services cost money, and other things equal, it can be concluded that an institution can increase enrollment only at an increased cost per student."

    14. Bishop, "Effect of Public Policies"; C. Shoup, Public Finance (Chicago: Aldine–Atherton, 1969), 130; Breton and Wintrobe, "Equilibrium Size," 197–98; W. Niskanen, Bureaucracy and Representative Government (Chicago: Aldine–Atherton, 1971). On cost functions, see also H. Bowen, The Costs of Higher Education (San Francisco: Jossey-Bass, 1981).

    15. Thompson and Zumeta, "Regulatory Model."

    16. Needs is a confusing word in this context because it is difficult to define as such. Perhaps educational service preferences is a better term by which to characterize student demand. The term in-service students as used here means students who are employed while they enroll in school.

Eight
Reform of University Academic Resource Management and State Government Budgeting

Preceding chapters have argued that three types of reform are needed in academic resource management and budgeting for universities. The first reform is development of the critical mass and core resource approach to academic planning, budgeting, and management at the university level. The second reform is a change in state government budgetary procedures to reduce budget management control through experimentation with enrollment-based per-unit subsidies applied equimarginally across all segments of higher education. The third reform is a significant reduction in state government academic program regulation in higher education, eliminating most state program review and control over market entry and interinstitutional competition.

The gist of the arguments presented is that institutions must be responsive to student demand in order to survive in an era of financial restraint. However, responsiveness should not remove from faculty and university administrators the responsibility for making essential decisions about how university curricula should be organized and presented. Institutional academic program and budgetary decision making must continue to be based on criteria that represent academic values about what should be taught in a university. In order to render curriculum decisions wisely and to defend them against external scrutiny, most universities need to make significant improvements in academic program resource management, particularly in adopting more systematic methods for information management. Further, it is argued that university efforts to improve internal academic resource management will be assisted if state governments reduce budgetary and regulatory control to permit universities to exercise greater resource management flexibility. Relaxation of state budgetary control could result from a simplification of budget decision criteria to place greater emphasis on marginal enrollment subsidies. States could also reduce control over how budget appropriations are spent by universities as they attempt to respond to changes in student demand and other characteristics of the external environment.

Disagreements over control appear inevitable as university strategies to seek resources based upon critical mass and core resource considerations conflict with state initiatives to fund institutions relative to marginal enrollment changes. However, the reforms advocated attempt to provide selective advantages to meet both institutional and state government decision maker needs in budgeting as presently performed in most state systems. Institutional academic management control capacity is intended to be strengthened partially as a result of simplification of state budgetary decision making to reduce budget and program control costs. At the same time, state officials will maintain their ability to influence higher education outcomes through clearer application of financial incentives to universities. The argument for critical mass is essentially that of increased budget and program flexibility and more systematic application of institutional academic management control. The reforms advocated in state budgeting and regulation are based on the view that a reduction of comlexity and cost may be achieved with no loss of financial control. Further, budgeting under the enrollment market approach would provide institutions stronger incentive to respond to student educational preferences.

It may be anticipated that if these reforms were implemented universities would argue for budget augmentation or against budget reduction based upon critical mass considerations irrespective of enrollment changes. In contrast, state decision makers would attempt to fund exclusively according to marginal enrollment change. The success of university strategy in gaining new revenues or resisting cuts independent of enrollment change will depend on political strategy and clout in the state budgetary decision process, as is the case presently. However, under the reforms suggested, both institutional budget maximizers and state budget minimizers will have stronger a priori strategic positions established from which to compete than is presently the case. Further, it is assumed that universities, state government, and the public will be better served by this competition than they are by current budgetary practices because universities will use their resources more effectively, states will achieve their objectives more easily, and the public will benefit from more responsive universities and government.

The reforms advocated in this book are viewed as necessary to improve university and state academic resource decision making and management during a period of stable student enrollment and financial restraint. This final chapter briefly addresses the context for reform, summarizes the arguments for budgetary and regulatory reform, and addresses some of the criticisms that may be anticipated for each of the changes proposed.

THE CONTEXT FOR REFORM: BENEFITS LOST UNDER FINANCIAL RESTRAINT

The challenge to colleges and universities during the next decade is maintenance of academic quality and institutional vitality in a period of slowly growing, stable, or declining student enrollment. Because public higher education institutions receive substantial portions of operating and capital outlay funding on the basis of student enrollment, prospects for academic program expansion as a result of increased public expenditure are limited in a period of enrollment stability or decline. Financial limits constrain the ability of academic institutions to provide new modes of instruction, research, and service. Reduced financial flexibility limits the extent to which institutions are able to meet social goals in a number of areas, for example, improving access for low-income students, stimulating student and employee affirmative action, providing salary and benefit compensation to faculty and other employees to match changes in the cost of living, and maintaining safe and healthy physical facilities and work environments.

Many of the implications of low or no growth in student enrollment in higher education have been thoroughly documented over the past decade.[1] However, much of this discussion has failed to differentiate the consequences of

financial restraint across institutions. The distribution of
losses under financial restraint are not equal. Predictions
of no growth should not be accepted as inevitable for all
universities and colleges. Institutions that continue to
provide educational services desired by prospective students are very likely to experience enrollment increases in
some areas during the next decade, for example, in computer science and related instruction. Numerous public
and private institutions that have provided programs and
services demanded by students have maintained enrollment
levels over the past ten years. Evidence that enrollments
do not decline across-the-board is provided by the trend
of continued growth in many off-campus, adult, and extended university programs.

The challenge to universities over the last decade
and in the next is to develop marketing strategies to respond to changes in demand, and also to stimulate demand
for new services. While some public institutions made
major changes in their marketing, financing, and program
review strategies in the early 1970s, it has only been
within the last five years that most institutions have
given serious attention to external marketing and the establishment of clear priorities over internal allocation of
resources among competing academic programs. Also, use
of program evaluation and analysis of production functions
and costs to guide decision making is a relatively recent
practice in most universities. It may be argued that the
end of an era of steady enrollment growth in some ways
has been beneficial to institutions in providing both the
impetus and the time necessary for rigorous self-examination
and program reorientation. This is, however, an optimistic
view of the results of stabilized or declining student enrollments and restrictive state and federal funding policies.

Where funding for higher education institutions has
been reduced due to declining student demand, resource
limitations have affected the texture of academic life. Even
though there has always been competition for resources
within institutions, it would appear that the degree of
discretion for institutional academic administrators and
faculty in allocation of resources has not been so limited
since the 1930s. Increased competition for scarce resources
has affected the quality of academic life in higher education institutions, a fact that has become all too evident to
many faculty, administrators, and students over the past
decade. Even if we accept that public higher education

institutions will use their resources more effectively, the extent to which limited resources will impede the achievement of educational goals must still be ascertained.

As noted in Chapter Five, limited resources initially reduce the incentive for institutions to implement new programs and modes of instruction. Although there is impressive evidence of the successful integration of instructional innovation in public institutions during the past decade, there are also numerous examples of promising programs that have not been proposed out of the expectation that new initiatives would not be supported. Many innovative programs have not been funded for more than short periods of time and have not found their way into institutional budget bases.

In addition to the inhibition of innovation, institutions typically have had fewer resources to provide financial aid and special opportunities for students from low-income families, or students with special needs such as the handicapped and elderly. Some success has been achieved in increasing low-income, minority, and disadvantaged student enrollments in higher education over the past 15 years. However, low-income and minority student enrollments have stabilized or declined in some states during the 1980s. Much of the previous success in enrolling minorities and the disadvantaged may be attributed to federal, state, and institutional financial support for these students, a commitment that unfortunately has not been maintained.[2] Further, we have learned that simply enabling low-income, minority, and disadvantaged students to enroll in higher education institutions is not sufficient for them to achieve their educational goals. These students must demonstrate the capability and persistence required to obtain a degree. Counseling, tutoring, and other special educational services appear to increase the persistence of students who, due to a variety of physical, economic, social, and other factors, do not receive adequate preparation for advanced learning. The constraints on student financial assistance and university budgets generally imposed by federal and state governments have led some institutions to reduce the provision of special educational opportunities to low-income and other students not sufficiently prepared for university study.

Another problem faced by universities under financial restraint relates to faculty composition and renewal, particularly in responding to demands for affirmative action

and equal pay for women. If public higher education objectives include stimulation of institutions to achieve "proportionality" in the sexual, racial, and ethnic composition
of faculty, it may be observed that this objective is much
less likely to be achieved under financial restraint. Using
accepted methods of projecting faculty vacancies and renewal opportunities, without substantial increases in the
numbers of positions available for hiring in higher education institutions, sexual and racial proportionality is unlikely to be achieved even if only female and minority faculty are hired. A financial steady state will tend to
maintain existing staffing patterns. Even if some existing
positions are freed through normal attrition and as a result of program evaluation and termination, it is likely
that steady-state resource limitations will prolong existing
problems in meeting affirmative action goals. In addition,
the ability of institutions to equalize salary levels so that
there is no discrimination on the basis of sex is severely
constrained under financial restraint. While legal resolution of this issue is emerging in court decisions, the willingness of state governments to provide funding necessary
to comply with demands such as those for equal pay for
women and comparable worth has not been established. At
least one state has explicitly resisted implementation of an
equal-pay-for-equal-work court decision.

The dilemma of managing human resources under restraint was explored in Chapter Four. The threats of
staff demoralization and loss of talented faculty under restraint are real, as are the risks and liabilities faced by
institutions that cannot maintain safe and healthy work
environments. It is ironic that in many instances universities have had to raise prices charged to students to receive an education while the quality of education and of
university facilities has declined. Reduced financial resources will limit institutional goal achievement in the
areas of instructional innovation, student educational access, faculty and student affirmative action, and faculty
compensation.

Without stating all the potential effects of financial
restraint, it may be concluded that institutions and state-
level decision makers should understand that static enrollment levels are not a certainty for all higher education
institutions in the next decade. As the past decade has
shown, some institutions will not survive under financial
restraint because of their inability to implement new pro-

grams and to reallocate existing human and financial resources so as to continue attracting students. The loss of
benefits in universities from resource constraint in the
next decade will depend considerably upon the terms under
which state governments fund off-campus degree and nondegree instructional programs, the responsiveness of institutions to the threat of enrollment loss, and whether state
funding continues to be enrollment driven.

State funding policies for off-campus, nondegree,
and other outreach programs will exert a strong effect on
institutional academic planning strategy, as noted in Chapter Five. State governments have generally not provided
financial support to universities in any way comparable to
that given to community colleges for degree- and nondegree-
oriented off-campus instructional programs. In part, state
policies may be attributed to differentiation of function
established in state postsecondary education master plans.
Also, reductions in state revenues caused by economic recession in the early 1980s and competition for state funds
from other public service areas such as health, unemployment compensation, and criminal justice have reduced state
funding for higher education. Perhaps as a consequence
of these factors most states have not pursued a policy of
increasing university access to students through off-campus
enrollment incentives in state-funding formulas.

The second set of conditions that will affect the financing of higher education institutions pertains to the
extent of reallocation of existing curricula. In a period
of stable or declining enrollment, academic program review
to curtail or eliminate some programs appears necessary in
order to establish new programs. Curricula offered by
many traditional public universities and colleges are intended to provide students with the opportunity to pursue
divers academic subjects in the arts and sciences, to prepare students for graduate study, and to enable students
to obtain employment after graduation. Although undergraduate curricula include some professional programs, the
primary focus of instruction has been on the liberal arts
and sciences. Motivated by student demand shifts and the
desire to maintain or increase state funding, many universities have shifted faculty resources to provide more
professionally oriented content in areas such as business
administration, engineering, agriculture, and computer
sciences. Nevertheless, many public research-oriented universities have not deemed it desirable to respond to student

demand in the same manner in which community colleges and some public and private institutions have responded. Given that state government funding comprises a major portion of the operating revenues of public universities, assuming that states will to some extent continue to provide funding to public institutions on the basis of enrollment, the decision to maintain existing curricula is tantamount to acceptance of stabilized or declining real financial resources.

The assumption that state funding will continue to be based on enrollment is questionable, since in most instances present funding is not provided entirely on this basis even though enrollment-driven formulas are used to calculate major components of public university and college budgets. Part I of this book has anticipated the need for institutions to propose marginal increases in funding that are not related strictly to changes in overall enrollment levels. Such proposals should focus attention on the impact of shifts in student demand and the desirability of maintaining minimum, or critical mass, levels of academic program and breadth quality. Part of the purpose of the critical mass resource management approach is to provide the academic planning and budgeting procedures needed to advance nonenrollment-driven resource maintenance and acquisition proposals at institutional, systemwide, and state government levels.

In summary, increased goal achievement in universities coping with financial restraint will in most instances require establishment of financial incentives by state governments. However, incentives to adapt will also have to be developed and sustained within institutions. Faculty, administrator, and student resolve to accept more responsibility for sustaining the vitality of academic programs and campus life while adapting to new conditions will be tested mightily by restraint. As noted in the following section, adaptation may be facilitated through the implementation of improvements in university academic program resource management.

CRITICAL MASS ACADEMIC RESOURCE
MANAGEMENT AND DECISION MAKING

The reform in university academic resource management proposed in this book is implementation of the critical mass and core resource approach outlined in Chapter Three. Part I has attempted to demonstrate that nonenrollment-based academic resource management is both appropriate and necessary to guide resource planning, program review, and budget allocation within universities. Further, it has been argued that the critical mass approach will have a favorable impact on how university plans and budgets are evaluated by multicampus university administrators and state budget decision makers.

The approach to academic program resource management presented here is essentially an effort in improved system design and implementation in the manner advocated by Michael, Churchman, and other planning and management researchers, that is, an interactive and participative coordination of management tasks.[3] The use of a rationalized management system for planning and decision making, as opposed to less formalized procedures, is viewed as necessary to guide both short- and long-term academic resource management. It has been posited that employment of a structured academic resource management process that includes the collection and analysis of data on academic unit organization and performance is useful in order to track the myriad of academic activities that characterize the contemporary university.

The purposes of the critical mass academic resource management model are to facilitate internal planning, negotiation, and priority setting of academic program resource utilization under financial restraint, and also to enable public universities to justify external resource acquisition on a basis other than student enrollment levels. The critical mass approach establishes an institutional academic planning process and an information base to permit establishing priorities in academic program development. These tasks are accomplished through analysis of existing breadth and depth of faculty expertise in instruction and research at the subdisciplinary level and through identification of subdisciplinary areas in which academic units would like to provide instruction and research in the future.

Critical mass program elements are defined as those portions of the curricular and research activities of a unit essential to achievement of instructional and research goals as defined by the academic unit. Critical mass denotes the level of curricular offerings and research that academic units cannot reduce and still maintain programs that fulfill their objectives within the overall mission of the uni-

versity. Critical mass program size and core resource requirements are established by academic unit faculty and
then negotiated with academic senate planning and curriculum committees and institutional administrations similar
to the manner in which academic plans and budgets are
presently reviewed in many institutions. However, under
critical mass, resources will be allocated on the basis of
clearer, better-defined, and more comparable academic
program and disciplinary characteristics.

Definition of critical mass requires careful examination of institutional academic programs to determine existing and desired subdisciplinary depth and breadth. This
is accomplished through analysis of existing curricular
offerings and future goals by areas of instructional and
research specialization. Core resource requirements are
based on the analysis of existing and planned breadth of
the curriculum, aggregate student enrollment, course enrollment, frequency of course offerings, course type (lab,
lecture, siminar), and faculty teaching workload. All
these factors are then related to academic unit and campus
academic missions. A summary of existing programs by
subdiscipline, with supporting statistical data, is employed
to establish methods for maintaining existing academic program strengths, priorities for future academic program development, student enrollment targets, faculty and staff
personnel plans, academic program review schedules, and
the allocation of budgets to academic units.

Critical mass provides a system for academic resource planning and management as opposed to less formalized procedures. It may be used for both incremental
program change decisions and for comprehensive development, modification, or termination of entire academic programs. The critical mass approach may be employed by a
single institution that has negotiated its mission with state
government or within a multicampus university system. Deployment of the critical mass and core approach in a multicampus university is intended to assist the development of
systemwide academic planning and resource allocation priorities. At the multiinstitutional level, critical mass planning can improve systemwide academic program coordination,
as well as program review and budgeting, and can reduce
the amount of central information collection and processing
necessary to carry out these functions.

It must be acknowledged that even though a number
of criteria were employed to test the critical mass approach

theoretically and also in pilot application in several institutions, as discussed in Chapter Three, the evidence presented for evaluation is incomplete. Careful empirical evaluation cannot be accomplished until the model is implemented thoroughly in a university or in selected academic units of an institution. Universities are encouraged to test the methodology presented here as a means of verifying the hypotheses and evidence presented in support of the critical mass methodology.

ACCEPTANCE OF CRITICAL MASS BY STATE GOVERNMENT

With regard to the potential impact of the critical mass approach on state-level budgeting, the advantages of shifting from enrollment-based resource generation criteria to nonenrollment program criteria in a period of stable or declining enrollment were argued in Chapter Three. Critical mass would attempt to justify financing on the basis of breadth and depth of instruction and research necessary in a discipline and minimum levels of resources required to provide essential curricula. Although the critical mass data base permits the analysis of student demand by level and mode of instruction correlated with a number of disciplinary and instructional variables, it does not concentrate upon shifts in student demand, except as one factor indicating change in disciplinary demand.

In evaluation of nonenrollment-driven budget strategy in Chapters Three and Five it was noted that state decision makers would probably prefer to continue using enrollment-driven methods to fund universities. However, in some cases in the past the "prices" or subsidies paid by states for different university enrollment mixes have changed. Consequently, there is some precedent for state government acceptance of university funding proposals based upon differential instructional costs. Even though critical mass facilitates cost analysis, as noted later in this chapter, the most important element in using the approach for resource negotiation is not cost but the nature of change in academic disciplines and the implications of change for faculty staffing and support funding.

The most obvious external application for critical mass in defense of existing academic programs is at the point where state review agencies threaten program reduction on the basis of enrollment decline. The critical mass approach argues that higher education institutions have to maintain academic unit staffing levels in order to meet university curricular objectives regardless of student-faculty ratios and formulas previously established to guide budget decisions. At the university level, it is not unreasonable to expect acceptance of this strategy for maintaining existing academic program strength and for new academic program development, given strong leadership and articulation from the executive (presidents and academic provosts). However, probabilities for acceptance of critical mass by state government will be affected by the willingness of institutions to place detailed academic program data in front of state officials. The risks inherent in such disclosure were discussed in Chapter Two, that is, that universities want to be very careful in the use of academic workload and performance data to guard against misinterpretation by state officials.

Acceptance of the academic program based arguments that support critical mass as a method for determining state funding by state decision makers and budgeteers will depend upon a number of factors, the most important of which is probably the impact on state funding levels. Critical mass may not always supply the strongest rationale for state budget negotiation. In some instances universities may find it easier to make budget augmentation requests based upon arguments such as the necessity for state fiscal allocations to keep pace with the rate of price inflation for goods and services (utility prices, faculty salaries, and so forth), the necessity for meeting projected average costs of providing programs to meet student demand, and improved efficiency and management of the university. Institutional decision makers may perceive the critical mass approach as unfeasible for state-level resource justification. Without rejecting its selective applicability in defense of specific academic programs, it may be concluded that the principal use of the approach is in institutional and multicampus academic resource planning, decision making, and management. However, where critical mass budgeting can be negotiated with state officials, it is clearly preferable to enrollment-based budgeting under conditions of stable or declining enrollment. Alternatively, where enrollments are increasing, critical mass may be useful in arguing for augmentations above the enrollment-driven base.

Part II of this book has presented the argument for per-unit subsidies (that is, strict enrollment-based budgeting) as a state budgeting methodology. Throughout this book it has been acknowledged that the critical mass and per-unit subsidy arguments are essentially competing paradigms, and that their use depends on the strategic financing benefits provided to universities and state government in competition over resources. Critical mass provides academic program and financial flexibility to institutions. The principal advantage of the per-unit subsidy approach from the institutional perspective is increased financial management flexibility, reduced costs of accountability, and greater opportunity for setting market strategies.

Judgment of the relative utility of these approaches assumes fundamentally that universities are spenders and state governments want to minimize spending. This may not always be the case. Consequently, in some instances state officials may be quite receptive to critical mass budgeting proposals. However, state budgeteer interests in expenditure minimization will be served best by the per-unit subsidy approach where specific enrollment conditions and funding conventions apply: where average costs are used to determine unit budget decrements under conditions of declining enrollments and where marginal costs are employed to set budget increments under conditions of increasing enrollments. These combinations enable the state to cut university budgets most easily. On the other hand, critical mass aids universities in resisting such cuts. Where the critical mass approach is applied exclusively for purposes of improving internal institutional management and is not employed in state budget negotiation, integration of critical mass into the institutional budget process is the key to its utility. While the critical mass approach can operate as a "stand-alone" academic planning system, the view presented in this book is that institutions should utilize critical mass integrally in budgeting. Successful implementation of critical mass and core resource concepts to reform institutional budgeting must comprehend the characteristics that typify university budgeting.

REFORM OF THE UNIVERSITY BUDGET PROCESS: WEAKNESSES OF BASE BUDGETING

In most universities budgeting takes place within a relatively centralized decision system. Budgetary planning, decision making, and control is generally performed in the university budget office under the authority of the president, assisted in some cases by faculty budget committees and institutional research and planning staff. In most instances key faculty personnel decisions that influence budgeting are made by a faculty committee and a provost after academic-unit review has been rendered. Annual budget preparation guidelines are generally issued centrally by the budget office and sent to academic units. Budgets are prepared according to guidelines, are reviewed by departments, schools, and colleges, and are then submitted to the university budget office. The central institutional budget office reviews academic unit budget proposals for faculty positions, academic and nonacademic support, supplies, equipment, and other types of proposed spending. The budget is usually arranged by object classification categories (for example, personal services, materials, and supplies) and may be explained by some accompanying narrative. Workload and other statistics may be included in budget justification statements. Budget requests normally are aggregated into an institutional budget by the chief budget officer for review by academic administrators and in some cases a faculty budget committee.

Key budget decisions are usually made by provosts and academic vice-presidents and then reviewed by presidents. Presidents seldom review academic-unit budgets in detail. However, budget processes vary considerably. In some universities the president plays an important role in budgeting; in others this is not the case. Likewise, in some universities faculty committees are very involved. In others, budget decisions are made by the provost and executive budget officers and are not reviewed to any degree by representatives of the faculty. Some universities employ an academic as the key budget officer, assisted by an administrative staff. Under most forms of organization the most important academic budget decision maker is the provost and academic vice-president or vice-chancellor. After institutional budget decisions have been made, systemwide budgets are prepared in multicampus systems. The budget is then advanced to the state government by the university board of regents or trustees. Once the state budget is enacted, the university's share is allocated internally according to the amount of spending authority received from the state, from the state board of regents or trustees, and from the executive budget staff of systemwide university offices in the case of multiinstitutional systems. Institutional budgets are allocated to academic units proportionally as submitted, except where decisions made at a higher level prescribe otherwise.

University budgeting does not conform to the standard model of public budgeting. The phases of the budget process that pertain in most government organizations are often not fully present in university budgeting. Budgeting may be defined generally as a planning and decision process that consists of two phases: (1) preparation and (2) execution. Each of these phases may be divided into four subcomponents. Within the preparation phase are (1) issuance of instructions and preparation of estimates, (2) budget analysis, (3) negotiation, and (4) decision and enactment. Budget execution consists of (1) allocation of the approved budget, (2) allotment and spending, (3) monitoring and controlling of expenditures, and (4) audit and evaluation. However, in many universities some of these subphases are truncated or have never developed. In fact, budgeting in some universities does not operate as a systematic decision process in the sense described by the above model. Rather, budget preparation often consists of issuance of instructions, preparation of estimates, and then decision making; that is, the subphases of analysis and negotiation are represented only partially or not at all. Likewise, in budget execution the components of monitoring and control and of audit and evaluation often are not present to any degree.

An explanation of why university budgeting deviates from the model is that academic budgeting is budgeting on the base in the extreme. Base budgeting may be defined generally as a procedure wherein annual budget increments, or decrements where revenues decline, are made as pro rata adjustments to the budget approved for the previous year. Budgeting on the base exhibits the virtues of simplicity and certainty. Negotiation and analysis under this system are given far less emphasis than under alternative budgeting methodologies such as program or zero-base budgeting. In fact, these other approaches were developed to improve analysis of program alternatives and decision making in budgeting.

Why does budgeting on the base persist in universities in particular? Is analysis unnecessary or merely unwanted? Universities may be characterized as very conservative institutions in terms of their decision-making

methods. This is true in part because the scholarly production of universities--research and instruction--results
from a process where slow, deliberate, patient attention is
rewarded. The very notion of the ivory tower is that of a
place free from the rush and noise of the rest of the world.
Insulation, and in some instances isolation, is viewed typically as a necessary condition for scholarly productivity.
And while university faculty may be liberal thinkers, they
generally behave as the most conservative of bureaucrats
in matters of organization. This is often revealed in a
most frustrating way in organizational politics and decision
making.

While a number of factors cause university decision-
making and administrative functions to be performed slowly
and cautiously, perhaps none is as prominent as the faculty
hiring and promotion process. Similar to the manner described by Kaufman in evaluating the hiring and development of forest rangers,[4] universities screen and select faculty extremely carefully to produce a professional cadre of
people who revere the virtues of introspection, carefulness
of thought and action, persistence, and a passion for exploration of complexity in relationships between ideas,
states of matter, and events. The organizational preferences of this professional class are for stability and certainty to facilitate rigorous experimentation, observation,
and documentation of findings, that is, scholarship. In
institutions where such working conditions are sought, it
is little wonder that strong preferences for stability and
certainty in resource decision making are present.

However, while university faculty and administrators
often behave as the most conservative of bureaucrats, the
activities of universities are not organized and do not operate bureaucratically. Scholarship is performed at once
in isolation and also with a high degree of interrelation-
ship between faculty working in separate disciplines, subdisciplines, and academic units. Scholarly relationships
develop conceptually as well as organizationally. While
universities reveal relatively stable patterns of communication and influence organizationally, the process of discovery of new knowledge itself is ofttimes highly unpre-
dictable. There is no clear and certain organizational
formula for success in discovery. Thus the scholarly educational production process exhibits the characteristics of
matrix rather than bureaucratic organization. The organizational form for university resource allocation is, however,

much more bureaucratic and emphasizes stability, continuity, and certainty. Resource stability and protection of the educational production process from external interference are the objectives of a bureaucratically organized resource allocation process. This helps to explain why universities are so difficult to change organizationally and also in their processes of production.

Another factor that helps to explain the preference for stability and also the degree of centralization present in university budgeting is that historically universities have sought to minimize their central administrative overhead. While the modern "multiversity" belies this observation with its cast of hundreds or thousands of administrative staff, throughout their history individual institutions have attempted to allocate most of their resources to scholarship and its support rather than to academic administration. The idea of managing scholarship in the sense of guiding it rather than administering to it as it occurs is anathema to most university faculty. Budget analysis, negotiation, control, and evaluation all require expenditure of considerable resources for information gathering and administration. The increase in allocation of university financial resources to these activities that has occurred over the past decade may be explained by accountability and competitive pressures exerted interinstitutionally in multicampus systems and from state and federal governments. However, these are pressures to which universities have yielded with reluctance. Further, as indicated in Chapter One, the historical development of universities gave the president responsibility for administrative functions such as budgeting. Resource allocation decision authority and external negotiation responsibility was concentrated in the person and office of the president. Given the weight of their external university responsibilities, and attempting to function without large or highly trained administrative staff, presidents could not afford much budget complexity. While resource allocation complexity has increased significantly over time, university budgeting and presidential involvement in it has not changed very much at many institutions.

All this appears to have caused university budgeting to be incremental and base-line oriented. Under such an approach, broad faculty participation, extensive negotiation of budgets, and comprehensive analysis of budget alternatives are not only unnecessary, they are unwanted.

Close budget scrutiny typically raises thorny issues such as need, justification, equity, efficiency, and productivity. These issues are expensive to address in terms of the cost of information, that is, as a result of the need for information systems design and comprehensive data collection and analysis. Budget issues are also expensive to address in the subphases of negotiation, decision, and evaluation in terms of time, task organization, and risk of conflict. Other things being equal, universities and most other complex organizations prefer to avoid such costs, continuing instead to use their financial and personnel resources in scholarly production, rather than in administration or management control.[5]

If university academic budget decisions are made incrementally in relatively stable adjustments to the base where moderate increases in resources are available and also as financial resources become more scarce, then what criteria are used in evaluating university academic budgets? Wildavsky explains that almost all budget decision making reveals certain characteristics, that is, budgeting is

1. historical and incremental in that the resource level possessed by a unit or organization is likely to be retained. Therefore, the criterion for allocating new resources or for reducing the budget is proration;

2. specialized in that the activities and budgets of academic units vary considerably in organization and performance. The criteria used to evaluate budgets are weighted, and criteria may be weighted differentially across academic units;

3. fragmented in that in evaluating budgets, different criteria are likely to be applied at different points by different participants. In addition, criteria applied to one type of decision may not relate well to other types of decisions, for example, a faculty budget committee decision on allocation of faculty positions in academic units may not be coordinated with budgetary decisions affecting library acquisitions or computer support;

4. repetitive in that budget functions are repeated annually and decision criteria are likely to persist from year to year, making it difficult to change the existing order of programmatic allocation and the disposition of influence in the budgetary process.[6]

The factors listed above indicate some of the characteristics of criteria used in university budgeting. The most prominent budget decision criterion generally is the size of the previous budget allocation, which, in turn, often is related to historical levels of student enrollment. However, secondary criteria may include the following:

1. Instructional performance as indicated in annual (or fall-term) student enrollment statistics and trends; instructional service load (instruction provided to students seeking degrees in other academic programs); faculty teaching loads; course size and mode of instruction (lecture, seminar, laboratory, and so forth); external factors that influence instructional demand such as the employment market for graduates.

2. Research cirteria measured by variables that include faculty publication record, levels and trends in grant and contract funding, scholarly recognition for research accomplishments (for example, Nobel prizes), amount and type of involvement in research organizations, and meetings and conferences.

3. Reputational criteria as measured by instructional and research performance and by faculty membership on important academic senate or other university committees; accreditation reviews; national academic program rankings; leadership in scholarly and professional associations; community, government, or business support; local or national awards for faculty and the academic unit.

4. Budget justification criteria including quality of budget presentation both in terms of clarity of written argument and the use of quantitative data to support proposals; relationship between initiatives proposed and institutional, system, and state academic master plan guidelines; the manner in which increased or sustained budget support would increase the satisfaction of institutional, community, or social objectives; and how indexes of program value noted under the three other sets of criteria are woven into budget justification, for example, student demand, job market demand, placement of graduates and starting salary levels, quality of scholarship, degree of community support, and ability to raise extramural research funding.

The mix and nonmutual exclusivity of secondary criteria employed in university budgeting is indicated by these sets of criteria. However, these criteria typically balance, rather than counter, the power of the two most important budget determinants, the size of the base and student enrollment demand. Consequently, they may be applied only at the margin, for example, in determining the allocation of new money or in budget reduction. Due to the conservatism of university budgeting, and particularly where financial crisis is not present, the base trends tend to remain relatively fixed, with small periodic adjustments made at the margin, that is, less than 5 percent. In this respect university budgeting is not unlike budgeting for the federal or state government. Budget critics have argued that stability is an important product of such a system of resource decision making.[7]

A significant problem resulting from university budgeting on the base is that it appears to impede adaptation to environmental change and may not respond well to state government demands for increased accountability. The nonanalytic character of base budgeting does not respond well in that it does not provide arguments or data in a manner that justifies maintenance of existing levels of support, much less appropriation of new funding. Other problems with budgeting on the base include the absence of faculty participation and budget negotiation, and weakness in budget control. As noted, base budgeting is generally highly centralized and in many universities does not operate within a systematic decision process. Additionally, there may be little negotiation with academic units during budget preparation or allocation. Rather, the budget is assumed by central decision makers to be proposed on the base, and spending authority, once received, is distributed to academic units without much analysis. Negotiation does not occur under this budget methodology. The absence of faculty participation reduces university budgeting to a sequence of exchanges of memorandums and forms, without much opportunity to argue for new initiatives. The advantages of certainty are assumed to outweigh those of analysis or redistribution.

Beyond problelms in budget preparation, university budgeting typically reveals weakness in execution. Academic units and institutional decision makers often are not able to evaluate spending as it occurs; in some cases neither can schools, colleges, or the central institutional budget office. While few critics would expect university budgets to be monitored and controlled as closely as budgets for city governments, for example, in many universities virtually no timely expenditure reporting and monitoring activity takes place. Even worse, clear expenditure records may not be available at the point when the budget for the next year is prepared. Such weaknesses in monitoring, control, and reporting reduce institutional capability for resource management and make it impossible to provide data for budget and program evaluation. Such analysis becomes more necessary as financial resources are constrained.

Budgeting without a satisfactory information base reduces an institution's ability to estimate the consequences of redistributing the budget, of implementing new programs, or of terminating existing programs. It also inhibits the systematic development and application of methods to reduce expenditures without cutting programs.

In a period of reduced or shifting enrollment demand and financial scarcity, the absence of information to justify the budget externally or to analyze how the budget may be reallocated internally are significant weaknesses revealed by budgeting on the base. These weaknesses supply part of the rationale for developing and implementing the critical mass and core resource academic management system. Where pressures for external accountability increase and when resources become scarce, a number of new and different issues must be addressed in planning and budgeting. The need for analysis of resource justification, equity, efficiency, productivity, cost, and performance challenges budgeting on the base. The pressures of accountability and resource competition predictably require universities to devote more resources to information gathering, to analysis of information, and to refinement of administrative planning, decision, and control procedures. Without such pressures there would be far less need to design and implement the critical mass and core resource management in universities. However, for better or worse, requirements for accountability and competition for resources characterize the contemporary environment within which public universities operate.

THE CRITICAL MASS INFORMATION SYSTEM:
BUDGETING AND COST ANALYSIS

The choice for university academic management under financial restraint appears not to be whether to plan, ana-

lyze, and control, but how to do these tasks systematically. The key element in planning, analysis, and management control is information, that is, how information is
collected, verified, filed, reformulated, manipulated, analyzed, compared, and utilized for decision. The critical
mass and core approach attempts to provide information
necessary for the maintenance and development of academic
programs to guide the allocation of resources and to permit evaluation of the outcomes of program and resource
decisions. Budgeting under the critical mass and core resource approach requires that budgets be prepared by
academic units and reviewed, allocated, and controlled according to critical mass subdisciplinary specialization. At
the institutional level, analysis is performed and decisions
implemented by curricular areas of specialization rather
than by the more general academic-unit categories used in
most academic budgeting. Critical mass subdisciplinary
classifications and core resource costs for maintaining, expanding, or reducing subdisciplines serve as the basis for
budget proposal and for budget allocation once decisions
have been reached.

The key use of critical mass as an academic program information system in budgeting is in setting priorities. The definition of existing and planned subdisciplinary specializations, critical mass size, and core resource
use serves the most important task in budget preparation
and decision making--determination of funding priorities by
programmatic area. In applying the critical mass approach in academic unit budgeting, faculty and other personnel costs, and all academic and administrative overhead
support, costs are allocated across the critical mass areas
of disciplinary specialization. All of the I&R (instructional
and research) budget is distributed by subdisciplinary area.
In this way the critical mass budget is similar in intent
to program budgeting in that all costs are captured by
program and subprogram classification rather than only in
object of expenditure categories. Each specialization may
be treated as a decision unit, that is, one that may be
ranked against existing or proposed units and funded or
not funded as a distinct entity. In this way subdisciplinary budgeting is like zero-base budgeting. However, due
to the interrelationships among subdisciplinary specializations in the curriculum, it may not always be appropriate
to treat each subdiscipline as a decision unit. Instead,
subdisciplinary clusters may be aggregated for this purpose.

While areas of academic specialization are normally closely related within the curriculum, the strength of ties between these subunits may be evaluated closely under the critical mass system.

Programmatic and cost relationships may be defined more precisely under critical mass budgeting. In some cases subdisciplinary specializations or clusters of specializations may be treated as cost centers for purposes of expenditure monitoring, control, and evaluation. This is particularly the case in budgeting organization research units. Subdisciplinary budgeting is intended to improve academic unit and institutional use of analysis in budget preparation and justification, and also control, evaluation, and reporting. For example, high- and low-cost subdisciplinary areas may be identified and explained more precisely. Instructional performance by academic unit may be evaluated more carefully in terms of workload, course mode, curricular and disciplinary organization, and cost.

Subdisciplinary organization of the curriculum permits each academic unit, or each subdisciplinary area or cluster, to function as a cost center for purposes of accounting and cost analysis. Direct costs of instruction and research may be determined by subdiscipline. Indirect costs for one or multiple academic units may be allocated by subdiscipline using rough estimation (for example, proration by FTE students or faculty), sampling, or comprehensive analysis of actual expenses to determine appropriate formulas. Analysis of costs and their distribution by academic unit and by subdisciplinary area can clarify and justify the relative costs of instruction and research. Such analysis also permits costs to be indexed by subdiscipline against various measures of performance such as student credit hours, faculty time, and numbers of courses taught. This information can improve budget projection accuracy, justification, decision, control, and evaluation. In circumstances where academic units are considered for termination or merger under financial stress, critical mass subdisciplinary data can indicate the budgetary consequences of termination or of merging subdisciplines into other departments, schools, or colleges.

Critical mass cost models for academic units may be developed, varying in complexity from simple algorithms for instructional costs to more complex models capturing all the instructional, research, and other activity of the unit. Such models enable comparison of the cost behavior of academic units under different conditions, or comparisons among different campuses in a multiinstitutional university. While all the caveats about noncomparability among academic units noted in Chapter Two and elsewhere in this book remain, comparative analysis can reveal more than the simple conclusion that one unit or subdisciplinary area is more expensive than another. Importantly, good cost data can demonstrate how and why units or subdisciplines are more or less expensive. The availability of expense and cost data by academic unit defines the core resources under the critical mass system, that is, the minimum resource level at which an academic unit can continue to function and still satisfy its own and institutional objectives. Where opinion differs between the academic unit faculty and the school, college, or institutional academic decision makers regarding the critical mass size of the unit, cost data may be used along with performance indexes to examine the assumptions made in defining critical mass.

In addition, expenditure data provided in the critical mass and core resource information system can improve institutional and academic unit budget control. Monitoring levels and patterns of spending during the fiscal year is possible where timely (computerized) expenditure reports are provided. Expenditure reporting of this type may require significant improvements in the institutional accounting process. Expenditure-monitoring capability provides the means for improving cost control and budget forecasting, elements of financial management that typically become more important under conditions of financial stress. Identifying fixed versus variable costs by academic unit and subdiscipline is possible where critical mass expenditure data are captured in the institutional accounting system.

Knowledge of cost behavior can be important to institutions in specifying core resource levels needed to support critical mass programs and in negotiating with state government, that sets budget increments or decrements on a marginal cost basis. As noted by Spence and Weathersby,

> Many states . . . are studying marginal-cost approaches and the more precise costing of continuing activities. . . . the marginal funding approach [adds] about one third of the state dollars that would

normally follow additional students if all
costs were assumed to increase at the same
rate as enrollments increase . . . when
only variable costs are considered, an institution [that] loses students loses only
one third of the average total cost per student. Perhaps the most basic problem is
how to define a "core curriculum . . .
what resources are necessary to provide
quality programs at various levels of enrollment? Is there an enrollment minimum
below which a program should be eliminated?
These questions . . . should be the basis
of costing practices.[8]

These observations are consistent with the objectives
of the critical mass and core resource methodology. From
the institutional perspective it is useful to have the capacity to specify fixed and variable costs as a means of developing a strategy in state budget negotiation. Without
this ability universities place themselves at a distinct dis-
advantage relative to state budget analysis that, in absence of defensible institutional data, is likely to mandate
costs based upon very general data and little curricular
analysis. Further, good cost data will defend institutional
and academic unit budgeting and resource management
where it identifies the core costs that constitute critical
mass program size under various academic program and
enrollment assumptions and conditions.

BUDGET NEGOTIATION, STRATEGIC MISREPRESENTATION, AND DECISION CONTROL

In budgeting the practice of strategic misrepresentation is commonplace. As noted in Chapter Six, one type of
strategy is misrepresentation of facts, and a second is mis-
representing the consequence of failure to fund at the
level requested. Numerous ploys are used in the budget
process to maximize budget proposals and to increase the
probability of receiving the level proposed.[9] Budgeting
under the critical mass system must anticipate such behavior, whether budgets are increasing or decreasing. However, under severe financial constraints, where institutions
declare financial exigency, it may be expected that faculty

would choose to define and justify critical mass inclusively so as to increase the probability that the curriculum would remain intact.

Responsibility for definition of critical mass rests with the faculty of each academic unit. This characteristic indicates the difference between the use of critical mass for planning versus its use in budgeting. Where each academic unit and subdisciplinary area is treated as a decision unit, that is, a "go" or "no-go" decision may be made over funding and survival of the subdiscipline, the size, cost, and priority of each decision unit may be negotiated in the budget process. Critical mass recognizes the interdependence of subdisciplinary units within an academic unit and discipline. However, where priorities for survival must be set as a result of financial stress, budgeting under the critical mass approach would cause very careful evaluation of alleged interdependence both in academic units and at institutional levels.

University budgeting has been characterized as incremental base budgeting wherein costs are not identified carefully, program priorities are not set, participation is limited, negotiation does not take place, analysis is not done, and ex post budget control and program evaluation are not performed. In contrast, critical mass budgeting would not only permit but require that priorities be set within and between academic units, that costs and priorities be defended in negotiation, that analysis be performed, and that control and evaluation be utilized. As is the case in applying zero-base budgeting, it would not be possible to review each year the entire institutional budget at the subdisciplinary level because of the high analytical costs of this endeavor. Rather, each year critical mass detail would be evaluated at the margin for most academic units, but in detail for a few, for example, where potential for substantial change to the base budget is requested by the academic unit or proposed from higher levels of authority.

Disagreement over critical mass definition would require academic faculty to negotiate with school, college, and institutional decision makers over what was to be included under critical mass. Such negotiation would require careful analysis of costs and expenditure claims of critical mass and of the future subdisciplinary composition of the academic unit. As noted in discussing critical mass as an academic resource planning tool, critical mass for an

academic unit would not be fixed. Rather, it would change
as the discipline changed. The timing and degree of
change would be determined by evolution in the discipline
and also by alteration in the composition of other academic units. Hiring, retirement, and other academic personnel changes and the financial incentives provided to
stimulate adaptation to new conditions in the external environment could also affect critical mass. Financial incentives to develop new subdisciplines or to drop existing
ones could be provided internally by institutional decision
makers, externally by state government as explained in
Chapters Five and Six, or as a combination of internal
and external action.

The critical mass approach has been characterized
in this book as a decentralized decision system because
subdisciplinary status and plans are determined from the
bottom up by academic unit faculty rather than from the
top down by institutional administrators. Does the practice of critical mass budgeting centralize the process by
requiring academic unit resource proposals to be negotiated
upwardly through the decision hierarchy? The answer to
this question is that budgeting does exert a centralizing
effect on the decision system as a whole, but the resultant
process is far less centralized than is the case for most
budgetary systems presently employed in universities. This
is so because the principal analytical elements and tools
of budget negotiation, decision, and control are the critical mass subdisciplinary units about which faculty know
far more than administrators. More importantly, subdisciplinary change (growth or reduction) priorities are set at
the level of the academic unit. While institutional budget
analysts and decision makers have to be aware of the potential use of strategic misrepresentation in budgeting,
such as ranking the most valuable and productive subdisciplinary areas lowest while ranking new proposals very high
to maximize funding, these are the types of ploys that are
always faced in budget negotiation.

Budgeting by any method including critical mass
will involve strategic misrepresentation, trade-offs, risks,
competition, and disagreement over priorities. Further,
institutional decision makers will almost always hold the
upper hand in any budgetary system where there is no
legislative review of the budget. Academic senate and
faculty budget committees sometimes review budget proposals
and make recommendations to presidents and provosts, but

rarely if ever are they permitted to vote as a body over budget allocations in the way that a state legislature or Congress appropriates a budget. Although this fact may indicate the need for basic reform in institutional budgeting, such a reform is not required under critical mass budgeting. The fundamental advantage to academic units in critical mass budgeting is in giving them the responsibility for defining current and future priorities, for arguing plans and budgets according to these priorities, and negotiating resources rather than having to accept budgets merely allocated on the base without faculty participation in defining the academic implications and merits of alternative budget decisions. Because the critical mass system would require budget and academic plans to be proposed according to subdisciplinary composition on a multiyear basis, the scope of budget participation increases opportunity for the use of strategy. It also causes faculty planning and budgeting to focus on curricular development in the medium term, for example, over five years, rather than in just one year--the next budget year, as is normally the case. It gives faculty the opportunity to reallocate resources among existing subdisciplinary areas or to new areas. While constraints to flexibility are predictable-- they include high tenure ratios, responsibilities for satisfying university instructional and degree requirements, and tight budgets--the potential for earning funds in the budgeting process by proposing subdisciplinary changes increases the likelihood that such changes will be sought.

Under the critical mass system, the extent of academic unit responsiveness to changes in student demand and other factors depends in large part on how institutional decision makers use the discretion afforded them in the budget process. If financial incentives are established to reward change proposals, such as the opportunity to gain funds reallocated from another academic unit, then strategic behavior and competition in planning and budgeting will occur. Critical mass and core resource definition enables budget priorities to be funded at the institutional level by subdisciplinary area. For example, decisions would be made to allocate new resources to augment either an existing subdiscipline in physics or one in business, or to create a new subdisciplinary specialization in economics, political science, or chemistry. The ability to set incentives at the institutional level to stimulate change is an important attribute of critical mass budgeting. However, budgeting under critical mass is far less centralized than that which occurs in most universities presently.

INSTITUTIONAL REFORM RESPONSIBILITIES

The capacity for basing decisions on critical mass subdisciplinary program and cost data represents a significant improvement in the articulation of programmatic considerations in academic budgeting. It enables proactive academic resource management and strategic budgeting in external negotiation. However, implementing the system requires strong executive and faculty support, as is the case with the adoption of virtually any new approach to planning and budgeting.[10] Initially, proposals to implement the critical mass academic resource management system may be resisted by faculty perceptions that it is a threat to the status quo. Given the preferences of faculty for stability noted earlier, this reaction may be anticipated.
Institutional academic decision makers attempting to implement the critical mass approach must be willing to explain the advantages of the system and how it will operate carefully and persistently. Presidents, provosts, and faculty alike should recognize that the minimum amount of time required to implement the system completely is about five years, and certainly not less than three years. Institutional leaders need to allocate funds to budget and planning staff under the provost to assist academic units in preparing their subdisciplinary and critical mass goal statements and plans. Substantial financial resources will be consumed in designing, implementing, and maintaining the accuracy of a computerized critical mass instructional and research data base. As noted in Chapter Three, a number of information system design and implementation problems, such as whether and how on-line system capability would be made available to academic unit deans, chairpersons, and faculty, have to be addressed. As the budgetary responsibilities of academic unit heads increase considerably under critical mass as compared to base budgeting, attention must be given to academic unit staff resources and training as well.
Wildavsky has described the reasons why traditional base budgeting persists, although in modified form, despite the advancement of various reform methods, including program and zero-base budgeting.[11] Preferences for stability

and the low costs of base budgeting are not limited to academe. However, the opportunity costs of base budgeting
are apparent for many public universities. The inability
to augment or reallocate the budget and to negotiate priorities, the absence of an identifiable budget process as
opposed to a system of centralized allocation from the president's office, and the inability to justify budgets according to academic and disciplinary considerations reduce the
value of base budgeting, particularly under conditions of
financial restraint.

The opportunity costs of base budgeting in academe
result from the inability to prepare and successfully market strategic academic plans and budgets to state government and to other external university funding agencies.
The internal opportunity costs of base budgeting result
from preservation of rewards for the status quo rather
than creation of incentives for evolutionary curricular
modification in response to changes in disciplines, student
demand, and other exogenous factors. The absence of rewards and positive reinforcement in budgeting causes a
loss of faculty vitality and relevance in research. Where
incentives to change are not present, reduced research productivity and marketability may result in the loss of important faculty, weakened ability to attract high-quality
faculty and students, a decline in prestige, and less extramural research funding. In short, the opportunity and
other costs of base budgeting and the absence of incentives to change are significant when viewed over the long
term.

A determination of the relative benefits and costs
of attempting to implement the critical mass system of academic resource management must be made by institutional
decision makers prior to commitment of energy and funding
to its development. Arguments for the system have been
articulated here and at greater length in Chapter Three.
Chapter Four analyzed the condition of financial scarcity
and the phases of recognition and management of financial
stress in universities. Among the conclusions of this book
are that under conditions of financial restraint, universities need to evaluate academic activity more carefully,
manage resources more flexibly, and market more successfully to governments and the public. Implementation of
the critical mass system is intended to serve these ends.
However, no matter how promising the system appears on
paper, reform in institutional academic resource management

will not occur without significant commitment from university executives and faculty.

A recent study directed by Clark Kerr concluded that most university and college presidents are not involved to any great extent in institutional academic planning and decision making.[12]   In summarizing the study Kerr noted that only about 2 percent of 3,000 presidents are "fully involved and play a central role in academic life," and that only approximately 20 percent have any substantial involvement. This research substantiates the observation that, typically, the provost or academic vice-president is the key decision maker on institutional academic affairs. Kerr opined further that "the curriculum is a disaster area [without] a sense of intellectual purpose. . . . I place responsibility primarily upon the president as having the central role in reforming the curriculum. . . . changes of merit usually come from presidential leadership."[13]

In reviewing Kerr's comments one critic voiced a different opinion regarding the responsibility for curricular reform, as follows: "The responsibility [for student learning] lies not with the schools or with college and university presidents, or with the politicians or with the people, but with the professors. They have the power to will great change in the undergraduate curriculum. They should not be allowed to get away with pointing the finger of responsibility elsewhere."[14]

Adoption of the critical mass approach to resource planning and management assumes that responsibility for curricular planning and change rests with faculty rather than academic administrators. However, as noted by Kerr, the impetus for making major curricular changes in the past has often been supplied by presidents. In many cases presidents translate the pressures for change from the external environment into action within the institution. Additionally, we have noted that executive commitment to implementation of the critical mass system is necessary to overcome predictable institutional resistance to change. Thus, the perspective of this book is not whether faculty or presidents should be responsible for curricular change. Rather, it is that participation of both faculty and institutional executives is required. Without leadership and planning from the office of the president, it is unlikely that any significant institutionwide change in resource management and control can be implemented. From this

view, the president's commitment to and articulation of
the goals of the critical mass academic resource management system is essential in order to elicit a willingness to
act on the part of faculty and academic administrators.
Presidential leadership in justifying the need for change
and in committing financial and staff resources to implement critical mass is also necessary in order to use the
approach successfully in external resource negotiation.

With regard to implementation of the critical mass
system, the argument may be made that mere participation
by faculty, presidents, administrators, students, and other
parties is not enough. Participation in academic planning
for faculty, for example, may involve no more than attendance at departmental meetings. Participation on the part
of administrative decision makers may involve no more
than meeting with advisory committees composed of "inner
core" faculty. Participation on the part of budget staff,
institutional researchers, and academic planners may involve no more than occasional contact with decision makers
and "inner core" faculty. This type of participation does
not lead to integration of a resource planning process into
the system of academic budgeting, resource management,
and governance of a college or university.

As discussed in Chapter One, many of the first universities were planned and administered solely by faculty.
The principle of shared governance, that is, that faculty
would share the administrative responsibilities for managing
an academic institution with nonfaculty, is, in itself, a
change from the traditional notion of faculty leadership.
In a contemporary university it is a routine presumption
that many or most administrative responsibilities will be
managed by executives and staff who are not part of the
institution's teaching faculty. Despite the existence of
academic senates and senate committees, program review
committees, and executive advisory committees, institutional
management decisions typically are made by administrators after consultation with faculty. Many administrators
have been active participants in institutional academic life
as faculty members before becoming full-time administrators.
However, the diet of administration alone tends to be bland
when compared to that of an active faculty member pursuing his or her research and institutional interests with
colleagues and students. For administrators, the problem
of participation in their institution's academic life is that
external demands and ceremonial and other pressures of

office often leave too little time for interaction with faculty and students.

One remedy to this circumstance might be to reintegrate presidents and academic administrators more fully in instruction and research in the institution. This requires considerable courage, intellectual aptitude, and willingness to spend energy on the part of administrators. It also requires that they spend less of their time on administrative matters. The argument may be made that the net productivity of presidents and academic administrators would increase as a result of continued research and teaching activity. However, this is supposition without knowing more about the backgrounds and inclinations of individual presidents and administrators.

On the part of faculty, perhaps the easiest way to maintain position within a university is to pursue research with dedication, ignoring as much as possible the matters of academic unit and university administration. Where the rewards system is weighted heavily toward the demonstration of scholarship, it is rational for faculty to dedicate themselves to research and leave administrative matters to others. This explains why in many instances it is difficult to find good faculty candidates to serve as department heads or deans. The pressures and activities of administration generally make such service unattractive relative to the intrinsic satisfaction derived from scholarship. Despite this, there is some evidence to suggest that active scholars are often active participants in institutional governance. A faculty survey conducted on behalf of the Carnegie Commission found a high correlation between number of publications and committee participation for faculty working in high-quality research-oriented colleges and universities.[15] However, participation on committees may represent an institutional service surrogate for significant participation in institutional administration for many faculty.

Under conditions of financial abundance, it may be relatively easy for faculty and academic administrators to relax into limited modes of participation in institutional administration and governance. Further, it may be easiest to fall into these modes of behavior where institutions employ routine and low-profile modes of academic resource planning and management. However, relaxing into a pattern of nonparticipation is not consistent with the concept of shared governance given such reverent lip service within

the academic community. It is also not likely to result in
the adaptive and competitive behavior conducive to survival
under conditions of financial stress. The point of this argument is not that faculty should attempt to participate out
of a belief that such action is ethical or socially responsible. To the contrary, the argument is that planning will
not work, that resource decision making will not lead to
desirable consequences, that goals defined for institutions
will be shortsighted or incorrect, unless faculty not only
participate in the academic planning and management process but, in fact, take control of it. This is true according to the rationale developed here because administrators
need information from faculty about the nature of development in subdisciplines and disciplines, and also about research activities and instructional innovation in order to
guide institutional resource decision making.

As discussed in Part I of this book, to implement
the critical mass system decision makers need more than
quantitative proxies, such as student credit hours per
full-time employment faculty (SCU/FTEF) or average unit
costs, to understand the complexity of the academic activities they must represent to other sectors of the institution
and to organizations external to the university. Presidents
and other decision makers need to understand the texture
and quality of institutional academic activity in order to
act effectively as "boundary spanning" agents in negotiating missions and resources within multiinstitutional university systems and with state governments. A dedication
to openness in communication and to discovery of what
Trow has termed deep knowledge about the numerous and
diverse academic activities of an institution by faculty
and academic decision makers will increase the probability
for sustaining institutional vitality in an era of steady-
state or declining student enrollments and public ennui
toward higher education.[16]

From this perspective, the critical mass approach
provides the means for developing an information system
to improve strategic planning and resource management in
universities. High-quality information that reveals the
character of academic activity is viewed here to be essential both for the purposes of internal institutional management and also for external marketing of the value of
the institution. Few modern private corporations would
attempt to make significant product development or marketing policy changes without engaging in market research

to define the nature of consumer preferences and behavior relative to product and service attributes supplied by the firm. Similarly, it would seem wise for higher education institutions to engage in market analysis as an important element of strategic planning. Good marketing does not attempt to sell products or services that do not meet consumer preferences. Rather, marketing consists of defining the nature of consumer preferences for particular attributes of products or services and meeting these preferences through product development, pricing, distribution, and other actions.[17] While many of the attributes of the services provided by universities should be determined by faculty and administrative judgment of what ought to constitute the curricular and research activities of the institution consistent with its mission, there is considerable opportunity in most universities for adaptation of services to better meet consumer preferences. Further, there are significant opportunities to improve the marketing of existing services through modification of existing policies that guide service pricing, distribution, advertising, promotion, and provision.

Resistance to the adoption of what may be termed the marketing concept in universities may be anticipated. However, a combination of threat produced by financial stress and changes in state funding methods for institutions appears to be stimulating some faculty and administrators to regard market research and policy as an important component of institutional strategic planning and management. The critical mass system is intended to supply the information necessary to engage in market research, service development, and marketing. While this approach to academic management is new to universities, the perspective of this book is that the critical mass system may be adapted to serve the information needs of both internal university academic management and external marketing for resource acquisition. This is the case under present methods of state funding for universities and even more appropriate where states adopt funding procedures such as equimarginal budgeting as outlined in Part II of this book.

Under the equimarginal unit subsidy methodology, marketing, strategic planning, and management become even more important to universities. If institutions are encouraged to compete more freely and are permitted to manage their financial and academic resources less encumbered by state government budget management controls and market regulation, the advantages of developing high-quality information for planning and strategic management are compounded. The critical mass approach encourages proactive resource planning, management, and control in universities to cope with constraints imposed by financial austerity and equivocal public support for higher education. Where state government funding practices encourage interinstitutional competition and adaptation, proactive responses to resource scarcity and public educational preferences will be rewarded.

CRITICISMS OF STATE GOVERNMENT ENROLLMENT MARKET BUDGETING

The second major area of reform discussed in this book is implementation of an enrollment market approach for state government funding of universities. The argument developed in Chapters Five and Six is that state government budget management control is often applied inappropriately to restrict university expenditure flexibility. Control is justified in part out of an understandable concern by state officials that the budget remain balanced and also because officials wish to retain discretion over university resource allocation. However, the close control by budgeteers sometimes appears a waste of public revenues, time, and energy both for state government and higher education institutions. Further, budget, institutional, and market controls inhibit the ability of universities to meet the instructional preferences of citizens in a cost-effective manner. The view was advanced that options for instructional service production would increase under a system where university services could be purchased by state budget officials using per-unit subsidies. Additionally, it was argued that the threat of reimposition of budget management control may substitute for actual control, given that state regulation restricting interinstitutional competition is removed.

The change in state budget control orientation advocated in this book could be implemented without substantial implication for the politics of the state budget process. For state budgetary control to be applied more effectively, permitting greater institutional spending flexibility and competitive behavior, it would appear necessary to educate executive and legislative decision makers and

control agency staff more completely as to the undesirable
and sometimes unintended outcomes of their decisions to
control. Of course, this is no small task, but since virtually no budget process reform is necessary, the system
described may have some chance for implementation over
time. This may occur particularly where public concern
over the effectiveness of government expenditure and other
exogenous factors reduce government revenues so as to
cause closer review of expenditure priorities and budget
control practices. However, before state budget and market control practices are evaluated in earnest, chief executive officers in state government will have to understand
that to leave budgeting to the budgeteers and regulation
to state higher education coordinating commissions is often
a mistake in management policy.

The enrollment market strategy and the arguments
for regulatory reform are based fundamentally on a set of
assumptions about the market for higher education services
and institutional behavior within this market. Recently,
David Breneman criticized the application of market principles to higher education.[18] Breneman argued the following:

1. Universities do not seek to maximize profits or to minimize costs for a given level of activity.
2. Educational services produced by universities are not
   priced to students at marginal costs, average costs, or
   full costs—a wide range of pricing strategies is employed "reflecting more than cost or quality differences."[19]
3. Information available to students about university services is incomplete and consequently inhibits optimiza-
   tion in student decision making.
4. Students usually buy only one college education. Consequently, substitution behavior is restricted as a
   means of improving student benefits; that is, student
   "shopping" and analysis of educational options is limited.
5. Some institutions receive substantial public subsidies
   while others are not subsidized. Consequently, prices
   differ among institutions and by geographic area for
   the provision of comparable services.
6. The market for higher education services is "fifty minimarkets" rather than national.
7. Total demand for higher education is relatively fixed;
   that is, competition among institutions at a certain
   level of demand and supply is a "zero-sum game."

8. An increase in institutional competition "tends to erode the division of labor among institutions"; that is, universities compete for students with community and state colleges.
9. Competition can produce destructive competitive practices, for example, "price warfare" among institutions.
10. Price competition provides greater benefits to higher-income students, as pricing discounts are not based on need.
11. Lower prices will in some instances result in the provision of lower-quality educational services.

As a result of these constraints on the operation of markets, Breneman recommends against competition as a means for allocating resources in higher education, advocating instead a "mixed strategy" combining elements of competition, planning, and regulation. In effect, Breneman advocates the system that operates presently in higher education. However, he concludes that "states could . . . examine financing formulas currently in use, to be certain that the incentives built into the formulas are consistent with intended state policies. . . . Designing formulas that do not put a premium on enrollment growth may be one of the best--and most equitable--ways to improve the market."[20]

The arguments made in previous chapters on the advisability of reforming state financing of higher education through use of equimarginal subsidies appear to conform in part with Breneman's prescription that states examine funding formulas to determine incentive effects on institutional behavior. However, his conclusion that financing formulas should not be based on enrollment is not consistent with the arguments advanced for enrollment market or equimarginal funding. Breneman's conclusions are, however, quite supportive of approaches such as critical mass as means for improving equity in the market.[21] In this context it must be noted that Breneman defines equity narrowly in terms of maintaining fairness in competition between public and private higher education institutions. Several problems with Breneman's arguments are that he doesn't supply much justification for recommending non-enrollment-driven budget formulas and his conclusions about the operation of the higher education market appear to justify the status quo. The first problem may be noted in criticism. However, we may examine Breneman's hypotheses

about the failures of the market more carefully in attempting to determine whether greater reliance on the market to
allocate resources in higher education is desirable, as discussed in previous chapters of this book.

Breneman's first criticism of market assumptions
("salient features of the market for higher education") is
that universities do not seek to maximize profits or to
minimize costs for a given level of activity. While it appears this observation is correct, the important point not
stated is that this behavior is part of the problem. Breneman notes, "It is not clear what objectives guide the behavior of colleges and universities . . . prestige, status
and quality."[22] However, that institutions do not behave
as rational economic agents may be explained by the absence of sufficient incentives for them to do so. Where
such incentives are present, the absence of effort to maximize revenues and minimize costs while seeking prestige,
status, and quality may be regarded as management,
rather than market, failure.

Second, it is entirely possible that Breneman's observation is simply incorrect for many public and private
institutions. In attempting to respond to partial enrollment-
based funding, institutions have sought to maximize revenues, as explained in Chapters Five and Six. For example,
some public institutions have attempted to increase or maintain their budgets over the past five years by compensating
for enrollment losses in the arts and sciences by increasing
students admitted to business and other professional programs. Internal cross-subsidization to prevent termination
of programs suffering from low enrollment demand is also
evidence that some institutions have attempted to make a
"profit" on one type of service in order to sustain another.
Further, the operation of self-supporting continuing education enterprises in public institutions supports the notion
that where profits can be made through market pricing and
cost minimization, such behavior will result. Breneman's
observation serves well as an apology for the unresponsiveness and managerial inadequacy of some public institutions.

Breneman's second point is that institutions do not
engage in marginal cost pricing and do not appear to employ rational or systematic pricing strategies. Again,
this may be regarded as an institutional rather than market failure and not an effective argument against greater
use of market incentives to allocate resources. In fact,
it is just the opposite. Breneman notes, "A wide range of

net prices exist . . . reflecting more than cost or quality differences. The crazy-quilt pattern of subsidies to institutions . . . must give pause to anyone who would argue that prices . . . perform the task of allocating resources efficiently."[23] This is exactly the argument for refining state government subsidy methods made in this book. However, enrollment market funding would rely far more on the market and far less on state planning or regulation than is the case presently. Breneman also notes that state governments may not wish to accept the distribution of enrollments produced by an unregulated market. While this is true, under the enrollment market approach the state could influence institutional enrollment incentives by changing the per-unit subsidy level, rather than by regulation of supply or access as Breneman appears to suggest. Again, unit subsidies appear consistent with his recommendation that state governments analyze financial incentives set in budget formulas to ensure institutional responsiveness to state policies. Improvements in institutional pricing strategy are likely to be made only where the "crazy-quilt pattern of subsidies" is straightened out. That institutions do not price correctly under existing systems of subsidy is not a sound argument against market-based allocation of resources. Rather it is a statement of a problem exacerbated by existing methods of state subsidy, control, and regulation.

The third and fourth observations made by Breneman are that information provided to students is incomplete and student choice is limited to a single purchase so that errors cannot be corrected easily. Institutions have progressed considerably over the last decade in providing prospective students with better-quality information about programs of study and other aspects of university activity. In addition, an industry has grown to provide information and to evaluate institutions for prospective students; it publishes numerous guides and manuals annually.

Seldom is there a market where information is provided perfectly. However, there appear no major constraints to prevent students from finding out about comparative institutional and academic program offerings. Breneman overstates the point of information failures and also the "one choice in life" educational purchase decision. In fact, students do shop for and switch between institutions. Attendance at more than one undergraduate institution is commonplace in higher education. Student choice of graduate schools appears to be quite selective relative to academic program offerings. There is no doubt that geographical location influences choice, but this is not a serious market failure, given the number of institutions and their dispersion in the United States. Further, in his argument Breneman seems to ignore entirely the large and expanding continuing education market. Where students can purchase individual courses and where geographical limits are leaped through on-site, study-by-mail, and other curricular offerings, students have plenty of opportunity to shop and substitute one service for another.

The market also fails to allocate resources efficiently and equitably, according to Breneman, because some institutions receive substantial public subsidies while others do not and, as a consequence, prices charged to students vary. First, rarely is it presumed that firms in the private sector operate with the same financial base. Some private firms are advantaged not only by public subsidies but also by regulatory, trade, tax, and other government policies that provide competitive advantage. Despite the fact that various instruments of government policy provide differential advantage across firms, competition and competitive pricing strategy occur. Government sponsorship of private sector firms does provide significant advantage in many instances, for example, direct regulation of supply, market entry, and prices or tax expenditures and other incentives. However, firms compete with each other not only for consumers and market share but also for regulatory and other advantages provided by government. In much the same way, public and private colleges and universities compete for public subsidies and other advantages provided by federal and state governments.

Beyond this point Breneman seems to ignore the tremendous amount of student-based financial aid and other forms of public subsidy provided to private institutions. Additionally, he overlooks the difference between gross and net prices in higher education. Private colleges and universities do attempt to be competitive in pricing through the packaging of student-based financial aid with institutional financial aid. Net prices in higher education probably vary only slightly, except as they reflect different service quality and other attributes we would expect to be represented in competitive markets; these attributes include prestige and alumni interaction opportunities that presumably result in higher private benefits in the form of future

income to students graduating from private institutions.
From this view the pricing behavior of public higher education appears highly competitive and efficient in the allocation of resources relative to perceived benefits of attendance at private institutions. Breneman also ignores the
tremendous private fund-raising advantage enjoyed by
many private institutions over their public counterparts.
However, most incredibly, Breneman fails to mention that a
great deal of public subsidy is provided for the purpose
of improving equity in resource allocation. He does so
even though stating that he is addressing the question,
"Does this market meet the tests of equity and efficiency?"[24]
Certainly one may argue that equity is not achieved satisfactorily relative to almost any set of measures one chooses
to develop. After all, equity is a value-oriented term—it
means whatever we choose it to mean personally, institu-
tionally, and politically.

We cannot ignore the extent to which government attempts to influence the market through provision of subsidies. Breneman would not disagree with this point. But
he overlooks the fact that just because governments provide
subsidies, for whatever reason, it cannot be assumed automatically that competition and competitive behavior are absent or that the higher education market inevitably fails
the tests of efficiency and equity. If subsidies are provided correctly, both market efficiency and equity are improved. Still, under this circumstance the reliance on market incentives does not lessen. Indeed, just the opposite
occurs; that is, the market becomes more effective in providing the amount and distribution of benefits desired by
individuals, and more nearly approximates the social opti-
mum.

Additional objections raised by Breneman are that
the market is constituted of "fifty minimarkets" (that is,
resources are not provided uniformly nor are resources in-
finitely mobile), that total demand is fixed (institutional
competition is a zero-sum game), and that competition
erodes differences among institutions. On the first point,
few industrial markets exist where there is absolutely no
geographic segmentation. Segmentation typically provides
differential advantage to some firms within an industry in
terms of pricing, distribution, advertising, promotion, and
sales. The presence of geographical advantage does not
preclude competition, and most certainly this is the case
in higher education. While geographical location is an

important variable, its value differs by type of institution
and region. Regional, national, and international competition among institutions does occur in higher education.
Further, competition in "minimarkets" is still competition--
unless there is government-sanctioned monopoly supply.
Although it cannot be argued that competition takes place
within many states to the extent that it should, to ignore
the amount of competition that does exist is an error.
Likewise, although some segments of the higher education
market reveal limited demand, so-called "zero-sum" competition does not allocate resources any less efficiently than
do growing markets. Market expansion is not a suitable
economic criterion by which to evaluate market efficiency
and equity. Finally, it appears that the market for higher
education services is expanding, for example, in continuing
and outreach education.

Perhaps Breneman's point is that zero-sum competition is more likely to produce anticompetitive behavior and
destructive competition. This would explain why he advocates state regulation to prevent "price warfare among institutions." In the first place, there appears to be too
little rather than too much price competition within segments of the higher education market. Second, price competition benefits student consumers, other things being
equal. Third, where price competition takes place, in the
continuing education market for example, student choice
and institutional responses generally work to create a
price-quality equilibrium after a period of time. Few institutions will price below marginal costs in order to drive
other institutions out of the market. And, where such attempts are made, consumers hold control in choosing the
service that provides the price-quality mix desired.

As noted in Chapter Seven, there does appear to be
a role for state regulation in preventing some types of
anticompetitive and anticonsumer behavior by institutions,
such as outright sale of degrees and misleading or fraudulent advertising. However, with regard to Breneman's
characterization of price competition as providing greater
benefits to higher-income rather than lower-income students,
we should ask how equity should be achieved in markets.
Does Breneman suggest that equity may be achieved exclusively through pricing? Surely this is not the case because this suggestion would overlook the importance of financial aid, government fiscal policy, and special institutional admissions practices as a means of achieving social

equity objectives. Price discounts do advantage wealthy buyers, but to argue that market pricing should be based exclusively on equity considerations seems misguided due to the supply-and-demand distortion that such practices would produce. Equity may be achieved through means other than government-regulated pricing unless institutions operate as "natural monopolies" (where production functions reveal decreasing marginal costs in service provision), which appears seldom to be the case in higher education. In addition, Breneman's point that lower prices will in some instances result in lower-quality service seems to be a case of swinging the wrong end of the bat. Lower prices may be charged for lower-quality services, but they do not necessarily "result in" low quality. Lower prices for lower-quality or less service is exactly what we should expect and desire in the higher education marketplace. Where a mix of services is offered, consumer choice over time will reveal the extent of satisfaction with consumption. Additionally, the demand for "cheap" degrees is a function of how future employers evaluate student credentials and competence. Most students are smart enough to recognize that low-quality degrees do not produce much benefit in employment competition. In cases where it appears to students that degrees purchased by mail might increase their probability of landing a job or getting a high starting salary, it is likely that little attention is actually given to the degree in hiring and promotion decisions. The instructional service value marketed in higher education is knowledge and competence, not just degrees.

Finally, Breneman warns that an increase in institutional competition "tends to erode the division of labor among institutions."[25] If there is evidence to support this point, not much of it is presented to substantiate the argument. Institutions with different missions, such as community colleges and universities, do compete for the same students in some instances. But should such competition not take place? The point is that student consumers are better off having a choice among institutions. Institutions should compete for students by offering different types of services in different price-quality configurations, and different distribution options, that is, timing and location. There is no substantial evidence that such competition is wasteful of either public or private resources, as noted in discussion of the duplication issue in Chapters Five, Six, and Seven. Competition requires some degree of service duplication. However, the degree of homogenization of product or institution that results from competition depends on the expression of consumer preference in the market. On the other hand, where government planning and regulation are employed extensively, it would appear that product and institutional homogenization results are in fact due to the absence of bureaucratic imagination and high-quality information, a preference for easy methods for expenditure and market control, and a disregard of consumer welfare.

CONCLUSIONS ON REFORM OF STATE
GOVERNMENT BUDGETING AND CONTROL

In conclusion it should be stated that there is less disagreement between the competitive market view articulated in this book and Breneman's position than appears to be the case in light of the critique offered here. Essentially, the difference is in the relative degree of dependence on market forces to allocate resources, rather than whether the market should operate. The mixed model advocated by Breneman and others places greater emphasis on government planning and regulation than does the equimarginal subsidy proposal. Both approaches acknowledge that government subsidies will continue. As noted in Chapter Five, the provision of subsidies by means of a student voucher system would increase the market orientation of government subsidy, as would use of enrollment market budgeting. Although vouchers appear to be one of the best approaches to subsidy because of their market orientation, they are not proposed as a necessary component of equimarginal state government budgeting because of the low political feasibility of the voucher option. However, the political feasibility of vouchers has found an improved climate in some states.

The principal area of disagreement with the mixed model for resource allocation in higher education is its excessive reliance on state-level planning and regulation. State government officials believe in the virtues of state planning and regulation far more than these activities merit. Chapters Six and Seven attempted to point out how and why the costs of state control of institutional arrangements for service supply, markets, and curricula in most instances appear to exceed the benefits derived from such control. This appears to be the case particularly during periods of stable or declining enrollment and financial austerity.

Based on this analysis of the criticisms of market assumptions, there appears to be little reason not to rely more on competition and market adjustment as the primary means for allocating state government resources in higher education. While there are numerous advocates of a mixed model of market competition, planning, and regulation, the arguments advanced in Part II of this book and in this chapter disagree substantially, but not entirely, with the mixed model. This model supports the practice of what is, in effect, the status quo approach to resource allocation. Previous chapters on budget incentives, control, and regulation have attempted to indicate the problems that result from present practices in higher education. Absences of incentives, competition, and resource management flexibility inhibit adaptation to changes in market demand for higher education services. They also exacerbate the constraints imposed by financial austerity and tight state budgets.

Problems with the status quo approach to the funding and regulation of universities and higher education have been explained in this book to have resulted from the failure to establish incentives to adapt, the absence of financial flexibility to stimulate strategic behavior by universities in competition with other institutions and in budget negotiations with state government, and the inadequacy of university academic resource planning, budgeting, and management practices. Reliance on market dynamics, rather than on high-profile state budgetary control and regulation, appears over the long term much more likely to achieve the ends desired by universities, by state government officials, and by society in general than will perpetuation of procedures employed presently in many state governments.

NOTES

1. For example, see M. Trow, "The Implications of Low Growth Rates of Higher Education," Higher Education 5 (1976):377-96; L. Glenny, "Demographic and Related Issues for Higher Education in the 1980s," Journal of Higher Education 51 (1980):363-80.

2. F. Thompson and L. R. Jones, "Distributional Equity in Student Subsidies in Higher Education: 1967-1977," Journal of Student Financial Aid 9 (1979):42-53.

3. D. Michael, On Learning to Plan and Planning to Learn. (San Francisco: Jossey-Bass, 1973); C. Churchman, The Systems Approach (New York: Dell, 1969).

4. H. Kaufman, The Forest Ranger: A Study in Administrative Behavior (Baltimore: Johns Hopkins Press, 1967).

5. The term management control is used here to describe a system of planning, decision, operations maintenance and control, and evaluation, rather than a method for influencing the behavior of organization units, organizations, or people. See A. Anthony and R. Herzlinger, Management Control in Non-Profit Organizations (Homewood, Ill.: Irwin, 1979), chap. 1.

6. A. Wildavsky, The Politics of the Budgetary Process, 1st ed. (Boston: Little, Brown, 1964), 57-61.

7. On these points see J. Pfeffer and G. Salancik, "Organizational Decision Making as a Political Process: The Case of a University Budget," Administrative Quarterly 19 (June 1974):135-51; G. Salancik and J. Pfeffer, "The Bases and Uses of Power in Organizational Decision Making: The Case of a University," Administrative Science Quarterly 19 (December 1974):453-73; L. LeLoup, "Discretion in National Budgeting: Controlling the Controllables," Policy Analysis 4 (Fall 1978):475. LeLoup draws this conclusion because in his view the most important decisions in budgeting are long range. Small percentages of discretion are therefore reasonable in an annual budget.

8. D. Spence and G. Weathersby, "Changing Patterns of State Funding," in Challenges of Retrenchment, ed. J. Mingle (San Francisco: Jossey-Bass, 1981), 228-29.

9. Wildavsky, Politics of the Budgetary Process, chap. 3; Anthony and Herzlinger, Management Control, chap. 8.

10. D. Singleton, B. Smith, and J. Cleaveland, "Zero-Base Budgeting in Wilmington, Delaware," Government Finance (August 1976):20-29.

11. A. Wildavsky, "A Budget for All Seasons: Why the Traditional Budget Lasts," Public Administration Review (November/December 1978):501-19.

12. K. Winkler, "Presidents or Faculties: Who Should Make Key Decisions about the Curriculum?" The Chronicle of Higher Education 27 (January 25, 1984):21-22.

13. Ibid.

14. Ibid., 21. The quote is from Frederick Rudolph's critique of Kerr's conclusion based on the study.

15. O. Fulton and M. Trow, "Research Activity in American Higher Education," in Teachers and Students, ed. M. Trow (San Francisco: McGraw-Hill, 1975), chap. 2.

16. M. Trow, "The American Academic Department as a Context for Learning," Studies in Higher Education (March 1976):11–22.

17. P. Kotler, Marketing for Nonprofit Organizations (Englewood Cliffs, N.J.: Prentice-Hall, 1975); C. Lovelock and C. Weinberg, Marketing for Public and Non-profit Organizations (Palo Alto, Calif.: Scientific Press, 1979).

18. D. Breneman, "Strategies for the 1980s," in Mingle, Challenges of Retrenchment, 16–31.

19. Ibid., 25.
20. Ibid.
21. Ibid.
22. Ibid.
23. Ibid.
24. Ibid.
25. Ibid., 27.

Selected Bibliography

Adams, C. and R. Hankins. The Literature of Costs and Cost Analysis in Higher Education. Washington, D.C.: American Council on Education, 1977.

Adams, W. "Financing Public Higher Education." American Economic Review, 1977, 67 (1):86–89.

Adizes, I. "Organizational Passages: Diagnosing and Treating Life Cycle Problems in Organizations." Organizational Dynamics, 1979, 8 (1):3–25.

Alfred, R., ed. New Directions for Community Colleges: Coping with Reduced Resources, no. 22. San Francisco: Jossey-Bass, 1978.

Allison, G. The Essence of Decision: Explaining the Cuban Missile Crisis. Boston, Mass.: Little, Brown, 1971.

Allshouse, M. "The New Academic Slalom: Mission, Personnel Planning, Financial Exigency, Due Process." Liberal Education, 1975, 61 (3):349–68.

Alm, K., E. Ehrle, and B. Webster. "Managing Faculty Reductions." Journal of Higher Education, 1977, 48 (2): 153–63.

Alm, K., M. Miko, and K. Smith. Program Evaluation. Washington, D.C.: Resource Center for Planned Changes, American Association of State Colleges and Universities, 1976.

American Association of University Professors. Statement on Financial Exigency. Washington, D.C.: American Association of University Professors, 1976.

_____. AAUP Policy Documents and Reports. Washington, D.C.: American Association of University Professors, 1977.

_____. "Academic Freedom and Tenure: The State University of New York." AAUP Bulletin, 1977, 63: 237-60.

_____. "Draft Statement on Institutional Mergers and Absorption." Academe, 1981, 67 (2):83-85.

Anthony, R., and R. Herzlinger. Management Control in Nonprofit Organizations. Homewood, Ill.: Irwin, 1980.

Argenti, J. Corporate Collapse. New York: Halstead, 1976.

Argyris, C. Interpersonal Competence and Organizational Effectiveness. Homewood, Ill.: Dorsey, 1962.

_____. Integrating the Individual and the Organization. New York: Wiley, 1964.

_____. Applicability of Organizational Sociology. New York: Cambridge, 1972.

Arns, R., and W. Poland. "Changing the University through Program Review." Journal of Higher Education, 1980, 51 (3):268-84.

Ashby, E. Any Person, Any Study. San Francisco: McGraw-Hill, 1971.

Ashworth, K. American Higher Education in Decline. College Station, Tex.: Texas A&M University Press, 1979.

Association of American Colleges. Statement on Financial Exigency and Staff Reduction. Washington, D.C.: Association of American Colleges, 1971.

Bailey, S. "Human Resource Development in a World of Decremental Budgets." Planning for Higher Education, 1974, 3 (3):1-5.

_____. "The Peculiar Mixture: Public Norms and Private Space." In W. Hobbs, ed. Government Regulation of Higher Education. Cambridge, Mass.: Ballinger, 1978.

Baldridge, J. Academic Governance. Berkeley, Calif.:
    McCutchan, 1971.

_____. "Images of the Future and Organizational Change:
    The Case of New York University." In W. Bell and
    J. Mau, eds. The Sociology of the Future. New York:
    Russell Sage Foundation, 1971.

_____. Power and Conflict in the University. New York:
    Wiley, 1971.

Baldridge, J., and M. Tierney. New Approaches to Man-
    agement: Creating Practical Systems of Management
    Information and Management by Objectives. San
    Francisco, Calif.: Jossey-Bass, 1979.

Banfield, E. "Ends and Means in Planning." In S.
    Mallick and E. VanNess, eds. Concepts and Issues
    in Administrative Behavior. Englewood Cliffs, N.J.:
    Prentice-Hall, 1962.

Barak, R. "Program Reviews by Statewide Higher Educa-
    tion Agencies." In J. Folger, ed. New Directions for
    Institutional Research: Increasing the Public Account-
    ability of Higher Education, no. 16. San Francisco:
    Jossey-Bass, 1977.

_____. "Study of Program Review." In B. Krauth, ed.
    Postsecondary Education Program Review. Boulder,
    Colo.: Western Interstate Commission for Higher
    Education, 1980.

Barak, R., and R. Berdahl, State-Level Academic Program
    Review in Higher Education. Denver: Education
    Commission of the States, 1978.

Bardach, E. "Policy Termination as a Political Process."
    Policy Sciences, 1976, 7 (2):123-31.

Barnard, C. The Functions of the Executive. Cambridge,
    Mass.: Harvard University Press, 1938.

Behn, R. "Closing the Massachusetts Public Training
    Schools." Policy Sciences, 1976, 7 (2):151-71.

_____. "Closing a Government Facility." Public Admin-istration Review, 1978, 38 (4):332-37.

_____. "How to Terminate a Public Policy: A Dozen Hints for the Would-Be Terminator." Policy Analysis, 1978, 4 (Summer):393-413.

_____. "The End of the Growth Era in Higher Education." Statement presented to the Committee on Labor and Human Resources of the United States Senate, Raleigh, N.C., 1979.

Bell, D. "The Pattern of University Costs." In A. Mood, ed. Papers on Efficiency in the Management of Uni-versity Higher Education. Berkeley, Calif.: Carnegie Commission on Higher Education, 1972.

Ben-David, J. American Higher Education. San Francisco: McGraw-Hill, 1972.

Bennis, W. Changing Organizations. New York: McGraw-Hill, 1966.

_____. Organization Development: Its Nature, Origins, and Prospects. Reading, Mass.: Addison-Wesley, 1969.

_____. "Who Sank the Yellow Submarine?" In G. Riley and J. Baldridge, eds. Governing Academic Organiza-tions: New Problems, New Perspectives. Berkeley, Calif.: McCutchan, 1977.

Bennis, W., K. Benne, and R. Chin, The Planning of Change. New York: Holt, Rinehart & Winston, 1969.

Bennis, W., and P. Slater. The Temporary Society. New York: Harper & Row, 1968.

Bentley, J. Philosophy: An Outline-History. Paterson, N.J.: Littlefield, Adams, 1964.

Benveniste, G. The Politics of Expertise. Berkeley, Calif.: Glendessary Press, 1972.

_____. Bureaucracy. Berkeley, Calif.: Glendessary Press, 1977.

Berdahl, R. Statewide Coordination of Higher Education. Washington, D.C.: American Council on Education, 1971.

_____. ed. New Directions for Institutional Research: Evaluating Statewide Boards, no. 5. San Francisco, Calif.: Jossey-Bass, 1975.

_____. "Legislative Program Evaluation." In J. Folger, ed. New Directions for Institutional Research: Increasing the Public Accountability of Higher Education, no. 16. San Francisco, Calif.: Jossey-Bass, 1977.

Bergquist, W., and S. Phillips, A Handbook for Faculty Development. Washington, D.C.: Council for the Advancement of Small Colleges, 1975.

Bergquist, W., and W. Shoemaker, "Facilitating Comprehensive Institutional Development." A Comprehensive Approach to Institutional Development. San Francisco: Jossey-Bass, 1976.

Berman, P., and M. McLaughlin, "The Management of Decline: Problems, Opportunities, and Research Questions." Rand Paper Series, P-5984. Santa Monica, Calif.: Rand Corporation, 1977.

Bess, J. "New Life for Faculty and Their Institutions." Journal of Higher Education, 1975, 46 (1):313-25.

Biller, R. "Converting Knowledge into Action: The Dilemma and Opportunity of the Post-Industrial Society." In J. Jun and W. Storm, eds. Tomorrow's Organizations: Challenges and Strategies. Glenview, Ill.: Scott, Foresman, 1973.

_____. "Leadership Tactics for Retrenchment." Public Administration Review, 1980, 40 (6):604-9.

Bingham, R., B. Hawkins, and F. Hebert. The Politics of Raising State and Local Revenue. New York: Praeger, 1978.

Bish, R. The Public Economy of Metropolitan Areas. Chicago: Markham, 1971.

Bish, R., and E. Ostrom. Understanding Urban Government
    Washington, D.C.: American Enterprise Institute, 1973.

Bishop, J. "The Effect of Public Policies on the Demand
    for Higher Education." Journal of Human Resources,
    1977, 3 (Fall):285–307.

Blau, P. Bureaucracy in Modern Society. New York:
    Random House, 1956.

_____. The Dynamics of Bureaucrcy: A Study of Inter-
    personal Relations in Two Government Agencies.
    Chicago: University of Chicago Press, 1963.

_____. "The Research Process in the Study of the
    Dynamics of Bureaucracy." In P. Hammond, ed.
    Sociologists at Work. New York: Random House, 1964.

Bouchard, D. "Experience with Proposition 13 and Other
    Retrenchment Conditions." Journal of the College and
    University Personnel Association, 1980, 31 (1):61–65.

Boulding, K. "The Management of Decline." Change, 1975,
    7 (5):8–9, 64.

Boutwell, W. "Formula Budgeting on the Down Side." In
    G. Kaludis, ed. New Directions for Higher Education:
    Strategies for Budgeting, no. 2. San Francisco:
    Jossey-Bass, 1973.

Bowen, F. "Dollar, Dollar, Who Gets the Dollar? Making
    Decisions in a Time of Fiscal Stringency." In M.
    Lavin, ed. On Target: Key Issues of Region, State
    and Campus. Boulder, Colo.: Western Interstate
    Commission for Higher Education, 1976.

Bowen, F., and L. Glenny. State Budgeting for Higher
    Education: State Fiscal Stringency and Public Higher
    Education. Berkeley, Calif.: Center for Research and
    Development in Higher Education, University of Cali-
    fornia, 1976.

_____. Uncertainty in Public Higher Education: Re-
    sponses to Stress at Ten California Colleges and
    Universities. Sacramento, Calif.: California Post-
    secondary Education Commission, 1980.

_____. "Enrollment Management." In J. Mingle, ed. Challenges of Retrenchment. San Francisco: Jossey-Bass, 1981.

Bowen, H. The Finance of Higher Education. The Carnegie Commission on Higher Education. New York: Random House, 1968.

_____. Financing Higher Education: The Current State of the Debate. Washington, D.C.: Association of American Colleges, 1974.

_____. Investment in Learning: The Individual and Social Value of American Higher Education. San Francisco: Jossey-Bass, 1977.

_____. The Costs of Higher Education: How Much Do Colleges and Universities Spend Per Student and How Much Should They Spend? San Francisco: Jossey-Bass, 1981.

Bowen, H., and G. Douglass, "Cutting Instructional Costs." Liberal Education, 1971, 57 (2):181-95.

Bozeman, B., and E. Slusher, "Scarcity and Environmental Stress in Public Organizations: A Conjectural Essay." Administrative Science Quarterly, 1979, 11:335-55.

Brazziel, W. "Planning for Enrollment Shifts in Colleges and Universities." Research in Higher Education, 1978, 9 (1):1-13.

Breneman, D., ed. "An Analytic Critique of Internal Pricing and Agenda of Issues for the Future." Internal Pricing Within the University, Ford Foundation Program for Research in University Administration, Office of the Vice President—Planning, University of California, Berkeley, Calif., Paper P-23, December 1971.

_____. "Education." In J. Pechman, ed. Setting National Priorities: The 1979 Budget. Washington, D.C.: Brookings Institution, 1978.

_____. "Economic Trends: What Do They Imply for Higher Education?" American Association for Higher Education Bulletin, 1979, 32 (1):3-5.

_____. "Strategies for the 1980s." In J. Mingle, ed. Challenges of Retrenchment. San Francisco: Jossey-Bass, 1981.

Breneman, D., and C. Finn, Jr., eds. Public Policy and Private Higher Education. Washington, D.C.: Brookings Institution, 1978.

Breneman, D., and S. Nelson, "Education and Training." In J. Pechman, ed. Setting National Priorities: Agenda for the 1980s. Washington, D.C.: Brookings Institution, 1981.

_____. Financing Community Colleges: An Economic Perspective. Washington, D.C.: Brookings Institution, 1981.

Breton, A., and R. Wintrobe, "The Equilibrium Size of a Budget-Maximizing Bureau." Journal of Political Economy, 1975, 8 (Winter):95-101.

Brown, D. The Mobile Professors. New York: Wiley, 1965.

Brown, D., and W. Hanger, "Pragmatics of Faculty Self-Development." Educational Record, 1975, 56 (3):201-6.

Brown, R., Jr. "Financial Exigency." AAUP Bulletin, 1976, 62 (1):5-16.

Brown, R., Jr., and M. Finkin, "The Usefulness of AAUP Policy Statements." Educational Record, 1978, 59 (1): 30-44.

Brown, W. Academic Politics. New York: Wiley, 1982.

Bryson, J. "A Perspective on Planning and Crises in the Public Sector." Strategic Management Journal, 1981, 2 (2):181-96.

Buchanan, J., and N. Develetoglou. Academia in Anarchy: An Economic Diagnosis. New York: Basic Books, 1970.

Buckley, W., ed. Sociology and Modern Systems Theory. Englewood Cliffs, N.J.: Prentice-Hall, 1967.

Burke, J. Trying to Do Better with Less: The Experience of the SUNY College of Arts and Science at Plattsburgh, New York. Atlanta: Southern Regional Education Board, 1980.

Burns, T., and G. Stalker. The Management of Innovation. London: Tavistock, 1961.

California Postsecondary Education Commission. Financial Support for the California Community Colleges. Sacramento, Calif.: State of California, 1976.

Cameron, K. "Measuring Organization Effectiveness in Institutions of Higher Education." Administrative Science Quarterly, 1978, 23:604-32.

_____. "Domains of Organizational Effectiveness in Colleges and Universities." Academy of Management Journal, 1981, 24 (1):25-47.

_____. "Strategic Responses to Conditions of Decline." Journal of Higher Education, 1983, 54 (4):359-80.

Cameron, K., and D. Whetten. Organizational Effectiveness: A Comparison of Multiple Models. New York: Academic Press, 1982.

Caplow, T., and R. McGee. The Academic Marketplace. New York: Wiley, 1958.

Carlson, D. The Production and Cost Behavior of Higher Education. Ford Foundation Research Paper P-36, Berkeley, Calif., University of California, 1972.

Carnegie Commission on Higher Education. The Capitol and the Campus: State Responsibility for Postsecondary Education. New York: McGraw-Hill, 1971.

_____. Less Time, More Options: Education Beyond the High School. New York: McGraw-Hill, 1971.

_____. New Students and New Places: Policies for the Future Growth and Development of American Higher Education. New York: McGraw-Hill, 1971.

_____. The More Effective Use of Resources: An Imperative for Higher Education. New York: McGraw-Hill, 1972.

_____. Governance of Higher Education. New York: McGraw-Hill, 1973.

_____. Toward a Learning Society: Alternative Channels to Life, Work, and Service. New York: McGraw-Hill, 1973.

Carnegie Council on Policy Studies in Higher Education. Selective Admissions in Higher Education: Comment and Recommendations and Two Reports. San Francisco: Jossey-Bass, 1977.

_____. The States and Private Higher Education: Problems and Policies in a New Era. San Francisco: Jossey-Bass, 1977.

_____. Fair Practices in Higher Education: Rights and Responsibilities of Students and Their Colleges in a Period of Intensified Competition for Enrollments. San Francisco: Jossey-Bass, 1979.

_____. Three Thousand Futures: The Next Twenty Years for Higher Education. San Francisco: Jossey-Bass, 1980.

Carnegie Foundation for the Advancement of Teaching. More Than Survival: Prospects for Higher Education in a Period of Uncertainty. San Francisco: Jossey-Bass, 1975.

_____. The States and Higher Education: A Proud Past and a Vital Future. San Francisco: Jossey-Bass, 1976.

Carter, V., and C. Garigan, eds. A Marketing Approach to Student Recruitment. Washington, D.C.: Council for Advancement and Support of Education, 1979.

Cartter, A. "A New Look at the Supply and Demand for College Teachers." Educational Record, 1965, 46 (2): 119–28.

_____, ed. New Directions for Institutional Research: Assuring Academic Progress without Growth, no. 6. San Francisco: Jossey-Bass, 1975.

_____. Ph.D.'s and the Academic Labor Market. New York: McGraw-Hill, 1976.

Caruthers, J., and M. Orwig, Budgeting in Higher Education. AAHE-ERIC/Higher Education Research Report no. 3. Washington, D.C.: American Association for Higher Education, 1979.

Centra, J. College Enrollment in the 1980s: Projections and Possibilities. New York: College Entrance Examination Board, 1978.

_____. "Types of Faculty Development Programs." Journal of Higher Education, 1978, 49 (2):151–62.

Chaffee, E. "Decision Models in University Budgeting." Ph.D. dissertation, Stanford University, 1981.

_____. Case Studies in College Strategy. Boulder, Colo.: National Center for Higher Education Management Systems, 1982.

_____. Environmental Decline and Strategic Decisionmaking. (Contract no. 400-80-0109.) Washington, D.C.: National Institute of Education, 1982.

Chaffee, E., and D. Collier. Strategic Decisionmaking and Organizational Results in Colleges and Universities. Boulder, Colo.: National Center for Higher Education Management Systems, 1981.

Chambers, G. "Private College Mergers and State Policy: A Case Study of New York." Case Study prepared for the Southern Regional Education Board's symposium on Public Policy Strategies for Higher Education, Atlanta, October 1980.

_____. "Negotiating Mergers between Institutions." In J. Mingle, ed. Challenges of Retrenchment. San Francisco: Jossey-Bass, 1981.

Cheit, E. The New Depression in Higher Education: A Study of Financial Conditions at 41 Colleges and Universities. The Carnegie Commission on Higher Education and the Ford Foundation. New York: McGraw-Hill, 1971.

_____. The New Depression in Higher Education: Two Years Later. The Carnegie Commission on Higher Education. New York: McGraw-Hill, 1973.

_____. "What Price Accountability?" Change, 1975, 7 (9):30-34.

Chronister, J. Independent College and University Participation in Statewide Planning for Postsecondary Education. Washington, D.C.: National Institute of Independent Colleges and Universities, 1978.

Churchman, C. The Systems Approach. New York: Dell, 1969.

Churchman, C., and F. Emery, "On Various Approaches to the Study of Organizations." In J. Lawrence, ed. Operational Research and the Social Sciences. London: Tavistock, 1966.

Clark, B. Academic Coordination. New Haven, Conn.: Institution for Social Policy Studies, Higher Education Research Group, Yale University, 1978.

Clark, B., and M. Trow. "The Organizational Context." In T. Newcomb and E. Wilson, eds. College Peer Groups. Chicago, Ill.: Aldine, 1966.

Clark, M. "A Practical Guide to Graduate Program Review." Findings, 1979, 5:1-4.

Clark, M., R. Hartnett, and L. Baird. Assessing Dimen-
sions of Quality in Doctoral Education: A Technical
Report of a National Study in Three Fields. Princeton,
N.J.: Educational Testing Service, 1976.

Cohen, M., and J. March. Leadership and Ambiguity: The
American College President. New York: McGraw-Hill,
1974.

College Entrance Examination Board. A Role for Marketing
in College Admissions. New York: College Entrance
Examination Board, 1976.

Collier, D. The Strategic Planning Concept. Boulder,
Colo.: National Center for Higher Education Management Systems, 1981.

Coordinating Council for Higher Education. Financial
Assistance Programs, no. 67-13, Tables I-2, I-3, I-9,
I-10, B-3, Appendix, Sacramento, Calif., October 1967.

_____. The Cost of Instruction, no. 74-I, Sacramento,
Calif., February 1974.

Cope, R. Strategic Policy Planning: A Guide for College
and University Administrators. Littleton, Colo.:
Ireland, 1978.

_____. "Qualitative Approaches to College and University
Planning." Paper presented to the California Association for Institutional Research, February 1978.

Corrson, J. The Governance of Colleges and Universities:
Modernizing Structure and Processes. Carnegie Series
in American Education. New York: McGraw-Hill, 1975.

Cothran, D. "Program Flexibility and Budget Growth in
Community Colleges." Western Political Quarterly,
1981, 34 (4):593-610.

Craven, E. "Information Decision Systems in Higher Education: A Conceptual Framework." Journal of Higher
Education, 1975, 46 (2):125-40.

_____, ed. New Directions for Institutional Research: Academic Program Evaluation, no. 27. San Francisco: Jossey-Bass, 1980.

_____. "Managing Faculty Resources." In J. Mingle, ed. Challenges of Retrenchment. San Francisco: Jossey-Bass, 1981.

Craven, E., and K. Becklin. "Student Access and the Quality of Instruction." Educational Record, 1978, 59 (1):105-15.

Crecine, J. Defense Budgeting: Organizational Adaptation to External Constraints. Santa Monica, Calif.: The Rand Corporation, March 1970.

Cross, P. "1970 to 1974: Years of Change in Community Colleges." Findings, Educational Testing Service, 1975, 11 (2):9-11.

Crossland, F. "Learning to Cope with a Downward Slope." Change, 1980, 12 (5):18, 20-25.

Crosson, P. Pennsylvania Postsecondary Education Policy Systems: Coping with Enrollment and Resource Declines. Pittsburgh, Pa.: Institute for Higher Education, University of Pittsburgh, 1981.

Crozier, M. The Bureaucratic Phenomenon. Chicago: University of Chicago Press, 1964.

Cyert, R. "The Management of Universities of Constant or Decreasing Size." Public Administration Review, 1978, 38 (4):344-49.

Cyert, R., and J. March. A Behavioral Theory of the Firm. Englewood Cliffs, N.J.: Prentice-Hall, 1963.

DeLeon, P. "A Theory of Policy Termination." In J. May and A. Wildavsky, eds. The Policy Cycle in Politics and Public Policy. Beverly Hills, Calif.: Sage Publications, 1978.

Deutch, J. "Retrenchment, Crisis or Challenge?" Educational Record, 1983, 64 (1):41-44.

Dill, D. "Tenure Quotas: Their Impact and an Alternative." Liberal Education, 1974, 60 (4):467-77.

Dill, W., T. Hilton, and W. Reitman. The New Managers. Englewood Cliffs, N.J.: Prentice-Hall, 1962.

Dooley, D., and R. Catalono. "Economic Change as a Cause of Behavioral Disorder." Psychology Bulletin, 1980, 87 (3):450-68.

Dougherty, E. "Evaluating and Discontinuing Programs." In J. Mingle, ed. Challenges of Retrenchment. San Francisco: Jossey-Bass, 1981.

Downs, A. Inside Bureaucracy. Boston: Little, Brown, 1966.

Dresch, S. "A Critique of Planning Models for Postsecondary Education." The Journal of Higher Education, 1975, 46 (May/June):245-86.

_____. "Demography, Technology, and Higher Education: Toward a Formal Model of Educational Adaptation." Journal of Political Economy, 1975, 83:535-69.

Dressel, P. Handbook of Academic Evaluation: Assessing Institutional Effectiveness, Student Progress, and Professional Performance for Decision Making in Higher Education. San Francisco: Jossey-Bass, 1976.

_____, ed. New Directions for Institutional Research: The Autonomy of Public Colleges, no. 26. San Francisco: Jossey-Bass, 1980.

Dressel, P., and L. Simon. Allocating Resources Among Departments. San Francisco: Jossey-Bass, 1976.

Dror, Y. Public Policymaking Reexamined. San Francisco: Chandler, 1968.

Drucker, P. The Practice of Management. New York: Harper & Row, 1954.

Dube, C., and A. Brown. "Strategic Assessment—A Rational Response to University Cutback." Long Range Planning, 1983, 16:105-13.

Durkheim, E. The Division of Labor. Glencoe, Ill.: Free Press.

Eckaus, R. Estimating the Returns to Education: A Disaggregated Approach. New York: McGraw-Hill, 1973.

Edwards, H., and V. Nordin. Higher Education and the Law. Cambridge, Mass.: Institute for Educational Management, Harvard University, 1979.

_____. Higher Education and the Law: 1980 Cumulative Supplement. Cambridge, Mass.: Institute for Educational Management, Harvard University, 1980.

Etzioni, A. The Active Society. New York: Free Press, 1968.

Flaig, H. "The Budgetary and Planning Options for Higher Education in a Period of Contraction." Planning for Higher Education, 1979, 8 (6):20-27.

Folger, J., ed. New Directions for Institutional Research: Increasing the Public Accountability of Higher Education, no. 16. San Francisco: Jossey-Bass, 1977.

Ford, J. "The Occurrence of Structural Hysteresis in Declining Organizations." Academy of Management Review, 1980, 5 (4):589-98.

Ford, L. "The Battle over Mandatory Retirement." Educational Record, 1978, 59 (3):204-28.

Frances, C. College Enrollment Trends: Testing the Conventional Wisdom against the Facts. Washington, D.C.: American Council on Education, 1980.

Frances, C., and S. Coldren, eds. New Directions for Higher Education: Assessing Financial Health, no. 26. San Francisco: Jossey-Bass, 1979.

Fuller, B. "A Framework for Academic Planning." Journal of Higher Education, 1976, 47 (1):65-77.

Fulton, O., and M. Trow. "Research Activity in American Higher Education." In M. Trow, ed. Teachers and Students. San Francisco: McGraw-Hill, 1975.

Furniss, W. Steady-State Staffing in Tenure-Granting Institutions, and Related Papers. Washington, D.C.: American Council on Education, 1973.

_____. "Retrenchment, Layoff, and Termination." Educational Record, 1974, 55 (3), 159-70.

_____. "Steady-State Staffing: Issues for 1974." Educational Record, 1974, 55 (2):87-95.

_____. "The 1976 AAUP Retrenchment Policy." Educational Record, 1977, 57 (3):183-89.

_____. "The Status of AAUP Policy." Educational Record, 1978, 59 (1):7-29.

_____. "New Opportunities for Faculty Members." Educational Record, 1981, 62 (1):8-15.

_____. Reshaping Faculty Careers. Washington, D.C.: American Council on Education, 1981.

Gaff, J. Toward Faculty Renewal: Advances in Faculty, Instructional, and Organizational Development. San Francisco: Jossey-Bass, 1975.

_____. "Current Issues in Faculty Development." Liberal Education, 1977, 63 (4):511-19.

Galbraith, J. Organizational Design: An Information Processing View. Reading, Mass.: Addison-Wesley, 1977.

Gardner, D. "Five Evaluational Frameworks: Implications for Decision Making in Higher Education." Journal of Higher Education, 1977, 48 (5):571-93.

Garvin, D. The Economics of University Behavior. New York: Academic Press, 1980.

Gillis, J. "Academic Staff Reductions in Response to Financial Exigency." Liberal Education, 1971, 57 (3):
364-77.

Glassberg, A. "Organizational Responses to Municipal
Budget Decreases." Public Administration Review,
1978, 38 (4):325-32.

Glenny, L. Autonomy of Public Colleges: The Challenge
of Coordination. New York: McGraw-Hill, 1959.

_____. "State Systems and Plans for Higher Education."
In L. Wilson, ed. Emerging Patterns in American
Higher Education. Washington, D.C.: American Coun-
cil on Education, 1965.

_____. "Politics and Current Patterns in Coordinating
Higher Education." In J. Minter, ed. Campus and
Capitol. Boulder, Colo.: Western Interstate Commis-
sion for Higher Education, 1966.

_____. Coordinating Higher Education for the '70s.
Berkeley, Calif.: Center for Research and Development in Higher Education, University of California,
1971.

_____. State Budgeting for Higher Education: Data
Digest. Berkeley, Calif.: Center for Research and
Development in Higher Education, University of Cali-
fornia, 1975.

_____. Presidents Confront Reality: From Edifice Com-
plex to University without Walls. San Francisco:
Jossey-Bass, 1976.

_____. "Demographic and Related Issues for Higher Edu-
cation in the 1980s." Journal of Higher Education,
1980, 51 (4):363-80.

_____. "Decision-Making in Panic Time." ABG Reports,
1982, 24 (3):20-24.

Glenny, L., and F. Bowen. Signals for Change: Stress
Indicators for Colleges and Universities. Sacramento,
Calif.: California Postsecondary Education Commis-
sion, 1980.

Gomberg, I., and F. Atelsek. Trends in Financial Indicators of Colleges and Universities. Washington, D.C.: American Council on Education, 1981.

Gray, J. "Legal Restraints on Faculty Cutbacks." In J. Mingle, ed. Challenges of Retrenchment. San Francisco: Jossey-Bass, 1981.

Greenhalgh, L. A Cost-Benefit Balance Sheet for Evaluating Layoffs as a Policy Strategy. Ithaca, N.Y.: School of Industrial and Labor Relations, Cornell University, 1978.

Greenhalgh, L., and R. McKersie. "Reductions in Force: Cost Effectiveness of Alternative Strategies." In C. Levine, ed. Managing Fiscal Stress. Chatham, N.J.: Chatham House, 1980.

Grinold, R., D. Hopkins, and W. Massy. "A Model for Long-Range University Budget Planning under Uncertainty." The Bell Journal of Economics, 1978, 9 (2): 396-420.

Gross, B. The Managing of Organizations. New York: Free Press, 1964.

_____, ed. Action under Planning. New York: McGraw-Hill, 1967.

Gross, E. "Universities as Organizations: A Study of Goals." In J. Baldridge, ed. Academic Governance. Berkeley, Calif.: McCutchan, 1971.

Habbe, D. "Future Faculty Employment Levels, Projected Problems and Possible Solutions: A Commentary." Journal of the College and University Personnel Association, 1980, 31 (1):31-37.

Haines, J. Merger Procedures for Colleges and Universities. Albany, N.Y.: Haines Associates, 1980.

Hall, D., and R. Mansfield. "Organizational and Individual Response to External Stress." Administrative Science Quarterly, 1970, 16:533-46.

Hall, R. "Contemporary Organizational Theory and Higher Education: A Mismatch." In J. Wilson, ed. Management Science Applications to Academic Administration. San Francisco: Jossey-Bass, 1981.

Halstead, D. Statewide Planning in Higher Education. Washington, D.C.: U.S. Office of Education, 1974.

_____. Higher Education Prices and Price Indexes, 1975 Supplement. Washington, D.C.: U.S. Office of Education, 1975.

_____. Higher Education Prices and Price Indexes, 1979 Supplement. Washington, D.C.: U.S. Office of Education, 1979.

Hample, S. "Future Faculty Employment: Projected Problems and Possible Solutions: Conclusions and Summary." Journal of the College and University Personnel Association, 1980, 34 (1):105-9.

_____, ed. New Directions for Institutional Research: Coping with Faculty Reduction, no. 30. San Francisco: Jossey-Bass, 1981.

Hannan, M., and J. Freeman, "Internal Politics of Growth and Decline." In M. Meyer, ed. Environments and Organizations. San Francisco: Jossey-Bass, 1978.

Hansen, W. "Regressing into the Eighties: Annual Report on the Economic Status of the Profession, 1979-1980." Academe, 1980, 66 (5):260-74.

Hanushek, E. "Regional Differences in the Structure of Earnings." Review of Economics and Statistics, 1973, 55 (2):204-13.

Harcleroad, F. "The Context of Academic Program Evaluation." In E. Craven, ed. New Directions for Institutional Research: Academic Program Evaluation, no. 27. San Francisco: Jossey-Bass, 1980.

Hartman, R. "Federal Options for Student Aid." In D. Breneman and C. Finn, Jr., eds. Public Policy

and Private Higher Education. Washington, D.C.:
Brookings Institution, 1978.

Hatry, H. How Effective Are Your Community Sources?
Washington, D.C.: Urban Institute, 1977.

_____. "Current State of the Art of State and Local
Productivity Improvement." In C. Levine, ed.,
Managing Fiscal Stress. Chatham, N.J.: Chatham
House, 1980.

Hays, G. "Perspectives from a Statewide System." Journal
of the College and University Personnel Association,
1980, 31 (1):14-21.

Hefferlin, J. Dynamics of Academic Reform. San Francisco:
Jossey-Bass, 1971.

Heilbroner, R. The Future as History. New York: Grove
Press, 1959.

Henderson, A. The Innovative Spirit. San Francisco:
Jossey-Bass, 1971.

Henry, D. Challenges Past, Challenges Present. San
Francisco: Jossey-Bass, 1975.

Hermann, C. "Some Consequences of Crises Which Limit
the Viability of Organizations." Administrative Science
Quarterly, 1963, 8:61-82.

Herzlinger, R. "Zero-Base Budgeting in the Federal Government: A Core Study." Sloan Management Review,
1979, 20 (2):1-14.

Hills, F., and T. Mahoney. "University Budgets and Organizational Decision Making." Administrative Science
Quarterly, 1978, 23:454-65.

Hobbs, W., ed. Government Regulation of Higher Education. Cambridge, Mass.: Ballinger, 1978.

Hodgkinson, H. Institutions in Transition: A Profile of
Change in Higher Education. New York: McGraw-
Hill, 1971.

Hoenack, S. "The Efficient Allocation of Subsidies to College Students." American Economic Review, 1971, 61 (June):302–11.

Hofstadter, R., and W. Metzger. The Development of Academic Freedom in the United States. New York: Columbia University Press, 1955.

Holloway, J. "Termination of Faculty Due to Financial Exigency." Journal of the College and University Personnel Association, 1980, 31 (1):84–93.

Hollowood, J. College and University Strategic Planning: A Methodological Approach. Cambridge, Mass.: Arthur D. Little, 1979.

Hoos, I. A Critical Review of Systems Analysis: The California Experience. NASA Report no. CR–61350. Berkeley, Calif.: University of California, 1968.

Hopkins, D. Analysis of Faculty Appointment, Promotion and Retirement Policies. Stanford, Calif.: Academic Planning Office, Stanford University, 1973.

Hyde, W. "Proved at Last: One Physics Major Equals 1.35 Chemistry Major or 1.66 Economics Major." Educational Record, 1974, 55 (4):286–90.

Iannaccone, L. "The Management of Decline: Implications for Our Knowledge in the Politics of Education." Education and Urban Society, 1979, 11:418–30.

Ihlanfeldt, W. Achieving Optimal Enrollments and Tuition Revenues: A Guide to Modern Methods of Research, Student Recruitment, and Institutional Pricing. San Francisco: Jossey-Bass, 1980.

Jackson, G., and G. Weathersby. "Individual Demand for Higher Education." Journal of Higher Education, 1975, 46 (6):623–52.

Janis, I. "Groupthink among Policy Makers." In N. Sanford and C. Comstock, eds. Sanctions for Evil. San Francisco: Jossey-Bass, 1971.

Jencks, C., and D. Riesman. The Academic Revolution. Garden City, N.Y.: Doubleday, 1968.

Johnson, L. Islands of Innovation Expanding. Los Angeles: Glencoe Press, 1969.

Johnson, M., and K. Mortimer. Faculty Bargaining and the Politics of Retrenchment in the Pennsylvania State Colleges, 1971-1976. University Park, Pa.: Center for the Study of Higher Education, Pennsylvania State University, 1977.

Jones, L. "Fiscal Strategies to Stimulate Instructional Innovation and Change." Journal of Higher Education, 1978, 49 (6):588-607.

_____. "An Historic Survey of Academic Development." Planning for Higher Education, 1979, 7 (5):21-27.

_____. "A Model for Academic Planning." Canadian Journal of Higher Education, 1979, 9 (1):1-10.

_____. "The Process of Policy Analysis." Eugene, Oreg.: Institute for Social Science Research, 1981.

_____. "Termination Gamesmanship: The Strategic Uses of Evaluation, Feasibility Assessment and Marketing." Eugene, Oreg.: Institute for Social Science Research, 1982.

_____. "Competition and Regulation in Postsecondary Education." The Review of Higher Education, 1984, 8 (3):38-51.

_____. "Phases of Recognition and Management of Financial Crises in Public Organizations." Canadian Public Administration, 1984, 27 (1):44-58.

Kahn, R., and E. Boulding, eds. Power and Conflict in Organizations. New York: Basic Books, 1964.

Kaplin, W. The Law of Higher Education: Legal Implications of Administrative Decision Making. San Francisco: Jossey-Bass, 1978.

_____. The Law of Higher Education. San Francisco: Jossey-Bass, 1980.

Katz, D., and R. Kahn. The Social Psychology of Organizations. New York: Wiley, 1966.

Kaufman, H. The Forest Ranger: A Study in Administrative Behavior. Baltimore: Johns Hopkins University Press, 1967.

_____. The Limits of Organizational Change. University, Ala.: University of Alabama Press, 1971.

_____. "The Direction of Organizational Evolution." Public Administration Review, 1973, 33 (4):300-7.

_____. Are Government Organizations Immortal? Washington, D.C.: Brookings Institution, 1976.

Kaysen, C., ed. Content and Context. The Carnegie Commission on Higher Education. San Francisco: McGraw-Hill, 1973.

Keller, J. Higher Education Objectives: Measures of Performance and Effectiveness. Ford Foundation Research Paper P-7. Berkeley, Calif.: Ford Foundation, 1971.

Kelsey, J. "Coping with Cutbacks." Education Canada, 1983, 23 (2):10-15.

Keough, W., Jr. "Enrollment Decline: The Dilemma from the Superintendent's Chair." In S. Abromowitz and S. Rosenfeld, eds. Declining Enrollment: The Challenge of the Coming Decade. Washington, D.C.: National Institute of Education, 1975.

Kerr, C. The Uses of the University. Cambridge, Mass.: Harvard University Press, 1963.

_____. 12 Systems of Higher Education: 6 Decisive Issues. New York: International Council for Educational Development, 1978.

_____. "Administration of Higher Education in an Era of Change and Conflict." In C. Kerr, ed. Conflict,

Retrenchment and Reappraisal: The Administration of Higher Education. Urbana, Ill.: University of Illinois, 1979.

Kershaw, J. The Very Small College: A Report to the Ford Foundation. New York: Ford Foundation, 1976.

Kimberly, J., and R. Miles, eds. The Organizational Life Cycle. San Francisco, Calif.: Jossey-Bass, 1980.

Knight, W. Revised Academic Plan 1969–1975. Berkeley, Calif.: The University of California, 1969.

Kohn, M., C. Manski, and D. Mundel. "An Empirical Analysis of Factors Which Influence College-Going Behavior." Annals of Economic and Social Measurement, 1976, 5:285–307.

Kotler, P. Marketing for Nonprofit Organizations. Englewood Cliffs, N.J.: Prentice-Hall, 1975.

Kotler, P., and P. Murphy. "Strategic Planning for Higher Education." The Journal of Higher Education, 1981, 52 (5):470–89.

Kuhn, T. The Structure of Scientific Revolutions. Chicago: University of Chicago Press, 1962.

Kurland, J. "Reducing Faculty Positions: Considerations of Sound Academic Practice." Liberal Education, 1972, 58 (2):304–9.

Ladd, E., Jr., and S. Lipset. "The Ladd-Lipset Survey: When Colleges Retrench, Where Should Cutbacks Come?" Chronicle of Higher Education, 1976, 12 (7):7.

LaLoup, L. "Discretion in National Budgeting: Controlling the Uncontrollables." Policy Analysis, 1978, 4 (4): 469–78.

Lasalle, J. "Appointment, Promotion, and Tenure under Steady-State Staffing." Notices of the American Mathematical Society, 1971, 19:69–73.

Leder, C. "Economically Necessitated Faculty Dismissals as a Limitation on Academic Freedom." Denver Law Journal, 1975, 52:911-37.

Lee, E., and F. Bowen. Managing Multicampus Systems: Effective Administration in an Unsteady State. San Francisco: Jossey-Bass, 1975.

Lee, J. Case Studies of Institutional Decline. Washington, D.C.: ABT Associates, 1981.

Leibenstein, H. "X-Efficiency vs. Allocative Efficiency." American Economic Review, 1966, 56:392-415.

Lenning, O., P. Beal, and K. Sauer. Retention and Attrition: Evidence for Action and Research. Boulder, Colo.: National Center for Higher Education Management Systems, 1980.

Leslie, D., ed. New Directions for Institutional Research: Employing Part-Time Faculty, no. 18. San Francisco: Jossey-Bass, 1978.

Leslie, D., and R. Head. "Part-Time Faculty Rights." Educational Record, 1979, 60 (1):46-47.

Levine, C. "Organizational Decline and Cutback Management." Public Administration Review, 1978, 38 (4): 316-25.

_____. "More on Cutback Management: Hard Questions for Hard Times." Public Administration Review, 1979, 39 (2):179-83.

_____, ed. Managing Fiscal Stress. Chatham, N.J.: Chatham House, 1980.

Levine, C., and I., Rubin, eds. Fiscal Stress and Public Policy. Beverly Hills, Calif.: Sage Publications, 1980.

Levine, C., I. Rubin, and G. Wolohojian. The Politics of Retrenchment. Beverly Hills, Calif.: Sage Publications, 1981.

Levy, F. "On Understanding Proposition 13." The Public Interest, 1979, (56):66–89.

Lipset, S. Political Man. Cambridge, Mass.: Harvard University Press, 1960.

Lovelock, C., and C. Weinburg. Readings in Public and Nonprofit Marketing. Palo Alto, Calif.: Scientific Press, 1978.

Lyman, R. "Federal Regulation and Institutional Autonomy: A University President's View." In P. Seabury, ed. Bureaucrats and Brainpower: Government Regulation of Universities. San Francisco, Calif.: Institute for Contemporary Studies, 1979.

March, J., and H. Simon. Organizations. New York: Wiley, 1958.

Mayhew, L. Long-Range Planning for Higher Education. Studies in the Future of Higher Education. Report no. 3. Washington, D.C.: Academy for Educational Development, 1969.

_____. Surviving the Eighties: Strategies and Procedures for Solving Fiscal and Enrollment Problems. San Francisco, Calif.: Jossey-Bass, 1979.

McCaffery, J., and J. Bowman. "Participatory Democracy and Budgeting: The Effects of Proposition 13." Public Administration Review, 1978, 38 (6):530–38.

McConnell, T. A General Pattern for American Public Higher Education. New York: McGraw-Hill, 1962.

_____. The Redistribution of Power in Higher Education. Berkeley, Calif.: Center for Research and Development in Higher Education, University of California, 1971.

McGee, R. The Academic Marketplace. New York: Wiley, 1958.

McPherson, M. "Quality and Competition in Public and Private Higher Education." Change, 1981, 13 (3):18–23.

Medsger, L., and D. Tillery. <u>Breaking the Access Bar-</u>
<u>riers: A Profile of Two-Year Colleges</u>. New York:
McGraw-Hill, 1971.

Meeth, L. <u>Quality Education for Less Money: A Sourcebook</u>
<u>for Improving Cost Effectiveness</u>. San Francisco,
Calif.: Jossey-Bass, 1974.

Meisinger, R., Jr. <u>State Budgeting for Higher Education:</u>
<u>The Use of Formulas</u>. Berkeley, Calif.: Center for
Research and Development in Higher Education, University of California, 1976.

_____. <u>Evaluating a Private College Request for State</u>
<u>Affiliation: A Case Study of Sullins College in</u>
<u>Virginia</u>. Paper prepared for the Southern Regional
Education Board's Symposium on Public Policy Strategies for Higher Education, Atlanta, October 1980.

Mencke, M. "Strategic Planning in an Age of Uncertainty."
<u>Long-Range Planning</u>, 1979, 12:27-34.

Meyer, A. "Legal Aspects of Merger." In A. Knowles, ed.
<u>Handbook of College and University Administration</u>.
New York: McGraw-Hill, 1970.

_____. "Adapting to Environmental Jolts." <u>Administra-</u>
<u>tive Science Quarterly</u>, 1982, 27 (4):515-37.

Micek, S., ed. <u>Integrating Academic Planning and Budget-</u>
<u>ing in a Rapidly Changing Environment: Process and</u>
<u>Technical Issues</u>. Boulder, Colo.: National Center
for Higher Education Management Systems, 1980.

Michael, D. <u>The Unprepared Society: Planning for a Pre-</u>
<u>carious Future</u>. New York: Basic Books, 1968.

_____. <u>On Learning to Plan--And Planning to Learn</u>.
San Francisco, Calif.: Jossey-Bass, 1973.

Miles, R., and C. Snow. <u>Organizational Strategy, Struc-</u>
<u>ture, and Process</u>. New York: McGraw-Hill, 1978.

Millard, R. <u>State Boards of Higher Education</u>. ERIC/
Higher Education Research Report no. 4. Washington,
D.C.: American Association for Higher Education, 1976.

Millett, J. The Academic Community: An Essay on Organization. New York: McGraw-Hill, 1962.

_____. "State Administration of Higher Education." In C. Wingfield, ed. The American University: A Public Administration Perspective. Dallas, Tex.: Southern Methodist University Press, 1970.

_____. Politics and Higher Education. University, Ala.: University of Alabama Press, 1974.

_____. Mergers in Higher Education: An Analysis of Ten Case Studies. Washington, D.C.: American Council on Education, 1976.

_____. New Structures of Campus Power: Success and Failures of Emerging Forms of Institutional Governance. San Francisco: Jossey-Bass, 1978.

_____. Conflict in Higher Education. San Francisco: Jossey-Bass, 1984.

Mingle, J., ed. Challenges of Retrenchment. San Francisco: Jossey-Bass, 1981.

Mingle, J., and R. Berdahl. Consolidation and Reorganization in Public Higher Education: A Case Study of Connecticut. Atlanta: Southern Regional Education Board, 1981.

Mingle, J., and D. Norris. "Institutional Strategies for Responding to Decline." In J. Mingle, ed. Challenges of Retrenchment. San Francisco: Jossey-Bass, 1981.

Mingle, J., and M. Peterson. Consolidation and Reorganization in Public Higher Education: A Case Study of Massachusetts. Atlanta: Southern Regional Education Board, 1981.

Minter, W., and H. Bowen. Independent Higher Education: Fourth Annual Report on Financial and Educational Trends in the Independent Sector of American Higher Education. Washington, D.C.: National Institute of Independent Colleges and Universities, 1978.

Minter, W., and P. Snyder, eds. Value Change and Power Conflict in Higher Education. Berkeley, Calif.: Center for Research and Development in Higher Education, University of California, 1969.

Mitnick, B. "Deregulation as a Process of Organizational Reduction." Public Administration Review, 1978, 38 (4):350–57.

Mix, M. Tenure and Termination in Financial Exigency. Washington, D.C.: American Association for Higher Education, 1978.

Mokwa, M., and S. Permut. Government Marketing. New York: Praeger, 1981.

Moore, M. "On Launching into Exigency Planning." Journal of Higher Education, 1978, 49 (6):620–38.

Moore, W., "Determinants and Outcomes of Departmental Power: A Two-Campus Study." Ph.D. dissertation. University of California at Berkeley, 1979.

Moos, M., and F. Rourke. The Campus and the State. Baltimore: Johns Hopkins Press, 1959.

Morrill, J. The Ongoing State University. Minneapolis: University of Minnesota Press, 1960.

Mortimer, K. "Academic Government at Berkeley: The Academic Senate." Ph.D. dissertation. University of California at Berkeley, 1969.

Mortimer, K., and M. Tierney. The Three "R's" of the Eighties: Reduction, Reallocation, and Retrenchment. AAHE-ERIC/Higher Education Report no. 4. Washington, D.C.: American Association for Higher Education, 1979.

Mosher, E., and J. Wagoner, Jr., eds. The Changing Politics of Education. Berkeley, Calif.: McCutchan, 1978.

Moynihan, D. Maximum Feasible Misunderstanding. New York: Free Press, 1969.

Murray, M. "Modern Management Applied to Academic Decisions." Academy of Management Review, 1976, 1 (1):
79–88.

National Research Council. Research Excellence through
the Year 2000: The Importance of Maintaining a Flow
of New Faculty into Academic Research. Washington,
D.C.: National Academy of Sciences, 1979.

Nelsen, W., ed. "Faculty Development: Key Issues for
Effectiveness." Forum for Liberal Education, 1979, 2
(1):1–4.

Nelson, S. "Financial Trends and Issues." In D. Breneman
and C. Finn, Jr., eds. Public Policy and Private
Higher Education. Washington, D.C.: Brookings
Institution, 1978.

Nevison, C. "Effects of Tenure and Retirement Policies on
the College Faculty: A Case Study Using Computer
Simulation." Journal of Higher Education, 1980, 54
(2):150–66.

Niskanen, W. Bureaucracy and Representative Government.
Chicago: Aldine-Atherton, 1971.

Oakland, W. "Proposition 13: Genesis and Consequences."
National Tax Journal, 1979, 32 (Supplement, June):
387–409.

Oliver, R. An Equilibrium Model of Faculty Appointments,
Promotions, and Quota Restrictions. Research Report
no. 69-10. Berkeley, Calif.: Office of the Vice
President for Planning and Analysis, University of
California, 1969.

O'Neill, J., and S. Barnett. Colleges and Corporate
Change: Merger, Bankruptcy, and Closure. Princeton,
N.J.: Conference-University Press, 1981.

Ortega Gasset, J. Mission of the University. New York:
Norton, 1944.

O'Toole, J., W. Van Alstyne, and R. Chait. Three Views:
Tenure. New Rochelle, N.Y.: Change Magazine Press,
1979.

Ouchi, W. Theory Z. New York: Avon, 1982.

Palmer, D., and C. V. Patton. "Mid-Career Change Options in Academe: Experience and Possibilities." Journal of Higher Education, 1981, 52 (4):378-98.

Palola, E., T. Lehmann, and W. Blischke. Higher Education by Design: The Sociology of Planning. Berkeley, Calif.: Center for Research and Development in Higher Education, University of California, 1970.

Parsons, T. "Introduction." In M. Weber, Theory of Social and Economic Organization. New York: Oxford University Press, 1947.

_____. Structure and Process in Modern Societies. Glencoe, Ill.: Free Press, 1960.

Patterson, F. "Institutional Planning in the Context of Change." Planning for Higher Education, 1977, 6 (4): 1-8.

Peat, Marwick, Mitchell and Co. Ratio Analysis in Higher Education: A Guide to Assessing the Institution's Financial Condition. 2 vols. New York: Peat, Marwick, Mitchell and Co., 1980.

Perkins, J., ed. The University as an Organization. The Carnegie Commission on Higher Education. San Francisco: McGraw-Hill, 1972.

Perrow, C. Complex Organizations. Glenview, Ill.: Scott, Foresman, 1972.

_____. Complex Organizations: A Critical Essay. 2nd ed. Glenview, Ill.: Scott, Foresman, 1979.

Peters, M. "Mergers of Institutions of Higher Education." College and University, 1977, 52 (2):202-10.

Peterson, J. "The Dismissal of Tenured Faculty for Reasons of Financial Exigency." Indiana Law Journal, 1976, 51 (2):417-32.

Peterson, M. The State-Level Performance Assessment
    Process: Concepts, Perspectives and Issues. Ann
    Arbor, Mich.: Center for Higher Education, University
    of Michigan, 1977.

_____. "Faculty and Academic Responsiveness in a Period
    of Decline: An Organizational Perspective." Journal
    of the College and University Personnel Association,
    1980, 31 (1):95-104.

Pfeffer, J. "Organizational Design as a Political Process."
    Organizational Design. Arlington Heights, Ill.: AHM,
    1978.

Pfeffer, J., and G. Salancik. "Organizational Decision
    Making as a Political Process: The Case of a Univer-
    sity Budget." Administrative Science Quarterly, 1974,
    19:135-51.

_____. The External Control of Organizations. New York:
    Harper & Row, 1978.

Pincus, J. "Incentives for Innovation in Public Schools."
    In F. Williams and R. Elmore, eds. Social Program
    Implementation. New York: Academic Press, 1976.

Pondrom, C. "Faculty Retrenchment: The Experience of
    the University of Wisconsin System." In S. Hample,
    ed. New Directions for Institutional Research: Coping
    with Faculty Reduction, no. 30. San Francisco:
    Jossey-Bass, 1981.

Pondy, L. "Toward A Theory of International Resource
    Allocation." In M. Zald, ed. Power in Organizations.
    Nashville, Tenn.: Vanderbilt University Press, 1970.

Poulton, N. "Strategies of Large Universities." In
    P. Jedamus and M. Peterson, eds. Improving Academic
    Management. San Francisco: Jossey-Bass, 1980.

Purves, R., and L. Glenny. State Budgeting for Higher
    Education: Information Systems and Technical Analy-
    ses. Berkeley, Calif.: Center for Research and De-
    velopment in Higher Education, University of Califor-
    nia, 1976.

Radner, R., and C. Kuh. Preserving a Lost Generation: Policies to Assure a Steady Flow of Young Scholars until the Year 2000. Berkeley, Calif.: Carnegie Council on Policy Studies in Higher Education, 1978.

Radner, R., and L. Miller. "Demand and Supply in U.S. Higher Education: A Progress Report." American Economic Review, 1970, 60 (2):326–34.

Riesman, D. On Higher Education: The Academic Enterprise in an Era of Rising Student Consumerism. San Francisco: Jossey-Bass, 1980.

Riesman, D., N. Glazer, and R. Denny. The Lonely Crowd. New York: Doubleday Anchor Books, 1955.

Riesman, D., J. Gusfield, and J. Gamson. Academic Values and Mass Education. Garden City, N.Y.: Doubleday, 1971.

Rivlin, A. Systematic Thinking for Social Action. Washington, D.C.: Brookings Institution, 1971.

Roethlisberger, F., W. Dickson, and H. Wright. Management and the Worker. Cambridge, Mass.: Harvard University Press, 1946.

Rood, H. "Legal Issues in Faculty Termination: An Analysis Based on Recent Court Cases." Journal of Higher Education, 1977, 48 (2):123–52.

Rubin, I. "Universities in Stress: Decision Making under Conditions of Reduced Resources." Social Science Quarterly, 1977, 58 (2):242–54.

_____. "Retrenchment, Loose Structure, and Adaptablity in the University." Sociology of Education, 1979, 52 (4):211–22.

Ruyle, J., and L. Glenny. State Appropriations for Higher Education. Berkeley, Calif.: Center for Research and Development in Higher Education, University of California, 1980.

Salancik, G., and J. Pfeffer. "The Bases and Use of Power in Organizational Decision Making: The Case of the University." Administrative Science Quarterly, 1974, 19 (4):453-73.

Sanford, N., ed. The American College. New York: Wiley, 1962.

Savas, E. Alternatives for Delivering Public Services. Boulder, Colo.: Westview, 1977.

_____. Privatizing the Public Sector. Chatham, N.J.: Chatham House, 1982.

Schick, A. "Control Patterns in State Budget Execution." Public Administration Review, 1964, 24 (2):97-106.

_____. Budget Innovation in the States. Washington, D.C.: Brookings Institution, 1971.

_____. "Budgetary Adaptations to Resource Scarcity." In C. Levine and I. Rubin, eds. Fiscal Stress and Public Policy. Beverly Hills, Calif.: Sage, 1980.

Scriven, M. "The Methodology of Evaluation." In R. Tyler, R. Gagné, and M. Scriven, Perspectives of Curriculum Evaluation. Skokie, Ill.: Rand McNally, 1967.

_____. "Pros and Cons about Goal-Free Evaluation." Evaluation Comment, 1972, 3:14-27.

Selznick, P. TVA and the Grass Roots. Berkeley, Calif.: University of California Press, 1949.

Shefter, M. "New York City's Fiscal Crisis: The Politics of Inflation and Retrenchment." The Public Interest, 1977, 48:98-127.

Shirley, R., and J. Volkwein. "Establishing Academic Program Priorities." Journal of Higher Education, 1978, 49 (5):472-88.

Shoup, C. Public Finance. Chicago, Ill.: Aldine-Atherton, 1969.

Shulman, C. University Admissions: Dilemmas and Potential. ERIC/Higher Education Research Report no. 5. Washington, D.C.: American Association for Higher Education, 1977.

Simon, H. "Administrative Behavior." New York: Macmillan, 1945.

_____. "Administrative Behavior." In The International Encyclopedia of the Social Sciences, Vol. 1. New York: Crowell, Collier and Macmillan, 1968.

Simpson, W. "Tenure: A Perspective View of Past, Present, and Future." Educational Record, 1975, 56 (1): 48–54.

Sinclair, U. The Goose-Step: A Study of American Education. Pasadena, Calif.: Upton Sinclair, 1923.

Singleton, D. "Zero-Based Budgeting in Wilmington, Delaware." Government Finance, 1976 (August):20–29.

Sloan Commission on Government and Higher Education. A Program for Renewed Partnership. Cambridge, Mass.: Ballinger, 1980.

Slote, A. Termination: The Closing at Baker Plant. Indianapolis, Ind.: Bobbs-Merrill, 1969.

Smelser, N. Theory of Collective Behavior. New York: Free Press, 1972.

Smith, D. "Coping, Improvising, and Planning for the Future during Fiscal Decline: A Case Study for the University of Wisconsin." In M. Kaplan, ed. The Monday Morning Imagination: Report from the Boyer Workshop on State University Systems. Aspen, Colo.: Aspen Institute for Humanistic Studies, 1977.

_____. "Faculty Vitality and the Management of University Personnel Policies." In W. Kirschling, ed. New Directions for Institutional Research: Evaluating Faculty Performance and Vitality, no. 20. San Francisco: Jossey-Bass, 1978.

_____. "Multi-Campus System Approaches to Academic Program Evaluation." In E. Craven, ed. New Directions for Institutional Research: Academic Program Evaluation, no. 27. San Francisco: Jossey-Bass, 1980.

_____. "Preparing for Enrollment Decline in a State System." In J. Mingle, ed. Challenges of Retrenchment. San Francisco: Jossey-Bass, 1981.

Smithies, A. The Budgetary Process in the United States. New York: McGraw-Hill, 1955.

Snow, C., and L. Hrebiniak. "Strategy, Distinctive Competence, and Organizational Performance." Administrative Science Quarterly, 1980, 25:317-36.

Solomon, L., and P. Taubman, eds. Does College Matter: Some Evidence on the Impact of Higher Education. New York: Academic Press, 1973.

Spence, D., and G. Weathersby. "Changing Patterns of State Funding." In J. Mingle, eds. Challenges of Retrenchment. San Francisco: Jossey-Bass, 1981.

Spitzberg, I. "Professors and State Policy." Academe, 1980, 66 (8):425-26.

Stadtman, V. Centennial Record of the University of California. Berkeley, Calif.: University of California, 1967.

_____. Academic Adaptations: Higher Education Prepares for the 1980s and 1990s. San Francisco: Jossey-Bass, 1980.

Stampen, J. The Financing of Public Higher Education: Low Tuition, Student Aid, and the Federal Government. AAHE-ERIC/Higher Education Research Report no. 9. Washington, D.C.: American Association for Higher Education, 1980.

Starbuck, W., A. Greve, and B. Hedberg. "Responding to Crisis." Journal of Business Administration, 1978, 9: 111-37.

Stauffer, T., ed. Competition and Cooperation in American Higher Education. Washington, D.C.: American Council on Education, 1981.

Steiner, P. Mergers: Motives, Effects, Policies. Ann Arbor, Mich.: University of Michigan Press, 1975.

Stone, J. And Gladly Teche. Berkeley, Calif.: University of California, 1975.

Strohm, P. "Faculty Responsibilities and Rights during Retrenchment." In J. Mingle, ed. Challenges of Retrenchment. San Francisco: Jossey-Bass, 1981.

Suchman, E. Evaluative Research. New York: Sage, 1967.

Thompson, F., and L. Jones. "Distributional Equity in Student Subsidies for Higher Education in California." Journal of Student Financial Aid. Stanford University, 1979, 9 (2):42-53.

_____. Regulatory Policy and Practices. New York: Praeger, 1982.

Thompson, F., and W. Zumeta. "A Regulatory Model of Governmental Coordinating Activities in the Higher Education Sector." Economics of Education Review, 1980, 1 (1):74-87.

_____. "Control and Controls: A Reexamination of Control Patterns in Budget Execution." Policy Sciences, 1981, 13 (1):25-50.

Thompson, J. "Decision-Making, the Firm, and the Market." In W. Cooper, H. Leavitt, and M. Shelly, eds. New Perspectives in Organizational Research. New York: Wiley, 1964.

_____. Organization in Action: Social Science Bases of Administrative Theory. New York: McGraw-Hill, 1967.

Toll, J. "Strategic Planning: An Increasing Priority for Colleges and Universities." Change, 1982, 14 (3): 36-37.

Tonn, J. "Political Behavior in Higher Education Budgeting." Journal of Higher Education, 1978, 49 (6):
575-85.

Toombs, W. "A Three-Dimensional View of Faculty Development." Journal of Higher Education, 1975, 46 (6):
701-17.

Trow, M. "The Campus Viewed as a Culture." In H.
Sprague, ed. Research on College Students. Boulder,
Colo.: Western Interstate Commission for Higher Edu-
cation, 1960.

_____. "Reflections on the Transition from Mass to Uni-
versal Higher Education." Daedalus, 1970, 99:1-42.

_____. "The Public and Private Lives of Higher Educa-
tion." Daedalus, Winter 1975, 104:113-27.

_____, ed. Teachers and Students. San Francisco:
McGraw-Hill, 1975.

_____. "The American Academic Department as a Context
for Learning." Studies in Higher Education, 1976, 1
(1):11-22.

_____. "Implications of Low Growth Rates of Higher
Education." Higher Education, 1976, 5 (4):377-96.

Veysey, L. The Emergence of the American University.
Chicago: The University of Chicago Press, 1965.

_____. "Stability and Experiment in the American Under-
graduate Curriculum." In C. Kaysen, ed. Content
and Context. The Carnegie Commission on Higher Education. San Francisco: McGraw-Hill, 1973.

Volpe, E. "Retrenchment: The Case at CUNY." In R.
Heyns, ed. Leadership for Higher Education: The
Campus View. Washington, D.C.: American Council
on Education, 1977.

Wanat, J. Introduction to Budgeting. North Scituate,
Mass.: Duxbury Press, 1978.

Weber, M., A. Henderson, and T. Parsons, eds. Theory of Social and Economic Organization. New York: Oxford University Press, 1947.

Weeks, E., and S. Drengacz. "The Non-Economic Impact of Community Economic Shock." Journal of Health and Human Resources Administration, 1982, 4 (3):303-18.

Weick, K. "Educational Organizations as Loosely Coupled Systems." Administrative Science Quarterly, 1976, 21: 1-9.

Weiss, C. Evaluation Research. New York: Prentice Hall, 1975.

West, R. "Tenure Quotas and Financial Flexibility in Colleges and Universities." Educational Record, 1974, 55 (2):96-100.

Whetten, D. "Sources, Responses, and Effects of Organizational Decline." In J. Kimberly and R. Miles, eds. The Organizational Lifestyle. San Francisco: Jossey-Bass, 1980.

_____. "Organizational Responses to Scarcity: Exploring the Obstacles to Innovative Approaches to Retrenchment in Education." Educational Administration Quarterly, 1981, 17 (3):80-97.

Wildavsky, A. The Politics of the Budgetary Process. Boston: Little, Brown, 1964.

_____. "The Self-Evaluating Organization." Public Administration Review, 1972, 32 (5):509-20.

_____. Budgeting: A Comparative Theory of the Budgetary Process. Boston: Little, Brown, 1975.

_____. "A Budget for All Seasons? Why the Traditional Budget Lasts." Public Administration Review, 1978, 38 (6):501-9.

Wildavsky, A., and N. Caiden. Planning and Budgeting in Poor Countries. New York: Wiley and Sons, 1974.

Wildavsky, A., and A. Hamann. Administrative Science
    Quarterly, 1965, 10:321-46.

Wilensky, H. Organizational Intelligence: Knowledge and
    Policy in Government and Industry. New York:
    Basic Books, 1967.

Wilson, L. American Academics: Then and Now. New
    York: Oxford University Press, 1979.

Wilson, W. College and State: Eductional, Literary and
    Political Papers 1875-1913. New York: Columbia Uni-
    versity Press, 1925.

Wing, P. "Monitoring the Financial Status of Nonpublic
    Institutions in New York State." In C. Frances and
    S. Coldren, eds. New Directions for Higher Education:
    Assessing Financial Health, no. 26. San Francisco:
    Jossey-Bass, 1979.

Zammuto, R. Cutback Management and Resource Allocation
    in Higher Education (Contract no. 400-80-0109.)
    Washington, D.C.: National Institute of Education,
    1983.

Zammuto, R., D. Whetten, and K. Cameron. "Environmental
    Change, Enrollment Decline and Institutional Response."
    Peabody Journal of Education, 1983, 60 (2):93-106.

Znaniecki, F. The Social Role of the Man of Knowledge.
    New York: Columbia University Press, 1940.

Zumeta, W. "Doctoral Programs and the Labor Market, or
    How Should We Respond to the 'Ph.D. Glut'?" Higher
    Education, 1982, 11 (3):321-43.

Author Index

Subject Index

academic resource planning and allocation, definition, 39–40; principles, 43
austerity (see retrenchment)

budgeteers, resistance to experimentation with competition, 165–67; roles, 157–60
budgeting, average cost inadequacy, 135–36, 207; balancing, 153–54, 160, 166; base budgeting weaknesses, 207–20; certainty, 158–60, 165–66, 186, 209–11; competition, 87 (see also competition); criteria for state funding, 206; criteria in universities, 213; enrollment and revenue change in California, 146–47; enrollment data computerization, 148; enrollment market approach, 132–33 (see also budgeting, equimarginal); enrollment market criticisms, 230–40; equimarginal approach, 132–43 (see also unit subsidies); ex-ante and ex-post controls, 139, 155–62, 165–71 execution, 161, 214–15 (see also budgeting, ex-ante and ex-post controls); flexibility in negotiation, 157; higher education, 126–27, 135–37 (see also budgeting, equimarginal);

input measures as output indexes, 168; marginal costs, 136–37, 181–82, 207, 217–19, 233; minimization preferences of budgeteers, 157–59; misrepresentation in negotiation, 219–23; need for certainty and stability, 209–11, 214; performance base and cost accounting, 168–69; per-unit subsidies (see unit subsidies); phases of budget process, 209, 212; program change, 127–30; proxie use, 25; reforms, 115–16, 165–66, 170–71, 195–97, 207–15, 223–28, 230–32, 239–40; roles, 157–60; salary limitation, 130–32; state government control, 115–16, 118, 122, 138, 141, 153–60, 168–70, 230–31 (see also control); state government objectives, 121 (see also state government intervention); strategies to influence instruction, 119–20, 126–33; subsidy levels and costs, 135–38, 164–65 (see also unit subsidies); trade offs, 127–29, 157, 166; zero-base, 142

California Community Colleges, 184
California Department of Finance, 128

287

government spending, 154
(see also budgeting, and
control)

Higher education budgeting
(see budgeting)
Higher education market
analysis, 230–40
historical development of
university administra-
tion, 7–19

information, accuracy in
budgeting, 136, 148;
critical mass information
system, 215–16, 228–29
(see also critical mass);
high quality, 67–68; mis-
interpretation in budget-
ing, 33–34, 228–29;
necessary for market ef-
ficiency, 234–35

layoffs (see retrenchment)
legislative preferences in
budgeting, 161 (see also
budgeting)
line-item veto, 154

management controls (see
budgeting, and control)
marketing, 176, 178 (see
also universities)
Morrill Act, 10–11

Oregon Educational Coordination Commission, 177–78
organizational rationality,
74–80

price behavior in higher
education, 233–35, 237–38
production functions, 25
(see also budgeting,
and universities)

rationalized management sys -
tems (RMS), 23–28
reductions in force (see retrenchment)
regulation, rational for continuation, 187
regulatory costs in higher
education, 179, 180, 183,
186, 231–39
restraint (see retrenchment)
retrenchment, AAUP guidelines,
98–100; austerity in long-
term, 90–91, 106–8; categories of scarcity, 90; centralized decisions (see decision making); faculty
personnel policies, 99–100;
fees and service charges,
91, 106–8; layoffs and reductions in force, 98–102;
marketing improvements
needed, 108–9; options for
management, 89–92, 106–8;
phases of recognition and
management, 93–96; plan-
ning evaluation and participation, 103–5; smoothing,
93, 97, 105; study of, 89;
termination of policy programs, 97–103; training
and education, 107

scarcity (see retrenchment)
state government intervention
in university management,
5, 31–32, 174, 180–83, 184–
92, 239–40 (see also
regulation)
strategic misinterpretation in
budgeting, 166–67, 219–22
(see also budgeting)

termination of policies and
programs (see retrenchment)

About the Author

L. R. JONES is Associate Professor of Public Management at the University of Oregon. He teaches public financial management, budgeting, and regulatory policy and is Director of the Graduate Program in the Department of Planning, Public Policy and Management. Professor Jones received his B.A. from Stanford University and M.A. and Ph.D. from the University of California, Berkeley. He has published articles in the Journal of Higher Education, the Review of Higher Education, Public Administration Review, Public Budgeting and Finance, Canadian Public Administration, the International Journal of Public Administration, Academy of Management Review, Sloan Management Review, and numerous other journals. He coauthored Regulatory Policy and Practices with Fred Thompson, published by Praeger Scientific in 1982. His current research interests are higher education budgeting and management, budgetary control theory, state government regulatory policy, public power financing, and comparative U.S.–Canadian budgeting. Dr. Jones also is director of the Center for Regulatory Evaluation, a nonprofit research organization, and has consulted and given speeches for a number of public and private organizations.

Professor Jones lives in Eugene, Oregon. He is married to Cynthia L. Jones and has two children, Alyson MacKay and Cameron Evan Jones. He is a sports enthusiast and enjoys jogging, swimming, tennis, skiing, backpacking, fishing, sailing, and whitewater kayaking.